ART TALK

Conversations with 12 Women Artists

by Cindy Nemser

ART TALK

CHARLES SCRIBNER'S SONS   NEW YORK

First of all, I wish to thank all the artists who participated in this book for their interest, enthusiasm, and cooperation. Every encounter turned out to be an enriching experience for me and I can only stress again my admiration for these monumental and courageous women. I particularly wish to acknowledge my debt to Lila Katzen and Audrey Flack who cheered me on from the book's conception and whose zealous support in the form of suggestions and discussion never flagged until it came into being.

I wish to thank my editor, Patricia Cristol, for being generous with her time, wise and flexible in her judgments, and always a delight to work with. My thanks also go to Jane Collins and Vibeke Levy of the Marlborough Gallery, Peter Chidekel and Nancy Ungar of the Pace Gallery, Terry Davis of the Graham Gallery, Helene Seeman Zucker of the Louis K. Meisel Gallery, Carole Gallagher of Fourcade, Droll, Inc., Manuel Gonzalez of the Sidney Janis Gallery, The Cordier and Ekstrom Gallery, The Max Hutchinson Gallery, Aberbach Fine Art, The Rose Art Museum, The Minneapolis Institute of Art, and Nancy Neel for their kind cooperation in providing me with photographs and historical documentation.

My special appreciation goes to Marcia Tucker, curator of the Whitney Museum, for her concise, perceptive foreword. Considering her courageous ongoing support of women artists, I am most gratified that she has consented to be part of this anthology.

Most of all I want to thank my husband Chuck Nemser, managing editor of *The Feminist Art Journal,* who listened patiently, day by day, to all my problems, offered suggestions, gave encouragement and criticism, provided photographic works, ran errands, and performed many more invaluable tasks too numerous to name. His whole-hearted participation and support are the very foundation on which this project is built.

Last, but never least, I wish to thank my daughter Cathy for her cheerful acceptance and encouragement of a mother who was always upstairs typing.

Portions of the interviews in this book first appeared in *Arts Magazine, Artforum, Changes,* and *The Feminist Art Journal.*

Library of Congress Cataloging in Publication Data

Nemser, Cindy.
   Art talk: conversations with 12 women artists.

   1. Women artists—Interviews. I. Title.
N8354.N45   709'.2'2 [B]   74–11302
ISBN 0–684–13984–7

Contents

ILLUSTRATIONS

n 1962, when I was a graduate student in art history, the classic textbook (H.W. Janson's *History of Art*)—one which is still used in most introductory art history courses—did not mention a single woman artist. What is seen today as a glaring distortion of history was scarcely, if at all, noticed ten years ago. Since the end of the '60s, under the impetus of the women's liberation movement, women in the arts have become conscious of the covert and overt suppression of the fact that women are and always have been a major creative force. Not only has the role of women in art history been ignored, but important works by women have been attributed to male artists on the assumption that if they were good, women couldn't have done them.

Contemporary women artists find themselves in an only slightly improved situation. In the past, the opportunity and motivation to make art were often lacking. Even given both, most women have found themselves making work which had little chance of being seen, much less bought. Many women artists have also had the additional hardship of raising families and holding jobs at the same time, as the twelve interviews in this book clearly indicate. As a sculptor friend of mine pointed out, "You get used to stirring the pot with one hand and doing your work with the other." Nonetheless, women have always made art, but only in the last few years has this work begun to be recognized, respected, exhibited and written about.

In this book of interviews with women artists, who range in age from thirty-four to eighty-nine, Cindy Nemser has added to our understanding of how, why and under what circumstances women make art. Here we are given enormous insight into the motivations, backgrounds, working habits and ideas of these artists. To each, questions of feminist consciousness are also posed; from each, there are different responses. Some of the younger artists, like Nancy Grossman or Eleanor Antin, are politically committed feminists; older artists, like Delaunay or Krasner, take feminism for granted. Louise Nevelson, questioned about the women's movement, says only, "I *am* a women's liberation."

Cindy Nemser explores such essential issues as how family background affects one's role as an artist and to what extent each artist considers her work to be substantially different from that of men artists; she also deals with the evolution of the basic ideas in each person's work.

Hepworth, Delaunay, Nevelson, Krasner, and Neel are well-known artists who have had long, difficult, and ultimately distinguished careers; Nevelson, for example, when asked about hardships in her life as an artist, says matter-of-factly, "Of course, I wanted to cut my throat for maybe forty years, but I didn't." Krasner's work was obscured by that of Jackson Pollock, to whom she was married, and only recently has she had her first solo museum exhibition in this country. Women in their forties, like Hartigan, Marisol, Flack, and Katzen are less self-conscious about the difficulties of being women artists, and in the interviews concentrate primarily on their work. As Hartigan comments, "One doesn't want to be one's own history. I just think about the next painting." The interviews with younger women —Hesse (who died in 1970), Grossman, and Antin—show how the changing social structure allows women artists today the freedom to live their own lives and to make art, a situation which did not exist twenty years ago.

The interview is to art history what the private journal is to literature. The informality of these interviews permits an exploration of those personal aspects of one's life which so radically affect the making of art; these aspects are most often expurgated or ignored in the traditional artist-interview. Some of the women are outspoken, some reticent, some funny, others deadly serious; with all, there is an intimate glimpse of personality, mannerism, character and thinking that cannot be found elsewhere. Hearing the artists speak for themselves, hearing them speak about their lives as women and artists to another woman, is unique. For them, the trial by gender is a key aspect of their lives, but by no means the only one.

Charlotte Whitten, the mayor of Ottawa in 1963, once wrote, "Whatever women do we must do twice as well as men to be thought half as good. Luckily, that is not difficult." Hopefully, the artists interviewed here will provide prototypes for younger artists, and will help to create a world in which Whitten's words can no longer apply.

Marcia Tucker
Curator, Whitney Museum

ART TALK

Cindy Nemser, 1974.

Introduction

Artists are fascinating people who, in their obsession to create, to stamp their unique vision on inert matter and raw experience, give form to the individual and collective yearnings of us all. I have always been drawn to artists; I have always enjoyed talking to them and have rarely found myself engaged in a conversation that was not in some way productive. In the late 1960's, I began to do tapes with artists; rather than employ the straight interview technique, where a short question is posed by the interrogator, answered by the interviewee and then on to the next question, I preferred a conversational format in which a real exchange of ideas could occur. As a reader, I find the typical question-answer format tedious as one can never answer back, get into the act, so to speak. One is talked *at* rather than talked *with*. I realize, of course, that my questions and comments are bound to be, at times, at odds with my readers' responses, but, at least, I give the readers a place and an opportunity to substitute their reactions for mine before moving on to the next topic. For me, the empathy and participation of the reader are essential elements of any written experience.

At the same time that I was participating in these taped dialogues with artists of both sexes, I became aware of the women's movement and discovered it had a deep personal meaning for me. I became conscious that women, myself included, had been for the most part treated as second-class citizens. We had been exploited and excluded whenever possible, from all areas of power and prestige. And whenever total ostracism was impossible, our efforts and valid achievements had been frequently demeaned and downgraded.

It soon occurred to me that the art world, my liberal, avant-garde art world, was no more exempt from this sexist behavior than any other world. I had to find out for sure, so I began to query women artists, old and young, recognized and unknown, to discover how they assessed their position within the art community. The outcome of this probe, begun in 1970, was an article, included in this book, entitled "Forum: Women in Art,"[1] and the results were depressing. Many of the women interrogated were ashamed of their sex, viewed women's work as inferior to men's, were torn between their roles as artists and wives and mothers; they experienced all sorts of discriminatory behavior from dealers, critics, curators, and male artists, and yet feared associations with other women artists. Only a handful showed any signs of awareness of their actual situation or were angry enough to denounce it verbally.

I was especially interested in the assertion on the part of the women themselves of the female artist's supposed inferiority. I wondered if it were really so. Were women essentially second-rate under-achievers? While rummaging through a book by Margret Breuning on Mary Cassat, a descriptive phrase caught my eye. Breuning declared proudly that Cassatt never merited that "ignominous appellation 'Lady painter.'" Here was an eye-opener. The author considered the catagory of 'Lady painter' ignominous, yet many women artists, including her own beloved Mary Cassatt, were depicted in and out of print in just such a fashion. Although the phrases differed, the attitude implied by such adjectives as *sweet, light, graceful, delicate, nursery oriented,*[2] and so forth to describe their work was apparent. I was thunderstruck. Could it be that the inferiority of women artists, an inferiority acquiesced to by other women artists as well as men artists, was a result of art historical and critical brainwashing? Knowing that the rest of society held prejudicial attitudes toward women, would it be unlikely that art critics and historians were any less bigoted than the rest of the people in our culture? Subsequently I discovered they were not. In an article called "Stereotypes and Women Artists," researched in the Spring of 1971 and published in *The Feminist Art Journal,*[3] I compiled many examples of prejudicial writings about women artists, in France, England, Germany, and the United States, throughout the nineteenth and twentieth centuries. Even the contemporary critics, liberals, spokesmen, and most progressive women showed no awareness of the sexist attitudes they had inherited from their predecessors.

At the same time that I was examining the stereotypical criticism that asserted over and over that women were non-creative, narcissistic, passive, narrow in range, Linda Nochlin published an article entitled "Why Have There Been No Great Women Artists?" in *Art News.*[4] In this essay she stated, uneqivocally, that women artists had never achieved a level of greatness to match that of the greatest of male artists. In a tone strongly tinged with sarcasm she wrote, "The fact, dear sisters, is that there *are* no women equivalents for Michelangelo, or Rembrandt, Delacroix or Cezanne, Picasso or Matisse, or even, in very recent times, for de Kooning or Warhol." She continued, in the same vein of ironic detachment, to proclaim that "the fault, dear brothers, lies not in our stars, our hormones, our menstrual cycles or our empty internal spaces, but in our institutions and education...."[5]

In the light of my recent research exposing the biased attitudes and evaluations of women artists written into art historical and critical texts, I was shocked to read this equally biased pronouncement from a woman art historian who calls herself a feminist. Without needing to delve into the past, we have before our eyes the awesome works of

Louise Nevelson, Barbara Hepworth, and Eva Hesse; how could Noch-lin, in good conscience, proclaim that there were no women artists to match a de Kooning or a Warhol? Nochlin proved herself to be as brainwashed as the rest of the male art historians except that she grounded her stereotyped judgments on cultural rather than biological clichés of sexual inferiority. She claimed that sexist educational and institutional practices had made it impossible for women artists to attain the necessary skills and attitudes requisite for greatness. From Nochlin's point of view, women artists were no longer to be con-demned as anatomically ill-equipped but rather as culturally under-nourished; but in either case, they were still incapable of producing first-rate art.

Nochlin at one point raises the possibility that there may be "hid-den" great women artists, but then mystifyingly declares that if they do exist, "If women have, in fact, achieved the same status as men in the arts, then the status quo is fine as it is," and "what were the femi-nists fighting for?"[6]

Well this feminist knew what she was fighting for. Although it was undeniable that male-controlled society had handed women a raw deal, there were, as I have noted above, women artists who were on a par esthetically with the most esteemed male artists. But none so far (with the possible recent exception of Nevelson) had been accorded the power and prestige of their top male colleagues. With the existence of such an inequitable situation, how could the status quo be fine as it is?

No, I could not accept Nochlin's judgment or illogical rationale. I knew I would have to fight it, to reverse it, to help win back for women artists their rightful place in the forefront of art history. And where better to begin than in my own time with the assistance of the great women artists of the twentieth century.

I chose my artists carefully, delighted that these women were not just artists great among women; they held their own with men as well. On my original list were: Georgia O'Keeffe, Sonia Delaunay, Barbara Hepworth, Louise Nevelson, Lee Krasner, Alice Neel, Helen Franken-thaler, Grace Hartigan, Joan Mitchell, Marisol, Bridget Riley, Eva Hesse, Lila Katzen, Audrey Flack, Eleanor Antin, and Nancy Gross-man. These were the women I saw as major contributors to the art of our century, each making a unique and influential statement from the first decade up to the seventh.

Considering the obstacles facing these women, the role conflicts, the discriminatory practices of the art community, the minimal encour-agement offered by their male peers, I saw these women as heroic in having the strength to transcend it all in the service of their art. I wanted to hear from their own lips how they had accomplished it, how they had fought their way into the male ranks, what hurdles they had had to face, and how they had overcome them. I also wanted to elicit from them interpretations of their art works, their sense of their place in art history, and their philosophical and esthetic views. From their own voices I hoped to secure the testimony that would point, once and for all, to the absurdity of the premise behind the insulting question, "Why have their been no great women artists?"

This selection is, of course, a personal decision based on my knowledge and experience as a critic and art historian; others may have included different artists and excluded others, but after weighing my choices over a long period of time, these are the names I kept coming up with and to these names I feel committed. Of course there are many other women artists of great merit and their work should be dealt with in relation to its own development and in connection with the work of other artists. I hope, at a future date, to have the opportunity to pursue in depth this line of research.

Unfortunately, out of the sixteen artists I selected, four were not available to be in the book. Georgia O'Keeffe and Joan Mitchell were adverse to being taped and so were not able to fit into the format of *Art Talk.* Bridget Riley made it clear that she was resistant to the idea of being included in a book dealing with women artists, and to several invitations to participate in the anthology she responded: "I wish you every success with your book of conversations with women artists, although it seems to have a slight ring of women's lib about it, in which I am not interested."[7] Helen Frankenthaler's exclusion from this collection has a special story behind it. I did do an interview with her on tape which was published in *Artsmagazine,* in November 1971.[8] However, when the artist was notified that this interview was to be incorporated into this anthology she absolutely refused to have the interview included, although she had reworked it at the time of its original publication completely to her satisfaction. Frankenthaler, I might add, has refused to be associated with most women-artist activities.

I regret deeply the omission of the above four artists. The primary purpose of this collection of conversations is to furnish, in their own words, an insight into the aesthetic achievements of the greatest women artists of the twentieth century which, in some cases (Delaunay's, Neel's and Krasner's), have until recently been disgracefully overlooked. It must no longer be possible for an historian or critic to ignore the contributions of women artists and to perpetuate the inequity of keeping them separate, isolated, unable to compete and take laurels among male peers. The presentation of as many monumental women artists as exist makes such an oversight all the more difficult. In the past, women of distinction were looked on as a strange series of accidents, oddities, freaks, exceptions. By bringing the outstanding women artists of our century together in one book, I believe it will become clear that the highest accomplishment, greatness, in female artists is a rule rather than an exception.

And certainly the women artists whose voices are recorded here exhibit the stuff of greatness in every sense of the word; fascinating, provocative, literate, awe inspiring are only a few of the ways to describe them. While, it is not always easy to deal with greatness which, for the most part, comes wrapped in a totally egocentric package, essentially all my subjects were extremely cooperative and kind. But some people were more challenging than others. Lee Krasner was alternately ferocious and fearful, voicing heated indictments against art world powers one moment and editing them out the next. Audrey Flack was painstaking in her approach, polishing up the transcript, refining concepts, pinpointing meanings until the interview shone with the diamond precision of one of her astonishing Photorealist paintings. The sessions with Krasner and Flack provided a learning situation with a wealth of information and a series of intellectual adventures only hinted at in the finished conversations.

Other artists were more relaxed in their approach to the interviews. Louise Nevelson, who I had never met before, was astonishing. Dressed in one of her Scassi costumes, complete with exotic headpiece and gigantic primitive jewelry, she had a grand time exposing the skullduggery of all the behemoths of the establishment New York art world. After she had gotten it off her chest, she called for a round of drinks to celebrate the occasion. I followed Alice Neel around with a microphone while she dragged out painting after painting stored in racks and stacked up against the wall of her turn-of-the century, long-corridored, upper west side New York apartment. During our second taping session, she lined up portraits of all the men in her life, her sons included, and proceeded to give me her deliciously unconventional/unedited illustrated biography. Nancy Grossman also spoke with startling directness while digging out drawings, paintings, and bas-reliefs piled one behind the other in the studio section of her casual Lower East Side loft, while a free-flowing recorded transcontinental telephone conversation between myself and Eleanor Antin was the means by which a large portion of our interview was obtained. Eva Hesse was frightened of the tape recorder at first, and had to have it hidden from her, but then proceeded to speak in a completely ingenuous manner. Under terrible pressure from the disease that was about to kill her, she persisted indomitably in finishing the interview which covered three different sessions.

Grace Hartigan, Sonia Delaunay, Barbara Hepworth, and Marisol were somewhere half-way between the extreme precision of Krasner and Flack and the spontaneity of the others. I had the feeling that they all knew beforehand just what they would say to any interviewer and with a few fascinating slip-ups, here and there, they stuck to their programs. I admired their control but would have liked to have pierced their aplomb more frequently. For example, when the decorous Dame Barbara Hepworth said, "It was the English who were terribly patriarchal in this country," I quickly rejoined, "What about the English men artists, were they patriarchal too?" Dame Barbara, caught off guard, didn't want to answer at first but then she said, "I'll say yes."

The history of the conversation with Lila Katzen, which took place in my study, is really in a class by itself. It was one of hundreds of stimulating, delightful talks that we have had over the past four years. I only wish I had recorded them all and could provide my readers with the same pleasure of her company.

At this point it is also interesting to note some statistics concerning these artists which, I think, make a telling point. Of the 12 women interviewed, 10 were married, 2 were not; 8 had one or more children. These statistics, tiny as they are in number (but then greatness is not found en masse either), certainly dispute the deeply rooted assumption that women cannot split their time between career, marriage, and children and still rise to the heights of their profession.

The aim of this book is not only to present the accomplishments of these outstanding women artists, to investigate their aesthetic and personal values and in certain instances to follow the course of their often turbulent careers, it also seeks to provide new insights into the art world milieu in which these artists functioned. Sonia Delaunay gives us a fresh glimpse of the decades which spawned Cubism, Futurism, and Dada, while Barbara Hepworth provides us with insights into the wartime community of besieged Britain. A corroborating view of Baltimore, Maryland, as an art world rivulet is depicted jointly by Grace Hartigan and Lila Katzen, both teachers at the Maryland College Institute of Art, while Eleanor Antin furnishes us with an artist's perspective of Southern California.

Most provocative of all is the view we get of the New York art world from the thirties to the present from the reports of Louise Nevelson, Alice Neel, Lee Krasner, Grace Hartigan, Marisol, Lila Katzen, Audrey Flack, and Nancy Grossman. Often, overlaps occur offering different evaluations of people and situations which make the interviews, as a total collection, fascinating and complex. Art world celebrities such as Clement Greenberg, Harold Rosenberg, Jackson Pollock, and Henry

Geldzahler are concretely embodied as a result of the multifaceted views of them presented by these artists. It is also enlightening and sometimes amusing to observe how these giant women evaluate each other, watch each other's moves, sometimes admiringly, sometimes enviously, but always with fascination and deep concern.

These interviews are documents which add to our knowledge of the era in which these artists operated and clearly indicate how much pertinent information has been lost because of the sexist exclusion of women from art historical texts. Many of the conversations provide new data which raise art historical questions of both a general and specific nature. How does a male chauvinist culture act to keep female innovation in the background? How does the pose a woman artist often assumes in order to be acceptable to men interfere with our reading of her art? How have women artists who refused to conform to a macho standard influenced the male art world? And more particularly: What was the relationship of Robert and Sonia Delaunay with regard to the creation of the original art movement known as Orphism? How did the interaction that took place between Krasner and Pollock influence the development of all-over abstraction? What part did the exchange of ideas between Katzen and Morris Louis play in the evolution of his color field painting? What was Audrey Flack's contribution to the formation of realistic narrative painting and how is sexism being used to keep her contribution to Photorealism from being credited?

Regarding the question of a common point of view or style among these women, the only link I found in their work was its essentially affirmative nature. I did not perceive any over-all female sensibility in their art. Although the idea is a stimulating one, I find it impossible to endorse any notion of a generalized woman's sensibility which would manifest itself in any woman's art; upon viewing an unknown artist's work, I cannot immediately recognize some distinctive female characteristic and exclaim, as did the legendary Alfred Steiglitz about the unidentified Georgia O'Keeffe drawing, "at last a woman on paper!" (This lack of conviction about a generalized women's sensibility would not preclude, however, my apprehension of a conscious feminist stance in art; but then feminism need not be practiced by women alone.) I take this position because, as I see it women have been too closely immersed within the total culture to evolve an exclusive art separate from male influence. On the other hand, neither do I believe that there is a pure masculine art which has escaped the female influence, although in certain eras, that of abstract expressionism, for example, a pseudo-macho attitude did rule the art world of New York. Moreover, I believe that art is a synthesis of the artist's multiple characteristics: physical traits, race, class, ethnic background, social circle, philosophical milieu, as well as gender, are all inseparably intertwined in the finished aesthetic product.

This view was seconded by all the women artists with whom I spoke, with the exception, in certain instances, of Audrey Flack who insisted that *Jolie Madam* could have only been painted by a woman. For the most part, they all agreed that art transcended gender (although not sexual concerns) and, as true artists, each asserted that she was too much of an individual to partake of a collective sensibility.

And indeed, if there is any other common bond between these great artists, apart from their basic endorsement of human existence, it is the magnitude of their achievements, their indomitable, often obsessive will to create, and their distinctly individual approach to art.

Cindy Nemser

NOTES

[1] Cindy Nemser, "Forum: Women in Art," *Artsmagazine,* vol. 45, no. 33 (February 1971), 18.

[2] E. P. Richardson, "Sophisticates and Innocents Abroad," *Art News,* vol. 53 (April 1954), 62.

[3] Cindy Nemser, "Stereotypes and Women Artists," *The Feminist Art Journal,* vol. 1, no. 1 (April 1972), 1, 22, 23.

[4] Linda Nochlin, "Why Have There Been No Great Women Artists?" *Art News,* vol. 69, no. 9 (January 1971), 22–39.

[5] *Ibid.,* p. 25.

[6] *Ibid.*

[7] Bridget Riley, Unpublished Letter to Cindy Nemser.

[8] Cindy Nemser, "Interview with Helen Frankenthaler," *Artsmagazine,* vol. 42, no. 2 (November 1972), 51–55.

UESTION: How do you feel about the position of women in the art world today?

Pat Adams. Gender is a lesser factor in shaping the artist than place, pals, art tradition, and dream capacity.

Eva Hesse. Excellence has no sex.

Marjorie Strider. Male and female artists do exist and are treated differently.

Louise Bourgeois. A woman has no place as an artist until she proves over and over that she won't be eliminated.

Sylvia Stone. For women there is little tolerance of mediocrity, whereas the male's mediocrity is accepted and the idea of "future growth" acceptable.

Beverly Pepper. The female artist inevitably finds she must fight harder than most males to gain an equivalent position.

Grace Hartigan. In our society any man has a harder time than a woman dedicating his life to art.

Jennette Lam. The helpful hand is seldom stretched out to artists, and I am certain it is offered less to women.

Rosemary Beck. My first position was offered to me because of my gender, not in spite of it.

Raquel Forner. As far as I am concerned, the problem of the sexes in art has never existed, and if it still exists for some women painters, they must look into themselves for the reasons, not into the society that surrounds them.

Statement by X12 (group of 12 women artists). Women are unliberated and held back from full self-realization because of their conditioning, which makes culturally transmitted characteristics such as passivity, dependence, softness, unassertiveness into innate female characteristics.

Miriam Beerman. I have never, never thought of myself as a "woman artist."

Jane Logemann. The position of women artists in the art world is an absurdity of words.

QUESTION: Why do women artists dislike being associated with other women artists?

Nancy Grossman. Female artists are taken less seriously than male artists.

Jo Baer. Women in all endeavors suffer a failure-oriented second-class outlook.

Sally Hazelet Drummond. In the past, women have not excelled in the visual arts. This situation seems true for the present as well.

Margrit Beck. There are virtually tens of thousands of women with time on their hands who have taken a couple of art courses and concluded that they are now ready to be received into the arms of the waiting art world.

Helen Pashigan. If women show together as women artists, the common denominator becomes "women" not "art."

Hedda Sterne. Most women are Uncle Toms and would rather be loved and accepted than admired and feared.

Alice Neel. Women in this culture often become male chauvinists, thinking that if they combine with the men, they may be pardoned for being a hole rather than a club.

Irene Moss. A woman who has achieved success in a man's world feels grossly superior and fears identification with weakness—other women.

Nancy Spero. The art world loves the adventurous male musky hero.

Suzi Gablik. I'd rather identify with the men.

QUESTION: As a female artist, have you ever experienced discrimination from the art-world?

Sylvia Sleigh. Though women have been granted their rights within the law, many of the cultural pressures that kept them in subjugation are still operative, but in half-concealed terms.

Sue Fuller. In earlier days when black tie meant just that, and if you didn't have one you rented it, there was a quaint custom of after-dinner segregation. When this was applied to art events, it had a curious effect. Because of the rarity of women artists, I invariably found myself banished from my colleagues and sequestered with their wives.

Julie Lamoe. When I graduated from art school in 1965, men instructors were still asking women students why they were painting and not getting pregnant.

Deborah Remington. The head of a university art department informed me that he hadn't hired a woman to teach since 1939.

Lil Picard. I had the experience twice of being refused as an artist by galleries—once in New York and once in Düsseldorf—and told bluntly, "We don't take on women."

Ruth Vollmer. People tell me constantly, "I've admired your work often, but I never associated it with a woman."

Dorothy Dehner. I have been told by collectors that they have been advised never to buy the works of a woman.

Audrey Flack. I used to sign my name A. Flack, then they couldn't tell a woman did it.

Theresa Schwartz. I'll never forget the night when a good friend (male sculptor) made a little speech in a group and pronounced that "no woman artist could ever rise to the level of a really good man."

Grace Hartigan. I find that the subject of discrimination is only brought up by inferior talents to excuse their own inadequacy as artists.

Lee Krasner. Any woman artist who says there is no discrimination against women in the art world should have her face slapped.

QUESTION: Would you introduce any reforms or do you have any suggestions for ways to improve the position of women in the art world?

Eva Hesse. The way to beat discrimination in art is by art.

Helen Frankenthaler. Reforms have to be made by women themselves. That is, they should just go on being people and proceed from there to make paintings, and the question of sex will take care of itself.

Miriam Schapiro. A woman who is an artist should be careful whom she marries. She should avoid in her professional and social life male chauvinists, just as any sensitive Black would avoid white racists.

Betty Parsons. A woman who dedicates herself to the arts should be ready to sacrifice wifely and motherly feelings.

Juliette Gordon. Create an alternate economic structure in the art world which will enable women artists to be women and wives, creative beings, colleagues, and mothers, and not find conflict between these roles.

Mary Frank. Woman's unique awareness and personal vision should be explored and felt.

Deborah Remington. Women artists must be encouraged to discover themselves as women and not feel obliged to imitate masculine art.

Agnes Denes. Women should stop producing timid work as a result of ages of suppression.

Alice Neel. All insults, all attacks on, all downgrading and exploitation of women should be fought by all women. To permit a psychiatrist to say you suffer from "penis envy" is like singing "Old Black Joe" to a Black Panther.

May Stevens. By all means reforms should be instituted. We may even be beyond the integrationist stage ("There are no women artists, only artists"). We may be at the "woman-artist is beautiful" stage. The details will be worked out.

WAR (Women Artists in Revolution) demands "A continuous non-categorized, rotating, non-juried show—exhibition in the museum proper—of works by women to be held by women." (Presented to the Museum of Modern Art.)

Lil Picard. Every commercial art gallery should take on as many female artists as male artists without racial or sexual discrimination.

Yvonne Jacquet. Change one's name to a man's, as Grace (George) Hartigan did when she first exhibited? Not today!

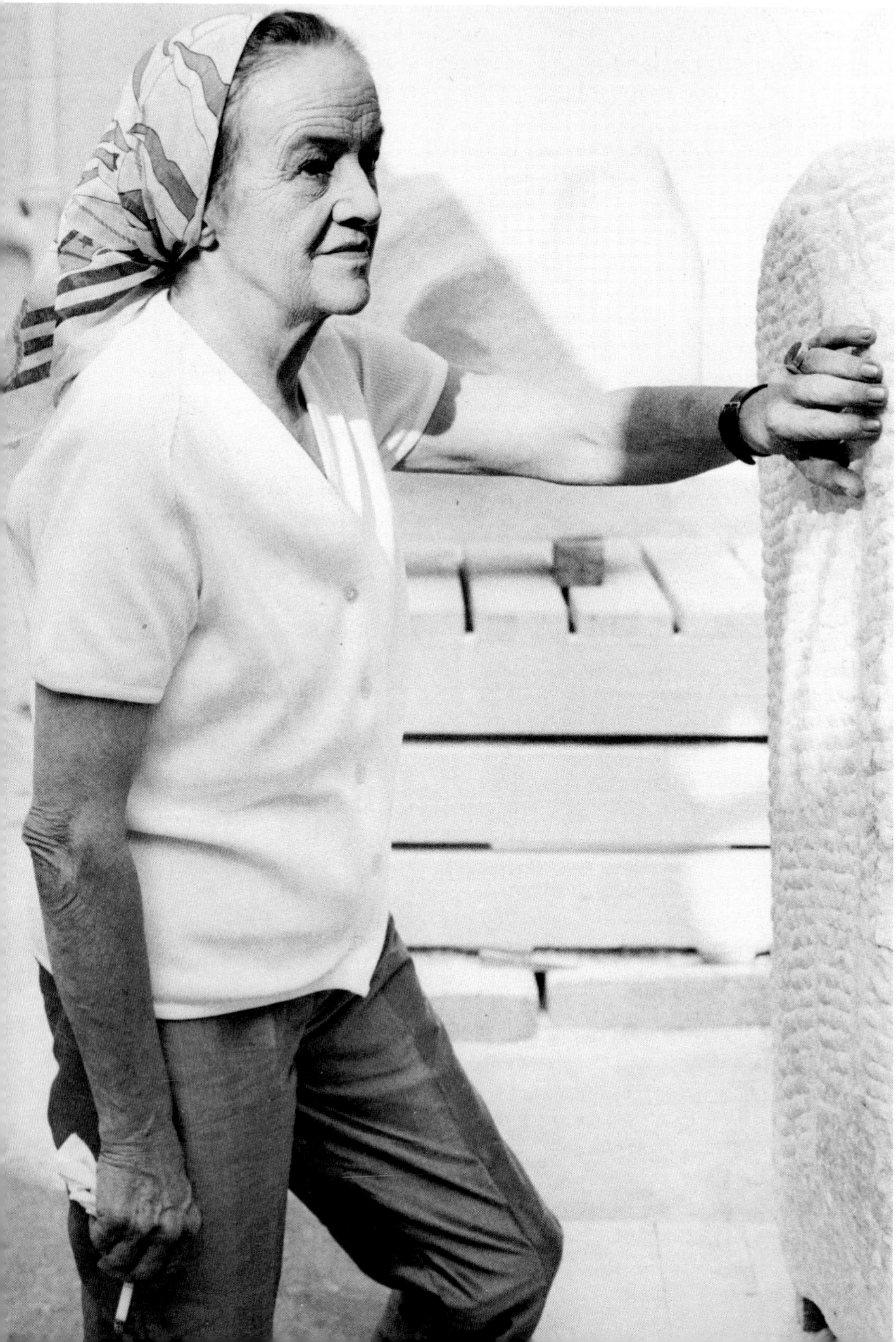

Barbara Hepworth, 1968.

BARBARA HEPWORTH is a world-renowned sculptor who lives in Saint Ives, a small community on the coast of Cornwall, England. She is surrounded by cliffs and sea and by her own walled-in, foliage-filled, sculpture garden.

Born in 1903 in Yorkshire, she studied, along with Henry Moore, at the Leeds School of Art and at the Royal College of Art in London. Then on a traveling scholarship to Italy Hepworth met her first husband, the artist John Skeaping, with whom she had a son, Paul. Later Hepworth married the painter Ben Nicholson and became the mother of triplets.

This artist is famous for the creation of what the historian Herbert Read termed "vitalist" sculpture. In the 1930's along with Henry Moore, among others, Hepworth infused new vitality into a sculptural tradition that had been languishing since Rodin. Drawing first on the carvings and castings of the early Greeks and Romans and then spurred on by her encounter with the work of Brancusi and Arp, Hepworth developed a form of sculpture which was at once pared down yet bursting with organic energy. Her doctrine of "truth to materials" came out of the need to deal directly and honestly with the sculptural media of wood and stone and to continually engage it in an ongoing dialogue.

An extremely innovative artist who sought to incorporate open space into the solidity of the closed form, Hepworth was the first to pierce the stone in 1931. Later, in 1938, she continued her investigations into space by integrating stringed configurations into the hollowed-out centers of her sculptures. Opting for the purity of basic geometric shapes consisting of rectangles, spheres, cones, and cylinders, this artist has managed to imbue these impersonal forms with organic, even anthropomorphic implications. Many sculptures made up of two squares or spheres—one large, the other small—are suggestive of the mother-child relationship. Other works consisting of scooped-out areas or sensuous flowing curves create in abstract terminology a visual metaphor for the human experience of the primary interaction of land, sea, wind, and air. On seeing these works the viewer becomes one with the natural elements and the artist who has made such a moving record of her visual response to them.

Eventually Hepworth, having revitalized monumental sculpture through her immediate contact with the stone and wood, was able to bring this spontaneous approach to bronze casting as well. In the fifties and sixties she incorporated her life-enhancing attitudes into many spectacular bronze works, among them her awesome

Barbara Hepworth

Single Form located at the United Nations plaza in New York City. Her ongoing concerns with natural elements have also appeared in her sensitively executed drawings and lithographs which form an essential part of her *oeuvre.*

Working throughout her lifetime, despite physical obstacles, family responsibilities, and, until fairly recently, limited financial means, Dame Barbara Hepworth is living proof of woman's ability to achieve greatness no matter what the odds.

CINDY NEMSER   You were married for thirty-three years and had four children. I find it astonishing that you could have done so much having such a large family to take care of and having so many financial difficulties.

BARBARA HEPWORTH   I found it was a great inspiration to me. I loved the family and everything to do with them. I loved the environment and the cooking. I used to cook and go in my studio. I had to have methods of working. If I was in the middle of a work and the oven burned or the children called for me, I used to make an arrangement with music, records, or poetry, so that when I went back to the studio, I picked up where I left off. I enjoyed it, you see; it was part of me.

C.N.   For myself I find it very hard to work if I have my little daughter around. I usually get someone to watch her. Did your husband help? He was an artist too.

B.H.   I had two husbands. Did they help me? Well, of course, because they were fond of children. But we lived a life of work and the children were brought up in it, in the middle of the dust and the dirt and the paint and everything. They were just part of it. But it is taxing if the children fall ill. That becomes a strain. I found the only way to resolve it in my mind was that it had to come out in the form of a new work. All my thoughts about the strain of the illness, all anxiety—this I think did discipline me in a way for which I'm deeply grateful.

C.N.   So it was in a sense overcoming an obstacle or a painful moment which made you strive in a different or almost harder way?

B.H.   I found that there was no point in giving in to anxiety and concern about illness. One had to retire and think about it and become affirmative inside oneself and then wait. And if one waited, good work came out of it. If one got into a terrible state, then bad work would come out of it.

C.N.   I can understand that. If you get too overwrought it's almost as if you can't do anything. If you resolve it and somehow calm yourself and accept, things begin to flow again. I feel there's a great balance and harmony in your work. Looking at it I feel that there's a great deal of the spiritual in it too. I was looking at the lithographs you did recently. There's so much space in them and the forms are enveloped in this space. One feels it's a cosmic vision.

B.H.   Well, I have to work that way. I have to dedicate myself. Do you understand? I don't feel conflict in myself because if I do my work doesn't go well. If there's conflict I have to sit down or go to sleep to solve it. And the only way to solve the whole problem is to produce really affirmative work which can only come—I can't make it come. I can't conjure it up. I can only go to sleep and hope it happens.

C.N.   You mean one can't work under terrible tensions.

B.H.   You have to digest it and if you digest you can contribute. This is where women are very good because they have great fortitude and on that they should draw. If they have the fortitude to raise families and go through life supporting this and that, surely they have the fortitude to use their blinking heads. I never had much patience with women who said, "Well, I can't work this week or next week or the week after, but maybe I'll work in six months time or maybe in a year's time." I found one had to do some work every day, even at midnight, because either you're professional or you're not.

C.N.   I know exactly what you mean. Coming down here on the train I met a woman who asked me what I did. I said, "I'm an art critic" and she said, "Oh I used to paint but then I got married and I haven't painted for thirty years and I suppose it's too late but I had all my family and children." I always feel sorry for people who don't do what they want or need to do.

B.H.   Well you need to know what to do and discipline yourself. I mean my home came first but my work was there always.

C.N.   Don't you think it would have been easier for you if it hadn't been that way?

B.H.   No. No, I was made that way—to incorporate family, children, and everything. I hadn't much patience with women artists trying to be women artists. At no point do I wish to be in conflict with any man or masculine thought. It doesn't enter my consciousness. I think art is anonymous. It's not competitive with men. It's a complementary contribution. I've said that and I do believe it, that one does contribute to art and that's nothing to do with being male or female.

C.N.   I noticed that when Adrian Stokes was writing about your art he said something about its being feminine.

B.H.   It's inevitably feminine because it's my experience.

C.N. But then we have to get into the problem of what the word *feminine* means.

B.H. We do, yes, because I don't think a good work of art can just be said to be feminine or masculine and I'm sure men would be very annoyed if they were called masculine.

C.N. Some would and some wouldn't. There was a big cult of the masculine at one point.

B.H. But art's either good or it isn't.

C.N. In our society masculine has always been the higher good and feminine the lower.

B.H. That's a stupid thing because the scales are out of balance. As far as I'm concerned, in my work and in my life, the scales are in balance.

C.N. Ultimately, we know that's true, but still I noticed that Stokes also used the word *complaisant* in reference to your work. That's a word that's also very often applied to women's art. I did an article where I put together a whole collection of words I call stereotypes which are often used to describe women's work. I think these categorizations are nonsense and I'm out to break down those stereotypes.

B.H. Well, that is marvelous. It has to be done but you have to back up a hundred years to George Eliot. Come to think of it I noticed from time to time that people look me up and down and say, "Oh we thought you'd be a very large, hefty woman." This irritates me vastly. The same way when I've been teaching, I've found opposition to my teaching because I said it's not the strength which does it, it's a rhythm. You don't need huge muscles, great strength. In fact, if you have that and misuse it, you're going to damage the material. It's absurd. It's a rhythmical flow of an idea whichever sex you are.

C.N. Linda Nochlin wrote a piece called "Why There Are No Great Women Artists," and I think that's a terrible title for an article about women artists because I don't think it's true at all.

B.H. But it isn't true. Looking back, women dancers and entertainers, singers, actresses have been accepted because they were entertaining. It's been hard for women architects, engineers, lawyers, sculptors, and so on to be left free, but I never accepted this point of view—never.

C.N. Right from the beginning of your career, you've done what you wanted to do?

B.H. Yes.

C.N. I read that you went to Florence on a scholarship and spent the time looking and didn't come back with any concrete work. I thought that was marvelous to have the nerve—the courage to have done that.

B.H.   I was in terrible trouble because the committee of men said they would never again give a scholarship to a woman. But if I'd done a lot of work and got married, they would have said the same.

C.N.   They assumed it was because you got married that you didn't do any work?

B.H.   They put two and two together—"Women are hopeless."

C.N.   It was amazing that they gave you the scholarship in the first place.

B.H.   Well, I was a bit of a fighter. Yes, it was really amazing looking back. Nevertheless, I've never been disturbed by this.

C.N.   What about the whole community of men artists that came in the 1930's, Mondrian, Gabo?

B.H.   They were marvelous. They were all my friends.

C.N.   And did they treat you like an equal?

B.H.   Absolutely. They did. You see it was the English who are terribly patriarchal in this country.

C.N.   What about the English men artists, were they the same? Patriarchal too?

B.H.   [silence]

C.N.   It's for posterity. The truth has to out.

B.H.   I'll say yes.

C.N.   Didn't you work with the men on a magazine called *The Circle?*

B.H.   It's been reprinted and it's now referred to as a classic. Well it is. But that was done by Ben Nicholson, Sir Leslie Martin, Gabo, and Leslie Martin's wife, Sadie Speaight, and me. We were sitting round the fire and we said, "Why shouldn't we do a book?" And so we started and now it's a classic and referred to as such. But we worked on it equally.

C.N.   Yet, I noticed they didn't put you down as an editor.

B.H.   There was no acknowledgment to the two women who did the dirty work.

C.N.   I noticed that right off.

B.H.   We did the layout, we did the corrections, proofing, everything.

C.N.   And the research and helped to write it too?

B.H.   Of course.

C.N.   That's the sort of thing I'm trying to pick up on.

B.H.   Men don't like being beholden to women. I quite like being beholden to men. I've no resentment. In fact I wouldn't be happy if I couldn't respect my husband or my men friends. I acknowledge that.

C.N.   The point is that women really don't want to destroy men. We just want them to treat us with the same respect that we have given to them.

B.H.   Precisely. I'd hoped I would live long enough to see a balance maintained without any friction because I can't see any point in it.

C.N.   I think people who are oppressed have to assert themselves. Nobody is going to do it for them.

B.H.   Yes, there's a difference which I think is silly between being a female entertainer, dancer, or singer, looking beautiful, and being a barrister or a sculptor. I don't find my forms menacing. I do them to please myself.

C.N.   Have people said that your forms have a certain menacing quality in them? Or an uneasiness?

B.H.   Well, either they're not menacing which is bad or they say they are and either way it's supposed to be slightly belittling. I don't care that the forms are stronger than they are.

C.N.   In the United States there was the minimal art movement and there was a reaction against Henry Moore's sculpture. There was a feeling that his work was too romantic, not austere enough. Your work seemed to me much more contemporary.

B.H.   I'm younger than Henry and I'm more in touch with the young people. I'm lucky. I have seven grandchildren and I watch them with great interest. I find there is still a tendency to give preference to the boys and that is rather heartbreaking because my father did not do that, so he was a damned sight more enlightened than people are now.

C.N.   Well, he was an extraordinary man I suppose?

B.H.   He was a very gentle, thoughtful person. He said my daughters will have the same freedom and the same everything as my son.

C.N.   Was that unusual for that time?

B.H.   It's a terribly long time ago. Sixty years ago. But he was true to it.

C.N.   He was an engineer, wasn't he?

B.H.   Yes. I learned a great deal from him. I inherited this aptitude, let's say, for form and construction largely through his gentleness. He didn't teach me; he just took me and I absorbed it. But he backed me up through thick and thin. I left home at sixteen.

C.N. You also had a headmistress, Miss McCroben, at your school who was devoted to you, didn't you? She gave you support and encouragement and recognized your talent.

B.H. She was marvelous. She was a very enlightened woman, much more enlightened than you find today. The only thing that worries me now—of course I shouldn't worry, life goes like that doesn't it?—but if the poor girls are going to be hemmed in and obviously preference for the male to be prolonged, I think it's a very sad thing. Honestly, looking round at my friends' grandchildren and at my own grandchildren I find that the girls are extraordinarily intelligent.

C.N. Yes. And now women are getting together to channel their intelligence and energy and creativity into a direction which will make it easier for them to gain recognition.

B.H. I'm actually not sure whether it should be channeled by women getting together or taking the whole picture.

C.N. That's a matter of a transitory stage. We have to do it at this point. Hopefully there'll be a point where women will be accepted just as people. After all, you haven't had a retrospective in the United States. I think it's a shame that they don't know your work in my country as well as they should.

B.H. It will come one day.

C.N. Earlier you mentioned certain works you did after periods of anxiety. Can you remember any of them specifically? Pieces that came out of any particular tensions?

B.H. There's an oval sculpture of 1943. I was in despair because my youngest daughter, one of the triplets, had osteomyelitis. In those days the war was on and you couldn't get anything. She was ill for four years. I thought the only thing I can do to help this awful situation, because we never knew if it would worsen, is to make some beautiful object. Something as clean as I can make it as a kind of present for her. It's happened again and again. When my son died, he was killed, it's the only way I can go on.

C.N. It's as if you as an artist instead of keeping in your anxiety and grief—letting it fester—you let it out and use it. And out of something bad comes something beautiful.

B.H. I have to.

C.N. It's like a rebirth.

B.H. Yes. And I'm quite sure I owe a lot to my upbringing, my parents, my background that was hard working but pretty emancipated in its thought. It was a fairly cruel background, industrial stagnation, poverty, but books and music came first and hard work.

C.N.   Were there artists in your family?

B.H.   No, no artists in my family but they loved life and music and literature.

C.N.   It seems as if everything fell into place for you. You seemed to have gone to the right places to meet the people who were right for you.

B.H.   I hope I've matured in my work. I had to wait many years to do my recent sculptures, *The Family of Man,* because I had to have money and space and time.

C.N.   You always wanted to work big didn't you?

B.H.   Yes. I worked big in '38, '39, but then the war came and then of course things were quite difficult.

C.N.   How large are the largest of *The Family of Man* sculptures?

B.H.   Up to eleven feet.

C.N.   They look beautiful on this hillside where you've photographed them. They make me think of prehistoric stone structures, placed on top of that hill as if by some giant hand. It makes one think of Stonehenge.

B.H.   Maybe I helped to make Stonehenge. I don't know.

C.N.   Are they welded together?

B.H.   Each piece is placed on top of the other.

C.N.   There is a certain sense of the minimal in them, in the contemporary sense of the word. And yet I never think of your work as minimal.

B.H.   I don't know what it means. Can you tell me?

C.N.   People who did that kind of art were interested in simplifying almost to the very bone all the objects that they made. They produced almost basic geometric forms and then placed the whole perceptual response on the viewer. The viewer has to bring so much to the sculpture that he or she has to get very involved with it. It's a kind of perceptual give and take.

B.H.   You wouldn't call Rothko minimal would you? He's all-embracing.

C.N.   The Minimalists took off from Barnett Newman. His very simple, stark kind of image. In fact before he died Rothko had rather gone out of fashion.

B.H.   I'm a great admirer of Newman's.

C.N.   Yet most of the work the Minimalists have done is very geometric. There's an emphasis on the geometric, on the intellectual. I think that's why theirs was such a violent reaction to Henry Moore. His work was so organic, so humanistic. It was too threatening. Yet I don't think that would ever bother you. Your work is very organic, too.

B.H.   It's meant to be. I'm organic myself.

C.N.   In your writings you've mentioned being very concerned with how people relate to your sculpture in an environmental way. You too wanted them to almost get into it, to react to it on a physical level.

B.H.   I've always felt this. You can't make a sculpture, in my opinion, without involving your body. You move and you feel and you breathe and you touch. The spectator is the same. His body is involved too. If it's a sculpture he has to first of all sense gravity. He's got two feet. Then he must walk and move and use his eyes and this is a great involvement. Then if a form goes in like that—what are those holes for? One is physically involved and this is sculpture. It's not architecture. It's rhythm and dance and everything. It's to do with swimming and movement and air and sea and all our well-being. Look at all the phrases that we use: "being on his toes," "bowed with grief." All those phrases to denote the human body in relation to its environment. In sculpture the main thing is to stand on your toes and become aware to the fingertips. You know it bores me to think people come in and say, "We'd thought you'd be a large woman," I mean it's so stupid. I did my largest works when I broke my leg. I was so hopping mad to have broken my leg, I found every means I could to surmount that improbable disaster.

C.N.   You seem to react to obstacles very well. They become a challenge, something to work against.

B.H.   Yes, but that's a part of the involvement. Touch, and poise, wind and water, everything. Sculpture is involved in the body living in the spirit or the spirit living in the body, whichever way you like to put it.

C.N.   Do you think, for the most part, people understand what your sculpture is all about?

B.H.   The comforting thing is that many people do. The ones who find it difficult are the ones who've decided that women artists are no damn good anyway and they stiffen up as soon as they see a work. So they don't communicate because they can't move. Their bodies are stiff. They don't go round; they can't touch.

C.N.   What do you think of Anthony Caro's work?

B.H.   I think all these new young sculptors—he's not all that young though—are taking a stand against abominable architecture since the war and I think rightly so. But again I feel it's not enough to be against something. You have to do something that will damn well replace it. Where do you put these sculptures? I mean if they don't work with architecture or culture what do these sculptors do with their work and what do we do with our heritage?

C.N.   There's been a great deal of anti-art being done now, out of Duchamp, as if artists want to tear everything down but they have nothing to put up in its place.

B.H.   I like to think that time is timeless and I wouldn't want to make a work which wouldn't last for more than ten years—nor a work that wouldn't go anywhere. It would make me terribly mad. Mind you, I have to wait to find a place for my work. It doesn't happen all that easily, but it does happen. It slips in somewhere. Before the war the architects were very much one with the sculptors, painters, everybody. We thought alike. Then the war was over and there was the economic unit. It was so ugly. Then the architects gave up coming to look at sculpture and painting.

C.N.   There has been a tremendous alienation between architects and artists?

B.H.   Tremendous, terrible.

C.N.   Then have you gotten many commissions like the one for the United Nations plaza where you actually knew where the sculpture would be placed?

B.H.   If an architect says, "Will you do a sculpture for here?" and I get an immediate reaction, I say "yes." If I don't and I stay blank, I say "no." Simple.

C.N.   The sculpture has to be right for the setting that it's going to be placed in? But very often the pieces are placed afterward?

B.H.   So far so good. I've got a new one they will unveil next month in Cheltenham which is thirty feet long. It's the longest I've done and I enjoyed it very much but I've had to wait two years for the architects. It's called *Theme and Variations.* It's kind of a musical piece.

C.N.   It's beautiful in St. Ives. I guess you always wanted to stay here once you got settled in.

B.H.   I couldn't get away.

C.N.   Don't you miss the big city? Or the art life?

B.H.   I tried to run two studios, one in London, one here. But whenever I was in London I wanted a piece of rock that was here. I couldn't work it. I think where you live as a sculptor is a very practical matter. You want space and light, materials, simple living, and everything. But one can't get it in London anymore. It doesn't exist.

C.N.   In New York everybody has lofts. They live in them and they're in the downtown section of Manhattan.

B.H.   But a sculptor can't live in a loft. How do they get the stuff up?

C.N.   A lot of people have their work fabricated now. They work from mock-ups or maquettes.

B.H.   I never liked maquettes much. I like to work to the size that I must. I like making small works but they are to be handled and they're different.

C.N.   Yours is basically a public art isn't it? It's trying to reach out and be part of a total environment.

B.H.   Absolutely. I have been asked to do a work for various things—commissions to do with things like lifeboats and wildlife and all kinds of things. I love this because I am part of this life. I can't be unpolitically minded. I'm very involved.

C.N.   In what way? You don't actually participate in political movements?

B.H.   I don't march.

C.N.   You feel you can express your involvements through your work?

B.H.   Yes.

C.N.   How do you do this specifically?

B.H.   Well, I'm involved in everything I read just as I was in the thirties during the Spanish War and Franco and everything. And after all there's not a great deal of difference between the *Monument to the Spanish War,* a group of things one on top of the other, that I lost and *The Family of Man.* I mean I've always been involved. I was involved in industry in my home town. I was involved in the distress and the strikes, everything. I wasn't marching but I was involved through my work.

C.N.   There's been a great deal of discussion about how an artist can become involved in a political way in the sense of doing something about problems that exist and how the work can say something about it. Some people say the work has to be a direct political expression which can be read by people to have any political impact.

B.H.   If that was true people wouldn't ask me to help with my work, would they?

C.N.   Evidently they feel that it's a very positive statement and that something that's strong and beautiful gives courage to people.

B.H.   If you wake up in the morning you have to have something strong and affirmative to start the day on. I don't mean you have to have a sculpture, but you have to have your eyes open, your body aware and receptive.

C.N.   Recently I saw your lithographs at the Marlborough Gallery in New York. I thought they were beautiful.

B.H.   I've done three lots. I'm just embarking on the fourth.

C.N.   I think the lithographs are a wonderful way of reaching people who could not afford to own one of your sculptures.

B.H.   Yes and I thoroughly enjoy it. I've always drawn as my exploration of forms and space, for what could *be* in a vague sort of way. I've never drawn a sculpture, though five years later you could say, "Oh my goodness, that's related to that."

C.N.   I also remember you saying that no work of yours is an accident. Do you mean by that that your work isn't a chance thing—that there's nothing whatever automatic about it?

B.H.   Oh no, there isn't, though, by the way, that is quite a useful contribution. But if you're looking after a sick child or a sick husband you use your intuition or sharp response to a set of conditions and this is simple providing one knows oneself. I would just hate it if I did things heedlessly. I would hate them so, I would set fire to the whole studio. I really would.

C.N.   I think very often one has to work very hard, do lots of research and lots of thinking, and then when you start to work, it's all there, waiting to come out—to flow out of you.

B.H.   It is. There's a beautiful book written by Stravinsky, *The Poetics of Music.* It's so beautiful because of the whole early description of the flow of the beginning and procedure to the end. You only have to change a word or two and it becomes form.

C.N.   I think all creative work is very similar but it's such a mystery at the same time. How do things really happen? What is the catalyst?

B.H.   One of the mysteries is how the human mind can hear a piece of music, a symphony from the beginning to the end, before beginning, or see a sculpture finished all the way round when it doesn't exist. Now these faculties are the sort of faculties which are needed in sciences, math, and medicine and all kinds of things. But if one has them, one has to learn to use them. You have to learn how to play the piano, don't you?

C.N.   Actually, what's happened in some of the recent art is that artists are trying to teach people *how* the process of creation evolves. How to *see* is the idea behind minimal art. There are modern composers who just make sounds. They just make noise as if they are trying to get people to understand that this is the process—this is the thing that has to go on. I think it's not enough for an artist to do. You have to get beyond the process.

B.H.   There are various aptitudes. I think carving or building or construction is perhaps nearer to composing music, and some painting and modeling and so on is much nearer to a more fluid interpretation, to film. But you can't start with a block and say, "Now it's going to dictate to me." You dictate to it.

C.N.   There's an interaction at the same time, isn't there?

B.H.   Oh yes.

C.N.   And you have said that you follow the stone. It speaks to you.

B.H.   Of course, but you can't put anything back.

C.N.   It's a high risk business you're in.

B.H.   I enjoy that.

C.N.   But still it's very scary. The thought of making one false move and then ruining it.

B.H.   I'm not afraid you see. I know how to carve. No credit to me. I was just born like that.

Barbara Hepworth's studio, St. Ives, Cornwall, 1972.

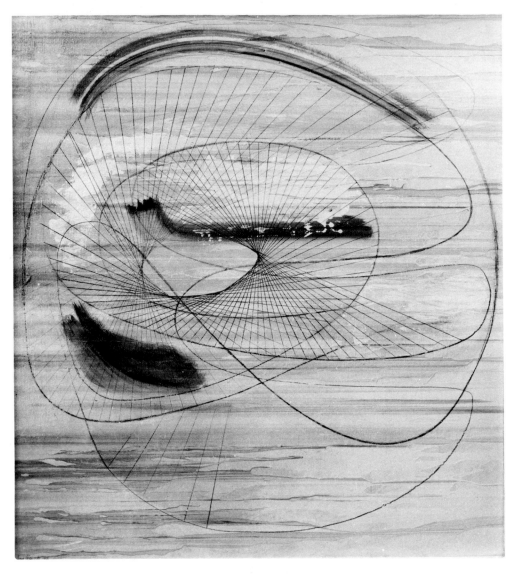

Curved Form (Orpheus), 1956.

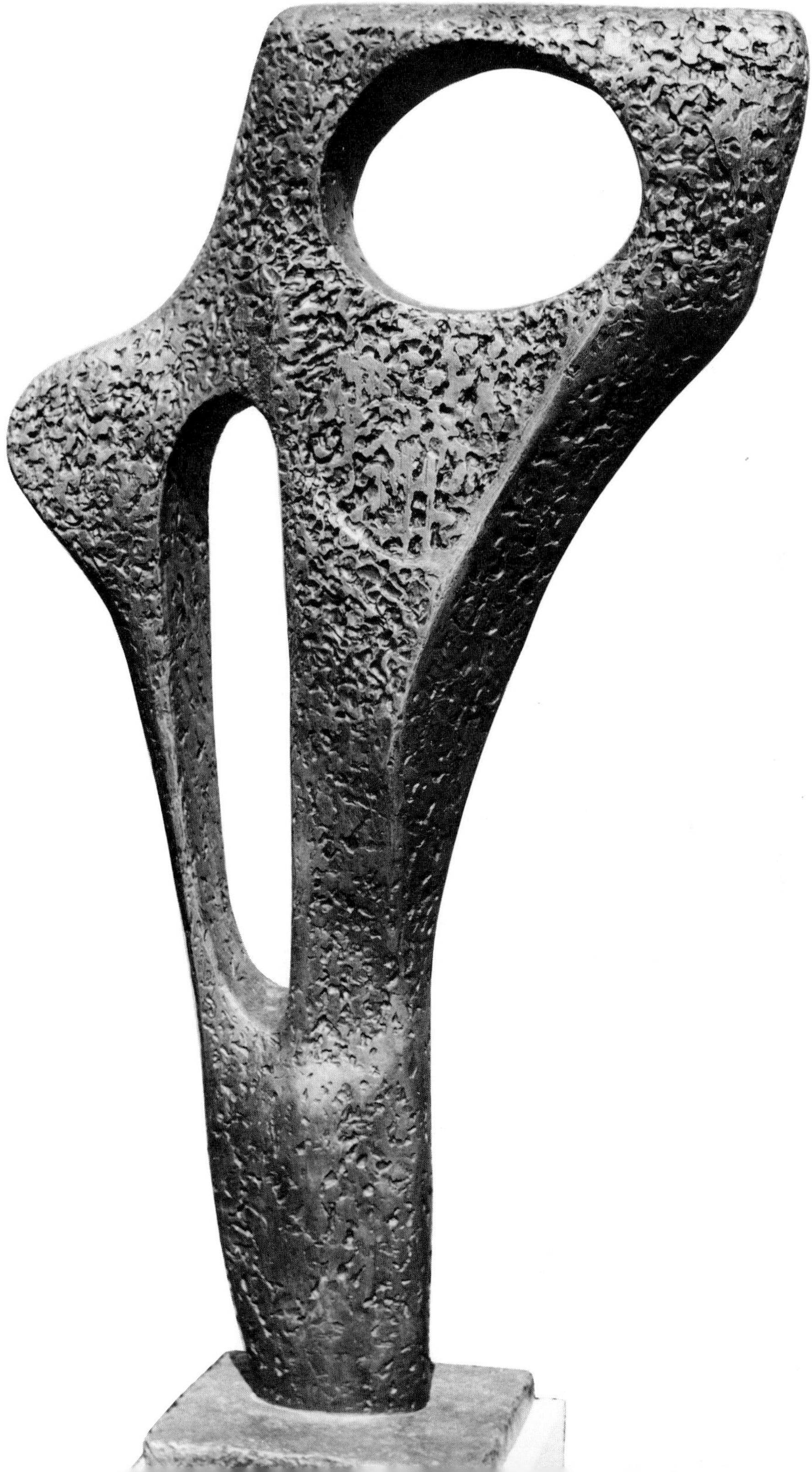

Figure (Archaean), 1959.

Single Form (Memorial to Dag Hammarskjöld), 1963.

Maquette, Theme and Variations, 1970.

Family of Man, 1970.

SONIA DELAUNAY-TERK was born in Russia in 1885. The daughter of a well-to-do landed family, she came to Paris in 1905 to study art and within a few years married the avant-garde dealer Wilhelm Uhde. Moving in a circle of artists, writers, and poets of all nationalities, she eventually encountered the intense and brilliant Robert Delaunay. The two were drawn irresistibly to each other both emotionally and esthetically and decided that their lives had to be joined. In 1910 she divorced Uhde to marry Delaunay.

Husband and wife worked constantly side by side equally developing and perfecting the art form their friend Guillaume Apollinaire christened Orphism. They were equally responsible for the introduction of the concept of simultaneity of color into the Paris art scene. In fact, it is openly recognized that Sonia Delaunay, with her Russian heritage of brilliant color and her desire, along with other Russian painters, to apply it to Cubist forms, was instrumental in bringing the bright planes of prismatic color to the collaboration that took place between herself and Robert Delaunay.

Her first simultaneous works appear in 1912 and in 1913. She painted *The Bal Bullier* which was the name of the café in which she and friends met to dance. Evolving out of her discoveries of the rhythmic capacity of color, the sensuous bodies of the dancers appear to move dynamically in and out of the intensely pigmented planes that form the backdrop to their activity. In a second version of that subject she shifted from recognizable configurations to totally abstract, ovular forms which anticipate the famous color discs that actually make their appearance in her work in 1914 in a painting called *Electric Prisms.*

In 1915 the Delaunays left Paris for Portugal and remained there until 1918. During this Iberian period Sonia Delaunay returned to recognizable imagery in such monumental works as *Market in the Minho* (1915) and *Flamenco Singers* (1916). However her more realistic subject matter is built out of her characteristic disc-like forms and her color is purer and more effervescent than ever.

Not content to relegate her stylistic discoveries to canvas alone, as early as 1909 she began to embroider her own abstract designs on to material, and when her only son, Charles, was born in 1911, she made him a traditional Russian patchwork blanket. This homely item with its play of color and geometric patterns foreshadowed her essay into pure dynamic color paintings. The artist was so intrigued by the idea of transposing the esthetic into the functional that she began to apply her painting principles to her entire environment, filling her home with patchwork cushions and lampshades of her own design. Then she reached out to others with her dynamic color compositions and circular motifs. In 1913 she collaborated with the poet Blaise Cendrars to illustrate his poem *La Prose du Trans-Sibérien et de la Petite Jehanne de France.* This was indeed an extraordinary endeavor, a poem in book form, six feet in length, that combined a revolutionary composition with original typography and color forms. The artist also carried out commissions with other poets, including Mayakovski, Joseph Delteil, and Apollinaire.

Due to the Russian Revolution, Sonia Delaunay lost her income after 1917 and the need to support her family forced her to extend her art even further than her own beloved circle of artists and poets. She met Diaghilev in 1918 and began to design sets and costumes for his ballets. Her creations for Cleopatra and Aida are among the most original costumes ever constructed.

Fashion houses commissioned the enterprising Sonia Delaunay to design materials, prints, dresses, scarves, and coats. In 1925 she displayed her wares in collaboration with Jacques Heim at a boutique at the Exhibition of Decorative Arts, published an album of her designs, and became the rage of Paris along with Chanel, Jeanne Lanvin, and others.

No project was too ambitious or improbable for the irrepressible Sonia Delaunay to tackle. In 1925 she planned an entire dining room in simultaneous color, in 1937 she executed large-scale murals for the Railway and Aeronautics pavilions at the International Exhibition, and in 1928 she even embellished the surface of an automobile with her ebullient patterns. Ceramics, tapestries, carpets, even playing-cards were vehicles for her fabulous motifs. Yet even as she dedicated herself to integrating her magical color forms into everyday life, this artist continued to create magnificent works on canvas.

Although Sonia and Robert Delaunay evolved their innovative art forms together, it was only after her husband's death that Sonia's part in this collaboration came to be acknowledged. This oversight can be attributed to both prejudicial social attitudes and to the painter's own reluctance to put herself forward. Happily, today at eighty-nine Sonia Delaunay is still a working artist and is enjoying a richly deserved international reputation for her truly astonishing accomplishment.

CINDY NEMSER   When I look in the art history books—those written up until now—I find there is very little written about women artists. Do you think that this is unfortunate?

SONIA DELAUNAY I'm against women's work being seen apart. I think I work like a man.

C.N. Do you mean that if people know you are a woman artist they tend to say of your work, "it's delicate, it's weak"—things that are not complimentary—whereas if people look at a man's work they say, "it's strong and intellectual"?

S.D. I think it's always people who say stupid things that say this. I don't believe it and I don't think of it.

C.N. Yet respected critics have said that women are not original or innovative. I think at this point it's important for the world to know that there have been women artists who were innovators. For instance, you as much as your husband Robert Delaunay are the originator of an important art movement—of Orphism.

S.D. Yes, but when we first were together I wanted to work quietly because he was very nervous. All my work was done at the same time and independently, but I didn't speak of it because I didn't take it so seriously—though it was quite serious.

C.N. In other words you didn't promote yourself. You didn't tell people what you were doing and therefore they didn't know about your accomplishments.

S.D. Yes. I didn't show—only in a very few exhibitions. Robert began the first. It was quite novel.

C.N. You mean he showed first, but actually you were together in the development of Orphism or simultaneity of colors?

S.D. Yes, the whole time we were together, and I have only begun to be known—because I didn't want to be known. It was my life and I worked the whole time, but I wasn't working—I was living—and that is the difference.

C.N. Isn't that one of the problems of being a woman artist? If you are married to a man who is an artist, you put his career first. You want him to prosper and then you have the tendency to efface yourself—to make yourself less important. Yet I read an account of your influence on your husband in a review by the American Arthur Craven in 1914.* Do you remember Arthur Craven?

S.D. Yes.

C.N. He said that Russian women were very intellectual and that *you* were an intellectual who was stuffing your husband's head full of new

*Arthur Craven, "L'Exposition des Indépendants," *Maintenant,* special issue, March–April 1914.

ideas. He seemed to imply that in the collaboration between you and Robert Delaunay you were the moving force.

S.D.   We were two moving forces. One made one thing and one made the other.

C.N.   Often your work looks very similar.

S.D.   Sometimes, but I was doing them alone. I made my paintings alone.

C.N.   You didn't show your paintings at the same time?

S.D.   No. I began to show twenty years ago.

C.N.   Only twenty years ago? Why did you wait so long?

S.D.   Well, people didn't speak of one of us without the other.

C.N.   You felt if you waited, then your works would be separate?

S.D.   First I didn't feel it was necessary to speak of my art. I made it very much for myself.

C.N.   Really?

S.D.   Yes.

C.N.   All the men were speaking of *their* art. They didn't keep it to themselves, did they? They told everybody about what they were doing. Don't you think it's strange that you didn't want to tell anyone?

S.D.   No. I didn't. Now it's the same.

C.N.   You mean you really don't care if your work is publicized or not?

S.D.   It's strange to me that people should speak of my art—because I *have* to do it. They asked to make an exhibition—there's an exhibition now in Nancy—there are some good pictures there. But I didn't go. I don't care very much.

C.N.   Yet you are pleased to have this big monograph published? [I point to the large book on the table on Sonia Delaunay with a text by Jacques Damase and herself.] Do you feel that in this book your work is being treated in a much more serious way?

S.D.   Yes. It's better. It begins to be better. There will be many other books. And one is coming out at the end of the year, a very big book like this one.

C.N.   The Arthur Cohen book being published by Abrams. Does that book deal fairly with all the accomplishments of your life?

S.D.   I haven't seen what they write. They had many talks with me but I don't know what they write.

C.N.   It seems extraordinary to me that you care so little about being recognized as a great artist. Certainly the men—like Picasso—cared about that.

S.D.   Well they have dealers. I have no dealer. I'm quite free.

C.N.   Sometimes you show at the Gimpel Gallery in New York?

S.D.   Yes.

C.N.   But you don't have a commitment with them?

S.D.   No. Because I want my freedom of thinking and living.

C.N.   You think dealers would stop you from that?

S.D.   Yes.

C.N.   Still, even before they had dealers, the men artists wanted people to write about them, didn't they? Apollinaire wrote about them and others did too.

S.D.   Apollinaire did it because it was conversation and it came out to be so. My husband didn't ask him to write.

C.N.   But he liked the idea?

S.D.   He liked not the idea but the effect of it.

C.N.   The effect?

S.D.   Yes, to speak to change ideas.

C.N.   Wouldn't you want the same?

S.D.   No, not always.

C.N.   Wouldn't you want your work to change people's ideas?

S.D.   It does.

C.N.   When you put an exhibition up people see it and it affects them.

S.D.   But I don't want it. It's a false idea you have—an American idea that artists must be famous. That's an idea of today. Artists form their lives. They don't live because they are thinking of it. And if you have thought enough it comes out. Very young people like me very much. Between me and painting there is nothing.

C.N.   I think it's important that you have always made your art a part of your total everyday life—the way you lived and the way you dressed.

S.D.   It's my life and I felt I needed to design the dresses and things around me.

C.N.   Many people don't seem to understand that. They think that it's less important to make designs for clothing than to do an oil painting. If you do decorative arts—furniture, books, dresses—it's not considered as important as if you do fine art, which is painting or sculpture. How do you feel about that?

S.D. One day you make paintings and one day you make clothing.

C.N. You've designed coverings for furniture and books as well?

S.D. Yes. And I made my furniture. When I have time, I make these things for myself now—but I haven't much time.

C.N. You don't think we should separate these things into categories such as fine arts and decorative arts? You see these things as really together?

S.D. Yes. I think it's all the same. If you are an artist you are doing pictures like you do furniture. You must do what you want and be ready not to sell. You can't be too ambitious for money. Artists are designing furniture today but they don't go at it the right way. They are too intellectual.

C.N. Do you mean the kind of thing that's going on at Documenta 72? It's actually Dada. The same old thing all over again.

S.D. Yes. But when Duchamp made Dada he was real. I went to see his first wife and I saw all the things that were in his house. He made them for his own amusement and people took it seriously. But that was many years after.

C.N. By taking it seriously they made Duchamp into a great celebrity.

S.D. It was his second wife who did that, and she makes money with it. I don't take her seriously. The first wife lived with his things and she liked them. She's free to like them. But the second wife, she made a business with it.

C.N. And your husband Robert, did he design household furnishings too?

S.D. He did nothing.

C.N. You also illustrated that wonderful poem by Blaise Cendrars* about the Trans-Siberian express. Did you like the idea of collaborating with poets?

S.D. Yes.

C.N. Your husband didn't collaborate with the poets did he?

S.D. No. But he was always with us. He loved poetry.

C.N. At this point it seems artists mostly make paintings. Paintings that sit on the wall and are decorations. But when you made a dress and wore it or when you designed a room and lived in it you really

*The Sequence of the Trans-Siberian and Little Joanne of France.

attempted to introduce the arts into the real living world. Do you think you succeeded at that?

S.D.   Yes. I sold many of them. We lived from all of my designs during ten years. I was asked to make prints and I sold many to houses. Then I made them for myself and they served as pictures. People are still living with them now and selling the material prints like paintings.

C.N.   I see. People buy your designs for paintings. But it's still only the well-to-do who have them, isn't it? It seems as if it's impossible to reach out to the larger world with them.

S.D.   No. My prints did more. My materials introduced painting into the home. My materials were like this [pointing to a new painting], but they were made in the form of material prints in the thirties. They copy them now.

C.N.   You don't do material prints anymore?

S.D.   No. Paintings, drawings, and lithographs.

C.N.   When did you make these material prints to sell commercially?

S.D.   After the First World War I had to make money.

C.N.   While you were doing your designing did you do paintings too?

S.D.   Yes.

C.N.   Was that hard for you?

S.D.   No. It was a good discipline. I made the designs and I learned very much.

C.N.   You had to go out into the world?

S.D.   Not very much.

C.N.   But you had to deal with business people?

S.D.   Yes.

C.N.   Were you supporting the family?

S.D.   Sometimes.

C.N.   What did your husband do?

S.D.   He painted.

C.N.   And you supported him. That often happens when both husband and wife are artists. The woman puts her husband's career before hers.

S.D.   It was because we lost all during the war.

C.N.   Yes, but what about your husband? He didn't do designs commercially did he?

S.D.   No. He couldn't speak with those people [shaking her head with low, incredulous laughter at the thought].

C.N.   I think that you were very protective of your husband and that you made it easier for him.

S.D.   No, not at all. I worked for him sometimes. It was quite natural. It is difficult to explain, because we lived—we had no time. We made friends and they loved to look at my work and they helped me. They let me into their houses and soon it became natural.

C.N.   These people bought your designs?

S.D.   Print designs—all the ideas for dresses—and afterward I made dresses.

C.N.   You also did theater sets later on, didn't you?

S.D.   Yes, for the Russian Ballet. For Diaghilev. He was a big friend of ours.

C.N.   You knew so many of the great people of the time. People like Apollinaire and Henri Rousseau. They were good friends of yours, weren't they?

S.D.   Yes and they were like myself and like my husband too—very individual and real artists. They don't think of the things like you say. You are speaking like somebody who writes about artists [laughs]. Artists have no time to make implications.

C.N.   Your husband wrote. He had very complicated theories, didn't he?

S.D.   No. It was not complicated at all—only in his work.

C.N.   But when he wrote about his work and when he spoke about it many people didn't understand him. When one reads a book about Robert Delaunay, such as this one by Gustav Vriesen and Max Imdahl, the authors go on at great length to explain his complicated theories.

S.D.   It was complicated in his head and he tried to make it simple and to understand what he wanted to say. But I have no such problems.

C.N.   That's interesting that your husband felt the necessity to tell people about his work, to explain it, and you didn't.

S.D.   Robert was not secure at all.

C.N.   Do you think that's why he wanted to explain?

S.D.   Yes.

C.N.   But you knew exactly what you wanted to do?

S.D.   Yes. If you play at something you don't think why you do it.

C.N.   I read that you and your husband went to the museums together to look at ancient works. Did you study the colors of the ancients—the Egyptians?

S.D.   Yes. But I really knew color through my work.

C.N.   You mean it comes out of your experience?

S.D.   Yes.

C.N.   And it's a kind of experiment?

S.D.   Experiment? No. It's more and more work. I make another work and so forth.

C.N.   Your work went back and forth from abstraction to recognizable images. Did you do that intentionally?

S.D.   I don't know. When I make these things up I *need* to make them. I don't think of it.

C.N.   I think of your abstractions as a kind of force, a universal force, a kind of energy of light and color.

S.D.   Yes. But it is more simple than people make it.

C.N.   Do you think people like to complicate things?

S.D.   They are too complicated and too intellectual. The very young people like me very much. Children like me. It's a big compliment.

C.N.   And all during these years you continued to work in your own way and developed the ideas you began with. Sometimes it seems as if your works have become simpler, more pared down. It seems as if the edges become sharper.

S.D.   I can't tell you this, it is not thought out.

C.N.   It strikes me, however, that you always knew just what you wanted to do.

S.D.   Yes.

C.N.   You were from a very good Russian family, weren't you?

S.D.   Yes.

C.N.   Was it customary for Russian girls to go and be artists and come to Paris by themselves?

S.D.   I think everyone makes his life.

C.N.   Your parents didn't mind?

S.D.   No. They helped me. They were very good people and they placed me in a good house with nice people in Paris.

C.N.   It was also extraordinary that you were married to someone else, to the dealer Wilhelm Uhde, before you met Robert Delaunay. And when you realized that you and Robert needed to be together, you just went ahead and asked your first husband for a divorce.

S.D.   Yes.

C.N.   I think you are a very unusual woman. So far the women artists I have interviewed have all been very unusual. I was in England and I went to see Barbara Hepworth the sculptor.

S.D.   Yes. I like her work. I have a sculpture of hers.

C.N.   She's a wonderful woman who's had a very hard life. In certain ways there is a close resemblance between you two. She also married twice and worked very closely with her second husband, Ben Nicholson. There's a resemblance in your personalities in the way that you work and think. She said that being married and having a family was an important thing for her. You feel that way about your child too, don't you?

S.D.   Yes.

C.N.   You also ran a large household?

S.D.   Well, you arrange these things.

C.N.   How about other women artists of the time? Was Marie Laurencin taken seriously as an artist?

S.D.   No. Well, she took herself seriously.

C.N.   Nobody else did?

S.D.   Some society people—but not the artists.

C.N.   Do you think she was a good artist?

S.D.   When she was with Apollinaire he gave her some ideas and she made some things.

C.N.   Do you think he's the one that gets the credit?

S.D.   Yes.

C.N.   You don't think she had talent?

S.D.   Well, she was modern. I think there will be nothing left.

C.N.   You think she was a social butterfly?

S.D.   Yes.

C.N.   I think there is value in her work.

S.D.   I hate it!

C.N.   The artists, the men artists, did treat *you* as an equal? When you spoke, they listened?

S.D.   Yes.

C.N.   And they considered you one of them?

S.D.   Yes. I was taken seriously because I didn't say stupid things.

C.N.   Yet there are women who are quite intelligent whom I have met and they have found it very difficult to be taken seriously. They have difficulty getting money to do projects. Women sculptors in particular have a very hard time and women artists have trouble getting galleries and museums to show their work. Even *you* haven't had a retrospective in New York.

S.D.   Well I had one in Paris, in Germany, and in Portugal.

C.N.   Do you see lots of people nowadays?

S.D.   No. Now nobody. The less I see the better I am.

C.N.   I guess it's difficult for you and tiring.

S.D.   Tiring and then the people don't say much now. They speak only of money.

C.N.   I was reading Roger Shattock's *The Banquet Years.* He describes life in Paris up until World War I. It seemed that people really enjoyed themselves then. They were a community of artists and they seemed so full of life and vitality and interest. Now we are looking for that kind of a world but we can't find it anywhere.

S.D.   Yes, before it was quite different. It was good. We never spoke of money and business.

C.N.   Did you know Gertrude and Leo Stein? Did you go to her house?

S.D.   Oh yes, my husband liked to speak with her. I, never.

C.N.   Why not you?

S.D.   Well, it was not necessary.

C.N.   I also remember reading that Apollinaire was accused of stealing the Mona Lisa and only you and Robert stood by him.

S.D.   My husband backed him.

C.N.   And you and your husband helped raise money for a grave for Henri Rousseau. It's amazing to think that you have known all those historic people and were a part of all that. Do you feel you are living in another world now?

S.D.   Yes, a poor world.

C.N.   Do you ever see any young people nowadays?

S.D.   No. I have no time. But the very young have the same ideas I do.

C.N.   And do you work everyday?

S.D.   Yes. One hour—two hours—the whole day. It depends, but I don't think of it as work. I prefer that to other things. That's my pleasure.

Embroidery, Foliage, 1909.

Le Bal Ballier, 1913.

Flamenco Singers, Opus #145, 1916.

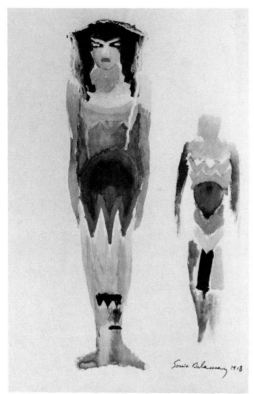

Study for the Decor of the Dining Room of the Boulevard Malesherbes Flat, 1924.

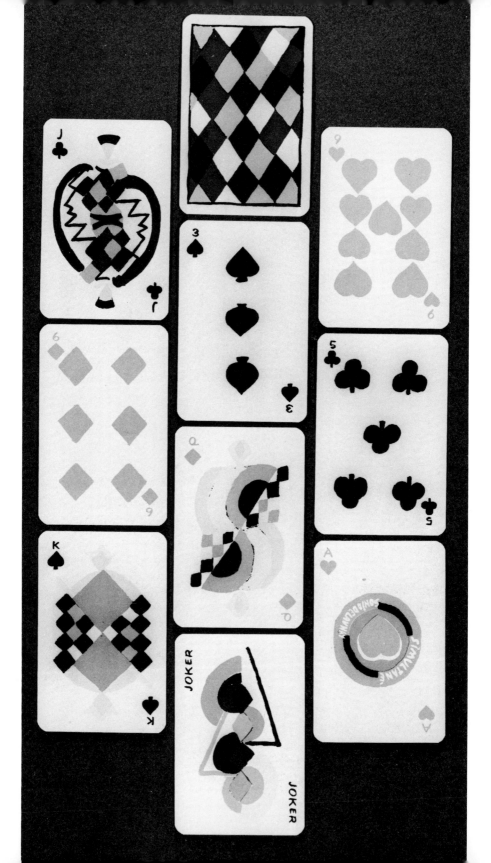

Textile Design, 1925.

Tapestry, 1970.

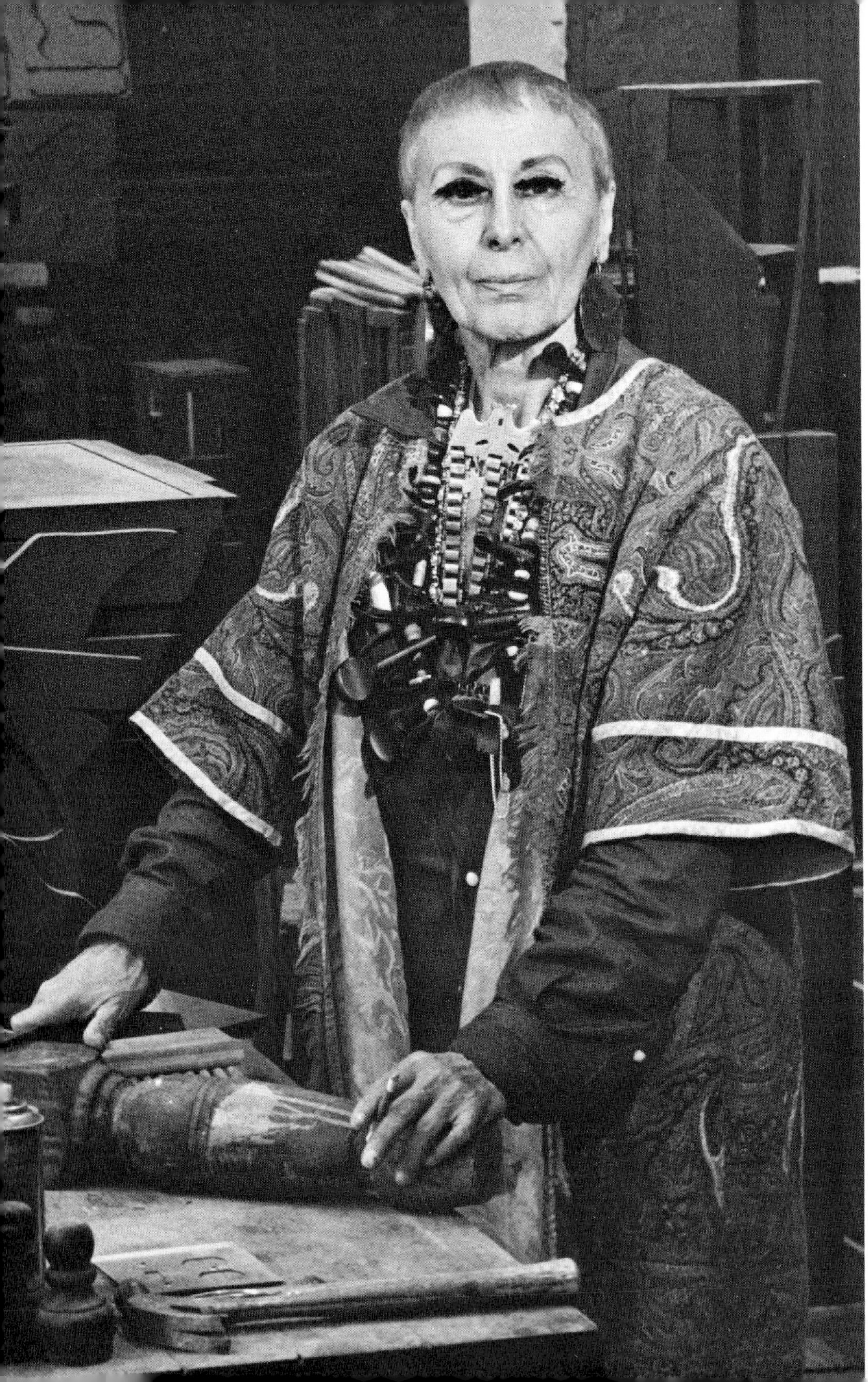

Louise Nevelson, 1972.

LOUISE NEVELSON was born in 1899 in Kiev, Russia, and was raised in Rockland, Maine. At the age of twenty-one she married Charles Nevelson and moved to New York City. Two years later she had a son, Mike, who today is a sculptor. Always believing that she was destined to fulfill herself as an artist, Nevelson studied all the arts during her married life which came to an end in 1931.

Next she went to Europe to study with the already famous art teacher Hans Hofmann and earned her keep as an extra in films in Berlin and Vienna. Disappointed with Hofmann's teaching, Nevelson returned to New York in 1932 to find Hofmann, who was forced out of Germany by the Nazis, holding forth at the Art Students League. She decided to study with him again and in his class she formed a friendship with the actress and painter Majorie Easton, who introduced her to the great Mexican muralist Diego Rivera and his equally gifted wife, the painter Frieda Kahlo. Nevelson became one of Rivera's assistants, although little besides the scale of his art influenced her mature development.

During the thirties and forties Nevelson struggled in impoverished isolation to continue to exist as an artist. She was on the Works Progress Administration for a short stretch, sold her jewels piece by piece, and lived on the money sent to her by her family. At this time she worked with clay, stone, and plaster, occasionally doing a bronze casting. Out of these materials she formed small anthropomorphic Cubist forms.

In 1942 she had her first one-woman exhibition at the prestigious Nierendorf Gallery in New York. Then in 1943 the artist exhibited a menagerie of animals and performers called *The Circus* made out of wood and metal and tacked together in Cubist collage fashion. These individual pieces all relating to a central theme were Nevelson's first intentional environment. It was also the beginning of her assemblages of mixed media—wood, metal and fabric—along with "found objects." Influenced by the European artists Masson, Matta, and Ernst who came to America in the forties, Nevelson brought to Cubist assemblage the Surrealist and Dadaist methods of chance meetings and spontaneous discoveries.

When Nierendorf died in 1948 Nevelson was once more cast adrift and began making totemic-like forms in clay. She also made some essays into stone sculpture but found the laborious carving and polishing process an unsatisfactory experience. Preferring to assert surface and frontality in her art, she turned to etching and in 1947 studied with the English artist Stanley William Hayter. In 1953 she turned the etching process to her own use, creating a series of original aquatints by etching lace and rag imprints into the copper plates.

In 1950 Nevelson visited Mexico and Yucatan, and the monumental steles which she saw there and at the American Museum of Natural History in New York were the final catalysts in the production of her own monumental environmental assemblages. In a one-woman show at the Grand Central Moderns Gallery in 1955, entitled *Ancient Places, Ancient Games,* many of the sculptures became indistinguishable from the base. To quote Arnold Glimcher, Nevelson's current dealer and the author of her monograph, "They were standing together like miniature Stonehenges."

From this period on, Nevelson's production rate became phenomenal. All sorts of "found objects"—milk boxes, lettuce crates, balustrades, hat forms, toilet seats, anything that came to hand—were painted black, white, or gold to erase their former identity and then commandeered into the service of her majestic vision. Great tableaux such as *Moon Garden Plus One* (1958), *Sky Columns Presence* (1959), *Tide I Tide* (1963), and *Homage 6,000,000* (1964), all painted black, created mysterious totalities filled with intriguing crevices and extrusions which drew the viewer into hundreds of shadowy three-dimensional plays. In contrast, the magnificent *Dawn's Wedding Feast,* which was shown at the Museum of Modern Art in 1959, was painted all in white, in an attempt to bring the mystery of creation out into the open. Composed of individual pieces which make up the entire ritual —the wedding chapel, the cake, the bride's mirror, etc.—the entire construction places the viewer in the center of the myth of innocence and unity where all is light and joy. The glowing surface of the resplendent *Sun Garden I* (1964), one of a number of gold-painted tableaux, conjures up visions of great Pre-Columbian palaces and temples.

Over the years the artist's work has alternated between an austere, classical presentation, composed primarily of pre-cut geometric forms, and assemblages of her favorite "found objects" connected in the most extravagantly Baroque fashion. Ever willing to explore new materials the artist has utilized Plexiglas, aluminum, enamel and Corten steel during the last ten years.

Nevelson has spent her life creating her own mysterious world of subtle contrasts and evocative relationships. Like her work, this artist is a complex mixture of contrasting elements. Flamboyant yet shy, imperious yet timid, idealistic yet practical, Nevelson is constructed physically and emotionally on a grand scale. Above all she is courageous, capable of throwing caution to the winds when her sense of injustice is aroused. Selfish in the most Emersonian sense of the word, she sums up the central goal of her life thus: "My interest is to reveal to myself the greatest possibility of life."

CINDY NEMSER   In an article written about you in the *New York Times* you said that you invented the concept of the environment.

LOUISE NEVELSON   I don't call it invented. It was a natural thing for me because I was doing it all my life. So it wasn't invention, it was an unfolding.

C.N.   In that article you described how you felt as a child. It seemed to me that you must have experienced the world as chaotic and threatening. It also seemed to me that you have taken this chaotic world and restructured it—given it an order.

L.N.   Well, the first part of your statement isn't quite the way I would say it. The last part is just the way I would say it.

C.N.   Even the way you live—you have made a whole world for yourself.

L.N.   That is true. Now, you see, we're public people, and I go out and I love people. Nevertheless, in my being I am a private person and live that way. I have lived, so-called, alone many, many years, almost all my adult life.

C.N.   That seems to be the condition of the artist in our society.

L.N.   I think it would be the condition of a being in any society. If you are going to spend your life, your total life, you cannot make compromises.

C.N.   And ultimately one is alone.

L.N.   One is alone of course, but even in daily living to have intrusions on the mind and awareness means that you are not finding your total being. Intrusions are like splinters. You have this hand, but if you have one small splinter in it, you can't function.

C.N.   It's true, but it's very difficult to keep those splinters out.

L.N.   Well, I don't think it's more difficult than having someone intrude on you all the time.

C.N.   I'm very interested in the way art relates to the culture—how the artist is expressing the culture in the work that she or he does. I think your work is extremely expressive of our time but most artists don't consciously say, "I'm going to express the culture that is around me." How do you feel about that?

L.N.   Naturally, the artist is a mirror for his time, and the times are a mirror for the artist. Consequently, you have to be expressing your time as you are alive and living in it. You can make the greatest work of art, and the greatest painting that has ever been painted, and if it is not in your time, who cares? It's not even valid. For me the culture, the physical or the visual world, is the mirror of my awareness.

C.N.   Yes, and you take the bits and pieces, the castoffs, the fragments of our society, which in themselves say something about our society, and you put them all together again in a new kind of order.

L.N.   Now I read the article in the Sunday *Times* on Genêt. I certainly have the greatest respect for him because he reversed things—it's like a piece of velvet and he turns it over and uses the inside. *Nevertheless,* he still is, for my kind of thinking, caught in the path of opposites: good and bad, black and white. I feel, for my kind of thinking and for my comfort, that I need a place where it's *one.* I don't need the paradoxes on any level and I don't even choose to make that distinction. It's like the difference between burning and white heat—where there is the degree of white heat, you see nothing. Or take an automobile—if it's going fast, you can't see the spokes, you just see a PHOOOMMM . . . where if it's going slowly, you can count every one of those spokes. So the person who wants to express something will cause a shift too. I like to think that where I am has all the intensity, the light, the speed, and the white heat that will burn you in a second. But it seems as if that is still, the final thing is quiet. That doesn't mean death; that means total life—no intrusions.

C.N.   The Zen ideal. You go up on the mountain and experience total enlightenment, and when you come down, you see everything is really totally a part of the whole, even though there are all these fragments.

L.N.   I haven't gone into Zen. I've never considered myself a student and I don't want to study *anything.* I don't want to *make* anything— that isn't where my interests lie. Where my true interest lies, is in myself, and to reveal to myself the greatest possibility of life.

C.N.   That would be the highest goal.

L.N.   Yes, but I feel that that is my true heritage. I'm willing to give my life for it. You're supposed to tap it somewhere, and I've tapped it enough for my kind of awareness. If one had a voltage of awareness, say, like those great geniuses Beethoven or Picasso, their awareness, their demand, then the objective would be what they have *done.* Mine will be what I have *done.* We are limited. But I don't want to reach for what they've done—that is their reflection. I might like to sing like Caruso, but that isn't my role and I don't want to imitate Caruso. I'm only doing the mirror of my own reflection.

56

C.N.   I used to read Emerson and he talks about each person having their own particular wonderful thing, their own potential. It's as if we're each a seed and it has to open up and develop in its own way. Each thing grows separately, and yet each thing is very much part of the total.

L.N.   You know, it's very interesting, because if you speak like this, people who are not aware of things think you are high and mighty or they think you are a little insane. But that is all in stupidity.

C.N.   To get into a more specific area, I understand that now you're working in metals and you're doing large pieces which will be outdoors. Evidently, most of your work has been for indoors. It seems to me as if you're reaching out into new areas by putting your work *outside* where it's more available. Did you think about that when you decided to do these large sculptural pieces?

L.N.   No, I didn't. Now I would really love to see the large pieces in a big public building indoors, where there are enclosures. I think putting a sculpture outdoors, which I'm doing, is a kind of carry-over, it's a romantic concept. I think that even those big, big pieces of mine would look magnificent indoors. A collector bought one of those great big things, we call them the *Trees,* for her garden, it's a penthouse with a patio on Park Avenue, and I said, "Please don't put it there. Take it and put it in the center of your living room and you will have a setting." She's intelligent and has an enormous layout, so she did that, and it changed her whole life. We make too much of that indoor-outdoor. Where is that palace in France?

C.N.   Versailles?

L.N.   Yes. Well, they have formal gardens; they give nature a structure. They don't let nature go wild—then I like it.

C.N.   I see, you always aim toward structure.

L.N.   One of our great sculptors had a show in the southern part of France. That work was beautiful, but it was spread all over the garden and you got the feeling of chaos. If I were to be invited to show there, I would have platforms built and then I would have plants in back of them, so that each piece would have its presence and would not be lost.

C.N.   Yes because when it's in nature it's without a structure.

L.N.   It's romantic and it's lost.

C.N.   A friend of mine who is an artist said for him art was a way to stave off the chaotic, to escape the terribleness of existence. He felt everything that an artist did was a response to this terrible sense of a void, a means of creating something that would protect him from this chaotic experience of the world. It's a kind of necessity out of fear.

L.N. I don't think it's a frightening experience. I think it's a whopping experience. But naturally we re-translate language because man needs language but we use it in the past sense. For instance, the romantic concept was that art is beautiful and that the artist is trying to make a masterpiece. You know, when I hear that it makes me sick. I don't demand that all work be a masterpiece. I think what I'm doing is the right thing for me—that is what I am and this is living. It reflects me and I reflect it.

Now you don't expect every child to be a master or a genius—who would want it—I think the concept is insanity. We're living and we are doing what we understand. We walk on two feet, we're vertical; we lie down, we're horizontal. Those are the two opposites. And if you go back to Emerson, you know that in between the eyes is the "I." All right, then comes Freud and he calls it the ego. Well, what's wrong with the ego? When anybody comes to me and says, "You're selfish," I'm so happy. I wish they would say, "You're the most selfish person on earth."

Look, darling, I didn't give birth to myself and you inherit a lot of stuff right on your back from birth. You're given a load of shit at birth. Now I don't want to inherit: I want to choose my life and build it to suit me. I have a theory for myself that everyone has a certain extension where they would like space. Some need more and some need less. It's the same with wealth. We have a yardstick. We can handle a certain amount, beyond that we go nuts. Some can handle a billion times more than others and they don't go nuts. Others go nuts if they *don't* have it. So you see, we have measurements within ourselves.

To go back to the work, I don't demand of it and I never did demand. I *hate* the word *intellectual*—that offends me. And I'll tell you another word that is poison for me, and that is *logic.* What has that got to do with life? You'd better use a yardstick. Well, why should we reduce or measure or take the time to measure? We're breathing. You don't measure your breathing and you don't stop your breathing. Life is life.

C.N. What about the idea of making qualitative judgments? In order to exist we make judgments all the time. We can't help that. It's true that every person does what he or she can, but still we say that some people do it better than others.

L.N. I don't know what you're talking about. Of course we make judgments—from the time you open your eyes in the morning until you go to bed. You cross the street, you're not going to have an automobile come and kill you. Not to go is a judgment. But that's a different judgment than the great intellectual judgments and that other word that I used that I don't like . . .

C.N.   Logic!

L.N.   Logic, where you ponder and, oh dear, it sounds so fancy—what in the hell do you need it for? It measures you and limits you. See now, take a word like imagination. What does imagination mean? Imagination means you've got it in a thinking moment. That's thinking. But why do you have to go through and take steps and steps and steps. If you walk to Bonwit Tellers you'd walk for a week. But now we have things that carry us. Well, we wouldn't have things that carry us unless there were people on earth that are already aware of them. They have given us the vehicles.

Imagination is not vague. Imagination is flash thinking, instantaneous. Now, happiness, what does happiness mean? I think that anyone who aspires to be happy is crazy. I think on earth you open your eyes in one fleeting second, and when you do this around the world and see the prisons and the dens and the dope and poverty . . . No! I can't conceive of anyone even aspiring to be happy.

C.N.   Well, it's a concept that you can't really pin down.

L.N.   That's right. It has no meaning. It has no validity. And I think that the sooner that language really re-structures itself and doesn't use those words the better we'll be. Suppose you are aiming for happiness and you define it; it can ruin your life. "I want this . . . I want that . . . I need this . . . and you give your whole life to it. You *pitch* your life to that goal and the rest of the things that come into your life, which could have meaning, are meaningless.

C.N.   Yet in terms of your own career, you've had many disappointments and hardships.

L.N.   I don't say that. You're saying it.

C.N.   Well, okay, you don't think you had any.

L.N.   Well, I didn't think like that. Of course, I wanted to cut my throat for maybe forty years, but I didn't. I didn't want to take one minute out of my time to not claim it. If I wanted to throw it away, I claimed it anyway. Someone didn't pull me out. Or if I chose to agree with someone, that was my motivation. When you are born a little ahead of your time—you're born in your time—but most people are living on different levels. We know that marriage, as we understand it, is hideous. Yet everyday you pick up the paper and everyone is getting married. So are they living in their times or aren't they? Some move faster in their time and some never move at all.

C.N.   I understand that very well. But sometimes when one is out of step with the times or feels that the culture needs to be changed or to be re-created, you have to fight to do that, you have to make an effort. When there are injustices you try to change them—even if they will always exist, you still have to try. It isn't always possible to accept what is. I want to get into the question of being a woman artist. Now you are a great woman artist and you were creating in a time when there was great prejudice toward women. Were you able to accept this? Were you able to live with it? Did you try to change it? Did you fight against it?

L.N.   Let me explain. From my earliest days, from four and a half, every teacher I had, knew that I was gifted. That gave me my *terra firma.* People, if you speak to them will say, "How arrogant she is, she's so sure." I've heard this. I'm not at all arrogant. When you see a thing and you recognize that that's yours, you know if it's within you. You have to have the equipment. Take a dancer. A dancer has to have the equipment of a body, a physical body, to manifest its fulfillment. Now, in what we call art, you have to have the equipment. You can run things, but you can't learn the well of life because you have to be born with that—that's your heritage. I am as sure as every breath I take, that that is my heritage. On earth, we humans live where we can afford— that isn't where we want to live. We eat what we can afford—that isn't what we want to eat. We marry whom we can get—not the ones we want to marry. And so, we are every day adjusting to placement. I had determined, very early in life, that I didn't want second best or below. I wanted something to reflect me and what I was aware of totally. And that's what I did, but I knew I had the price to pay.

C.N.   Yes, the price.

L.N.   I had the energy. I think sometimes we really generate our own energy to fulfill this.

C.N.   But you as a woman artist had a greater price to pay.

L.N.   All right, but many men artists don't have the equipment to pay what I did. So, for me, living in a man's world was difficult, because we ourselves were conditioned. If we were ill, we'd get a man doctor, if we needed legal advice, we went to a man. We felt their physical brawn was our support. I recognized that, but I also felt that men were no challenge to me personally.

C.N.   Yet, you are a great supporter of women's liberation.

L.N.   Of course, because I *am* a woman's liberation. But that doesn't annihilate anything, just because I was aware of this. I felt I could handle *myself,* but as a body in the universe, I think one has to take a stand. Now another thing is, I feel totally female. I didn't compete with men, and I don't want to look like a man! I love being a lady and dressing up and masquerading and wearing all the fineries. I'm breaking down the idea that the artist has to look poor, with berets. I think that artists should have anything they want. If you have studied anything, you know goddam well that we don't make price tag imagery. We should take and wear what we like, and not, "I can't wear this, I can't wear that," or "what'll she say, what won't she say." I just got myself a chinchilla. So fuck 'um. Yes, the fur's on the outside. I like fun, and I like men. I've always enjoyed them and I also enjoy women. But what I mean is *leave* men where they are, *leave* women where they are. The point is that men are as enslaved as women are and it's only after they recognize it that they *too* will be free. Human beings, every individual, has the hope of their life. If they have the organs of a female, let them be totally that. If they have the organs of a male, let them be that. Once you become aware and free, you will give freedom to somebody else.

C.N.   It seems to me that you have a great deal to offer other women artists, young women who are aspiring. After all, there have been people who have been gifted and have fallen by the wayside because, for one reason or another, they didn't have the support; they didn't have the confidence.

L.N.   That is the flaw within those people. They hadn't the confidence. You see, a gift is not enough, a gift has to be supported. We are like a building. You can put up the most beautiful building in the world, but if it hasn't the structure to hold it up, it collapses. I feel that it's a flaw within people that they don't *dare* to take what belongs to them—that total true heritage.

C.N.   Sometimes the barriers are so great!

L.N.   I'll tell you what I think. I've taught, and the first thing I did when I taught art, was not to teach art. I taught the students to clean their minds, to take that mind and polish it daily, to throw out what they don't need and not to clutter it. Don't remember every telephone number, don't remember every address, don't remember every name. Keep it open and keep it empty, so that when you see something, you see it totally. Don't go around with a bunch of things in your head that you don't need. The richest people in the world drive those big cars with chauffeurs and all and they never carry anything. But go down here at the Bowery and the poor men and the poor women, particularly, always have bags of rags and bags of things. Somehow it supports their nothingness. You see it in the reverse. The mind is the same.

C.N.   The richer you are, the less you need.

L.N. Exactly, the richer you are the less the mind needs to carry so much. It's the carrying that breaks us down over this and that hurt and all those everyday contacts. It is true that every religion and all institutions give us formulas—formulas. Be modest. Be puritan. Be—ugh—clean. All these things. And we get caught in them. But people that come to the surface see through it and cut through it. They don't permit these teachings to load them down. That's what I meant earlier about language. You get *caught* all your life in a phrase or two which is *deadening.* That's in prison! Physically a prison has bars. We have our animals in bars, even at Central Park or anywhere. Some day we are hoping to do away with that. But people who haven't conformed on a certain level are put behind bars—we reduce them to animals. But we humans, through our awareness, free ourselves. We clean out.

C.N. Very often we need others to guide us.

L.N. Oh yes! that's right.

C.N. Mostly by the example that they set.

L.N. Well, yes, but also by what they want themselves, and it isn't easy. But when I think that living a life to conform to everything is dead—so who needs that? So you deaden everything and you have no more desires—you're like a robot. Where you really understand, of course, you'll pay a price. But, it seems to me, that that's a dear, *delightful* thing to do even if it kills us—because the other is death anyway.

C.N. And you really went ahead and did what you had to do.

L.N. You bet your sweet life. I didn't ever give myself credit for whether I'm bright or not bright—that doesn't interest me. But the young people have begun to call me *Mother Courage* and I accept it, because I got very curious about life. I wanted to live life and I didn't want to restrict it. I wanted totality—what life is all about—and I threw myself into it.

C.N. But when you talk about art having a gender, do you look at it in an objective way? When I look at works of art, I can't tell the sex of the person that did it. Do you think that you can do that?

L.N. No, I can't do it, and I don't think it matters. I'm prolific, you know, because I don't demand perfection, and I feel that the doing of it is where I'm living, not looking and hunting for something. Consequently, I feel that my work is very powerful, and therefore people might think it's a man's work. Well, don't you think that's a false premise? I feel that women *and men,* but I mean the *individual,* can be totally feminine and still be totally powerful. But I do feel my work is feminine. I don't think any man would ever execute work as I do. For instance, I take a scissors and cut certain woods. I've never heard of a man doing that—a man would know the mechanics. I have less tools than anyone in the world. I'm *primitive* that way, but that's probably what gave me what I have.

C.N.   And yet there are male artists who are using stitchery and sewing and so on.

L.N.   Well, that's all right! Who said it belonged to females?

C.N.   A man could take a scissors too.

L.N.   He would now. Now, you see, it's freed itself, but I'm talking about when I did it, maybe thirty years ago. Or, if I wanted, bent wood, I'd get some wood and put it in my bathtub and let the water in there. I didn't know what would happen. Since then, I've learned that it has been done—but I didn't know—I just instinctively did these things.

C.N.   But would you say that that really should be attributed to your femaleness, or maybe it's the total *you*?

L.N.   Exactly! I feel that in my being there's a bit of originality. What does that mean, *originality*? Away from the norm? I don't mean that. I mean that's where *Mother Courage* comes in—I'll try it! Before I read a book or telephone to find out, I'll try something immediately. That's why I produce so much—usually you can make things work. For instance, I'll find a piece of wood with nails in it and I'll use it. Now one day, many years ago, I said, "Well since I like these nails that are in wood, I'll do it." So I hammered them into a piece of wood. It became so *self-conscious* and regimented; I couldn't use it. You see, I *recognize* this and this. Now, to go back to the concept of male, female. No matter how we will meet, male-female, we mustn't want men to be women or women to be men. They must be what they are. But in thinking and developing, they will be free! Freedom, we need.

C.N.   It seems to me that the supposed attributes of male-female are really universal attributes and that women have all the qualities that men have and vice versa. We are all male and female together.

L.N.   Of course, but I do feel, as I said, that my work is feminine. I can't conceive of it being anything else, because I feel so feminine. How could I want to do anything but mirror myself?

C.N.   What do you mean by feminine?

L.N.   When I say *feminine,* I don't want to superimpose out of my shell. For instance, when I speak to people, male or female, I speak to them pretty much the same, if they have the capacity to communicate with me. I don't make this distinction and that distinction. Where a woman knows a person—knows that totality—and that person knows her, they meet and they may even almost neutralize each other.

What I think we have to recognize, as we've already said, is that we were educated all wrong—to be puritan, and to bow to the elders, and to never offend another person. For Christ's sake, if you do all that, there is nothing left of you.

C.N.   That's true. But now, let's take a specific incident. I was outraged at the exhibition that Henry Geldzahler put on because he set up a certain premise and he . . .

L.N.   He didn't include me! Henry Geldzahler had a profile in the *New Yorker* about six weeks ago and he came out and said that Greenberg is the greatest critic of our time and that he looks to Greenberg for his analysis. He trusts Greenberg. It was a very interesting article because while the author praised, he tore. He called Greenberg and his group the Jewish Mafia. He said how Greenberg has established, in painting, a little Mafia group. There's Michael Fried at Harvard, where he holds seminars, and there's that girl—what's her name—Rosalind . . .

C.N.   Krauss.

L.N.   Yes. Now, I have never met Michael Fried, nor have I ever met Rosalind Krauss, but let me tell you what happened. I have collectors, and their children go to Harvard—I could say almost a dozen young people, who are very *bright*. They wanted to write their theses on me. Well, Michael Fried telephones Greenberg every day, and Greenberg calls up Michael Fried every day. So Fried says to the students, "Why do you want to write a thesis on *her?*" Now, I've never met the man, so it isn't *personal;* I have never met this Krauss, but the same thing happened. These people have studied and they want to write a thesis and Krauss says, "*What* do you want to write a thesis on *her* for?" Now, I tell you candidly, that at my age—I'm past seventy, I'm a great-grandmother—I'm not going to get excited over that. I have made a reputation.

C.N.   And what's exciting is that you have surfaced without them.

L.N.   Not only that, but not even David Smith, Rothko, de Kooning nor any of my good friends, have the reputation that I have in Europe—and in Japan. I have an international reputation. When I say that, dear, I don't want you to think that I am boasting about myself. I am only saying that my mind is a bit more universal—it isn't chauvinistic, it isn't local, it is universal—and so they recognize it. Actually, I was recognized in Europe long before I was in America and I'm in all the museums from all the countries—I don't even know where I am. And I mentioned it because I don't want to fight Greenberg. I'm too old! And I don't want to fight Henry Geldzahler. I don't want to fight anyone because I'm still the creator sitting on my arse and they're only critics that I don't respect. Now that's true, I have called my shots on earth. I have had a blueprint on my life and that's why I am positive about it. Now you can see that I'm a bit shy and I can get hurt by dropping a handkerchief—I can croak or something—but where my creation is, I am totally one piece. When they didn't include me, I didn't even know. I don't know half of the places I'm in. So someone says, "You know Louise, you're not included." So I called my gallery and I spoke to Fred Mueller, and I said, "Fred, I hear I'm not included at the Met." And he said, "Yes." I said, "How long have you known this?" And he said, "Several months," and he was so apologetic. I said, "Oh look sweetie, I'm older than you are. I've been around. I'll get more publicity out of this." And it happened.

C.N.   By excluding you Geldzahler pinpointed the discrimination which exists not only against women, but against any artist who is not of the Greenberg persuasion. You became a *cause célèbre.*

L.N.   Today we received a magazine, *Artforum,* and it's "Greenberg said, and Greenberg said." And it's photographs of Morris Louis whose hand Greenberg held to paint his pictures. Then there's Noland—it's a whole magazine about Noland and Olitsky. He's been pounding the balls off those boys since he got hold of them.

C.N.   You mean that he tells them what to do?

L.N.   He holds the brush that paints the picture.

C.N.   Don't you feel sorry for them?

L.N.   To hell with them! When I saw Noland get a prize from Brandeis, some time ago, Greenberg was there—he walked like a puppy dog behind him. Now wait, now wait, there's a gallery in Toronto, Mirvish, and they came to New York and cultivated me through my gallery and we had a show there. The next year the calendar came in this form—Olitski, Louis, and Frankenthaler and the gang—and I'm not in it. I didn't give a *shit* about that. That's fine with me, because I don't want to join anybody.

I'm a soloist, I'm on my two feet, and I got *good,* big feet. So here I am. But look at it. You go to London and you know, Greenberg is a king, the great authority, people are afraid all over the world. Now if I had been caught in any of that, I'd have been finished. I saw through them and they don't interest me. You say, well, don't they harm you? I think they do. I'd like to sue Harvard for having Michael Fried as a puppet for Greenberg. I'd like to take a gun and shoot that other little snot-nose up there for calling Greenberg every minute. "Can I write," and "Can't I write?" Hasn't she got a brain of her own? Hasn't she even got an ear of her own? But what I'm telling you is this: sure, they undermined me.

Now, at the moment they are what you call underground, but that doesn't mean that they're dead. Why should I, one woman, undertake to fight those monsters? I'd rather go into a bear's den. But I can't accept them anyway—though I'm past seventy and my career's set. But I feel that it is so undemocratic. And I think that it is choking creativity. I've always been independent from childhood and I would never accept, in any walk of my life, that kind of a performance.

C.N.   It can't last.

L.N.   *Can't last!* It's been lasting! The government sends these monsters to lecture. Look at what little Henry did in Washington—give prizes. The thing is, that this is more deadly than a bomb. When you take the spirit from people, the creative spirit, what are you going to have?

C.N.   Puppets, robots. Well, it's time to start fighting back.

L.N.   Yes, but Greenberg, Michael Fried, Krauss, hold the power. They have had the power for maybe a dozen years. I've never met these people, but they teach seminars. They have power—just like the Mafia. I think it has to be fought, and I can't understand why the art world, as a body, has permitted this Mafia to thrive.

C.N.   I think it's largely a question of the artist's position which is very shaky, very tenuous. So artists have given up their autonomy to a large degree, and they have delegated it to these people who speak well. They think they are good salesmen, and that's really where it's at.

L.N.   And at a good percentage. Now look. A friend of mine, Edward Paolozzi, wrote me a letter and said, "Anthony Caro is going to America and would you see him?" and I said, "Yes." So they came to this country, he and his wife, and I invited them for dinner because of Edward. Caro brought photographs of his work, and they were fat, ugly women—that was his sculpture. And so we became acquainted. The next day, he met Greenberg and David Smith. They put him in Bennington to teach so he made a living right away and the next day he was making those sculptures that he does today. Now, no mind can be transformed in twenty minutes. So I have no use for Anthony Caro even though he may be a great one in London with his stuff. Greenberg put him there and he took off. But Greenberg and his friends, they're a dangerous bunch.

C.N.   Everybody's been afraid to do it. Things are changing now. But it's going to take a while.

L.N.   I don't think it should take a while. It should come out in the open, but you, me, we're not enough! If people would support us.

C.N.   I think it's happening, I really do, it's just that the art world is scared. They're really frightened little people. But our whole society is changing. Our kids, especially, are rocking the boat and there is no way to stop them. You can't keep people quiet anymore. There are artists who have been ignored because they didn't fit into the mold; they're angry—everybody's angry and they've had it. Who are these people to tell us what we have to do and what we have to think? It's a much more democratic thing that is beginning to happen. It's a surge that's coming through. I write for *Arts Magazine;* they are changing their policy. The *Feminist Art Journal* will help do it. We don't give a damn. We're underground. There are possibilities. You know, most of us have had it!

L.N.   But look, let me explain what Harold Rosenberg did. When we were in Mexico this lovely, noted, beautiful young woman sculptor—she's the head of the museum too—gave a dinner. I had seen a poster in the museum because Mexico paid Harold, I don't know, a thousand or two, to select five of our noted painters and sculptors to have a show in the museum—which he did. He picked out de Kooning, from the Hamptons, which was wonderful, and then David Hare, who no one knows about anymore, and a few others. I said to the museum director, "Couldn't he have done better since you paid a couple of thousand dollars and he came to lecture and all?" She answered, "Well, I must say, Mrs. Nevelson, since you're having dinner at my home, I was disappointed you weren't in it." She might have said it for gracious-ness, that can happen, so I said, "Fine." When I got back, at some party, I said, "Harold, I saw who you selected for your show in Mexico. Aren't there any greater artists than David Hare? I mean he's a forgotten man."

C.N.   Well, they don't care. It's art politics. It's who you know. It's washing each others' hands. It's a little group. But you know there's a great Unwashed which is coming together. There is an insurrection taking place now.

L.N.   And it's necessary.

C.N.   It's got to happen. Lawrence Alloway just wrote in the *Nation* that it's time that the Whitney Annual was opened up. He says let's have everybody in, because who is doing the picking anyway? What are their criteria? Who the hell are they?

L.N.   And *why* are they doing the picking? Look at the Whitney's film department. Diana MacKown and I make movies, we're incorporated, and our title is *Iron Crystal Films.* We've made quite a few—the one that we'll be showing this fall, when my own show goes on in October, will be the one that Diana made on me. It's surrealistic, and certainly the language and the positions of the movie are very unique, very special, very different. We showed it, for the first time in public at the Minneapolis Walker Arts Center. So we're here; we're a whole thing by ourselves.

C.N.   You're terrific because you go into every area. You don't stay put for a minute.

L.N.   I made a hundred collages last summer. They'll be in the show in October. We'll have both floors of the Pace Gallery for a month. Then there's the metal things. I go to Lippencott and work with the men there. I can even project into time and say there may come a time when we may not even need visual art as such.

C.N.   You are in the forefront. You talked before about the fact that you are a person who was born ahead of your time and it's very hard to be in that position. But eventually, people catch up with you and know that you've been in the forefront.

L.N.   You mentioned before that you interviewed Helen Franken-thaler. You know, when I met her, there was a girl trying to lead a woman's group, and Helen came and a few others. I said hello to Helen a few times. I didn't really know her, and she didn't know me more than hello. She turned up her nose, she was younger, and said she would never have any part of a woman's group—that was years ago. Now that was so stupid. I mean art is art.

C.N.   She's a very unhappy woman I believe.

L.N.   I have no sympathy for her. She got everything along the way. She's used Greenberg. She's used everything in an abominable way. So why should I be sorry for her?

C.N.   But she pays a price too.

L.N.   Well, everyone pays a price. That is what she wanted. That's her price. It's alright, if she had the price to pay, and she did. That's her business. Look, they had incomes, all of them. That sister of hers, Gloria Ross, is enormously wealthy and her husband was a broker. And Helen, she deserved Motherwell as an artist, and he deserved her. He's twice her age and they have great fortunes and wonderful prestige. Helen's father was a Supreme Court Justice, plenty of money. Motherwell's a Wells Fargo heir, his father's a big banker out in San Francisco. So here are these two families. Well, I'll tell you, I wouldn't give you two cents for either one. And if you ever hear him speak, so pedantic, and he doesn't know what's happening. He wouldn't know how to talk to you.

I was called up by Israel Shenker from the *New York Times,* and he said, "Mrs. Nevelson, tomorrow there's a panel, five people are meeting, and we hope to include you. You'll be the only woman to celebrate Picasso's ninetieth birthday." And I said, "Who are the other people?" (It was to be at the Academy of Arts and Letters.) He answered Motherwell, and another monster, the curator William Rubin from the Museum of Modern Art, and some goddamn cartoonist, David Levine.

C.N.   He's my neighbor.

L.N.   Well, you should hear how he talks about Picasso, as if *he's* the genius and Pablo is shit. And wait, the other is Thomas Hess. Now here's what happened. I said, "I don't think they'd like to have me because Mr. Hess has always blackballed any of the critics that have written about me, plus the fact that I've never been in his magazine." I also said, "Motherwell, I'm very unsympathetic with." Shenker says, "I just spoke to Mr. Motherwell, and he doesn't want to be in it because he and Hess don't get along." "Wait," I said, "well, under those circumstances, it's alright, I'll go." So I go. Of course Hess kept us waiting half an hour saying he couldn't get a taxi. Then they sat here and I sat here —I must say Rubin behaved nicer toward me—but those other two men didn't say hello or anything. They didn't even see me. And have you ever seen me when I go out of the house?

C.N.   You can't miss you.

L.N.   I put on a show. You can't miss me, you're goddamn right! I had a Scassi on. Well, anyway they sat here and I sat down and then this monster Levine—who I could really throw right into the Hudson River —and this monster Rubin began to have a love fest. They're not talking about Picasso, they're talking about Homer and they get very erudite —both of them, you see, are classics students of the first order. So they're exchanging, they're just exchanging, exchanging. Finally, I'm just sitting, they don't say hello even, and so, I said, quietly (I figured with these monsters, I'm in good company), "Mr. Shenker, I thought we came here to pay homage to Mr. Picasso? Well, what is this? You have to make a statement don't you? What you think about Picasso, that was the question wasn't it?" Then, I said, "Picasso is eternally young, and even now, at ninety, he is still young because creativity has no age." I went on a bit like that—which is true. I could be dying, and I'd go downstairs. I do it because I'm moved to do it. It has no age. Of course, the physical body isn't as powerful as we go on, but still we regenerate our own image. Then this monster Rubin says that he thinks that Matisse is the great genius of our times or something like that. I said, "Even Matisse took a great deal from Picasso," and as far as I can feel, in my long life, when Cubism came into being it gave us a structure and then we moved from there. That was our root. Just like Mary Wigman in the dance. Martha Graham was a great genius, but she couldn't have been Martha Graham without Mary Wigman. You see, as independent as we are, we have to have roots.

C.N.   True.

L.N.   I feel that if you have certain convictions (we are not living in a vacuum) and if you go to foreign places, to schools where no one knows you and you're recognized—that's some convictions. You see, in our being we put and establish something.

C.N.   And it has nothing to do with power or politics or any of that nonsense. It has to do with what you feel.

L.N.   Well, anyway, I am an optimist and that's a funny thing. I went to an analyst to ask about somebody else who was in my life and while I was there I said I might as well ask a few questions. He was a very noted analyst and he said to me, "You know you are the most masochistic person I have ever met."

C.N.   Did he say why?

L.N.   Well he said, "because most people are aware that, to use a corny phrase, 'dog eats dog' by the time they are in their teens, and you've conducted yourself as if the world is rosy." So I said to him, "How is it (this wasn't too many years ago) if I am like that, that I am where I am in my work?" And he said, "That is in spite of you."

C.N.   I think you really knew everything and went ahead despite it.

L.N.   Well, you know why, I told you that earlier, I said my life is mine. Was I to allow them not to let me fulfill my life?

C.N.   I understand, because it's just what Emerson says. You don't owe anyone anything. The highest obligation a person has is to be themselves. There is nothing in this world that should stop you from being yourself.

L.N.   It's not easy and some people don't recognize themselves.

C.N.   You can be called selfish but you know what's right for you and you have to have the courage to say, "I will do it!"

L.N.   And if you fall down by the wayside, you pick yourself up. I never went through it like some of them, but I worked hard. Of course it's hard.

C.N.   But you fought a battle against overwhelming odds.

L.N.   And I raised my son, and my son's a sculptor and he's a good sculptor, but it's been a little hard for him. I wasn't maternal.

C.N.   You know that's a whole lot of bullshit, because you gave him something that many mothers, most mothers, couldn't give. You gave him a sense of pride in you. I can understand how you must have felt at times, how alone, because everything was against you, but to rise above it—that took so much. You were asking for everything. You knew you were entitled to everything.

L.N.   I wouldn't want to live for a home. I think that we must put matter in it's place. That is Emerson too. You know, darling, we don't die from lack of food. We die from lack of devotion.

C.N.   But it's not easy to be one of the strong people.

L.N.   I wouldn't call myself that. I saw myself as a playgirl. I had diamond bracelets, I had a little snap with clothes. I found myself attractive and I liked having a ball—I still do. I never thought of myself as strong, as a fighter. If I fought it was out of despair—drinking and despair.

C.N.   And you didn't give up anything. You didn't give up being a mother, you didn't give up being a woman, and you remained an artist. I don't believe in those choices. There are women who say you can't have it all.

L.N.   I wanted to see how people function. Coming from the country, I was sold a bill of goods. Women were forced not to know anything. That's what made them neurotic. They were half dead, you see, and shackled mind and body according to the law. You know what I can't stand—a man and woman who live together for fifteen, twenty, forty years and they get a divorce (she wants good alimony if she can get it), and she'll say, "I wasted all my life." Well, this kills me. If I had had two million dollars, I would have given it to my ex-husband to get rid of him. I wanted my freedom.

C.N.   You regret your marriage to him?

L.N.   There were two major things that I did in my life that were flaws, but I made those choices with my eyes open. If I had been freer and older, I would not have gotten married at that given time. I wasn't ready. But I didn't believe in myself when I was extremely young because I was brought up in the country and in the country you're limited from every point of view. So I didn't believe that anyone could be that emancipated. People get married. And so I got married. Then I went to Janis. I knew I shouldn't have gone, but I went and it nearly killed me. I have no guilt about everything else I did with men, liquor, or anything.

C.N.   What interests me is that because you were a woman you were forced into the marriage situation. You were convinced that you needed a man to take you out of that setting.

L.N.   I think that if I had been a little older—I was seventeen—I hadn't even graduated yet and I couldn't believe my own self—that was so new. So I didn't trust it.

C.N.   Later on you studied with Hans Hofmann?

L.N.   I studied with him in Germany and I never cared for the man. He was a good teacher, but that isn't the point. Every student that came to him said "Herr Doctor." He never looked at them. They were all Americans and they came there. I never saw him. He had already been in Berkeley that summer and the next year he came to America. That was in 1931, and he came to America in 1932, so I saw what was going on. He was kissing the asses of the rich ones and that made me mad. He had come to America and was a little frightened and he was playing up to them. I didn't cross the ocean to go to his school to see it and that always offends me anyway. So I wouldn't let him touch first base with me. I just couldn't stand it.

I have a sister who has a private house on Eleventh Street, Fifth and Eleventh, and one evening, some years ago, she had Greenberg and Rothko and Hofmann over. So Hofmann, whom I hadn't seen (I never looked him up in Provincetown—I never go there anyway) looks at me (I have a wall at my sister's) and says, "You know you are an original. This is magnificent." And Greenberg didn't like that. For no reason he says, "Hans, you are a great artist." Then, Hofmann, whom I never cared for said, and I'll never forget this, "This is original, I gave too much for teaching and I have to live longer to find myself. I have not found myself."

C.N.   He conceded that!

L.N.   Yes, he conceded that, and that killed Greenberg. That contradicted Greenberg, because he was writing a book on him. I don't know whether it had been published or not at that point. But I thought to myself, Hofmann was in America, he was successful, he made money, and finally he said that he had not yet found himself. He became more honest and confronted himself. That's worth something. We'll have to give him that.

C.N.   What led you to Diego Rivera?

L.N.   Marjorie Easton, she's a movie actress now, a society girl from San Francisco, wonderful girl. Girl? She's my age now. Marjorie was in Hofmann's class, and as much as I wasn't crazy about him in Germany, I still went to his class at the League. One day he picks up my drawing of a nude and says to the class, "This is bigger than life." Well, all the students began looking at me. So, Marjorie Easton became my friend. She had already done work with Diego in Mexico and she said, "Would you like to be Diego's assistant?" and I said, "Yes." So we combined, we took two studios with Diego and his wife Frieda—the four of us. And we entertained every evening—Diego and Frieda had open house. In that house you'd see a king and you'd see a laborer. He never made a distinction—never. There was nothing he wouldn't give you. He didn't have lines like "I can't," "I don't."

One day he took me to Leighton's when they were on Eighth Street. He knew Leighton from Mexico, and he said, "Take these things, I want you to have them." Well, I'm a friend of Frieda, and I'm conventional yet, so I can't take things from him. Well, he insisted, so I took something. Then I gave Frieda an antique piece of jewelry. The thing is, if I had said, "I want the moon," he'd have said, "All right, I'll get the moon for you." When he got finished with Radio City, they gave him $5,000. Everyone knew; they smelled it. There was a stream for a week. There were two doors, the service door and the front door in the building right off Thirteenth Street, 810 West Thirteenth Street, and every day there would be a line that would be ringing the service door. He never turned anyone away. He always gave, but he didn't just hand you the money, it would be in an envelope—and that was given. Now, that is the truth and I observed it. Then he had to get tickets to go on a boat and of course he had no money after that to get his tickets. So his friends collected money, bought his tickets, took him and his Frieda bodily and put them on the boat. And that's the truth.

He always wore overalls, he never liked to dress up, maybe a little in the evening, but not much. We would walk, and you know, the little pushcarts on Fifth Avenue—they have cherries, twenty cents a bag— he would buy them, no washing or anything, and he'd eat them. If someone would come along, a laborer, and say, "Are you Diego Rivera?" He'd say, "Yes. Oh, have some cherries." He was always like that.

C.N.   That's security—a person who knows who he is doesn't have to prove anything.

L.N.   His wife Frieda—she was the same. She was his pupil, but he didn't believe in marriage, and while he was married to Frieda, he was going with her sister and oh, they were busy—busy all the time. He just loved Mae West and Gypsy Rose Lee. That was the dream.

C.N.   That was before women's liberation.

L.N.   But he was liberated. He didn't feel this boundary line, never, never.

C.N.   I suppose he felt that people should come together freely because they care about each other.

L.N.   If you want to analyze it, we're all born out of a cunt. We dress up to go to the king's palace to eat and then we go to the bathroom. What is this goddamn thing if you want to face it? It's our stupidity. And if two people want to communicate, that's their business. But we have so many things we cannot really communicate until we free ourselves.

Dawn's Wedding Feast, 1959–60.

Moon Garden Plus One, 1958.

Tide I, Tide, 1963.

Atmosphere and Environment V, 1966.

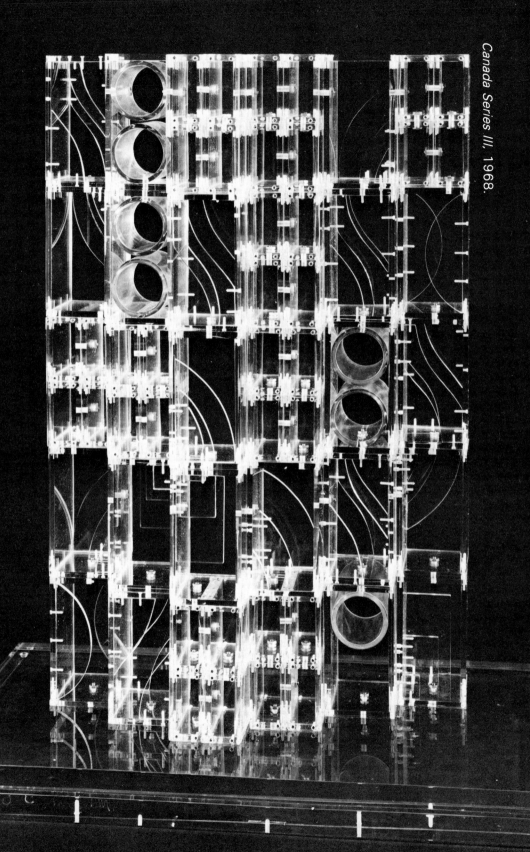

Canada Series III, 1968.

Tropical Trees II, 1972.

Night Presence IV, 1972.

LEE KRASNER is sixty-six years old and lives in New York City. A passionate woman of great determination, she has devoted her entire life to her art, never faltering even in times of great stress.

Krasner studied art at Women's Art School, Cooper Union, and at the National Academy of Design. After leaving school she worked on the Public Works of Art Projects and the Works Progress Administration from 1934 to 1937. From there she went to study at the Hofmann School, developing her own unique brand of Cubism which shifted from a Matissean concern with color to a Picassoesque emphasis on line.

In 1941, upon being invited to exhibit at the MacMillan Gallery in an exhibition called "American and French paintings," Krasner came into contact with the paintings of Jackson Pollock. Her response to both the man and his art was overwhelming and soon she was living with Pollock and plunging alongside him into uncharted esthetic territory.

In 1943, as Pollock slowly worked his way deeper and deeper into archetypal imagery, Krasner characteristically threw herself head first into the abyss and thrashed about for three desperate years building up on canvases only masses of gray paint out of which an image refused to emerge. Finally, in 1946, an all-over network of thickly applied strokes of pigment appeared on the surface and what she called the "Little Image" broke through. Paintings made by dripping paint from a can followed in 1947 as well as the hieroglyphic motifs which reappear frequently in works thereafter. Looking back, it is clear that Krasner simultaneously with Pollock had taken the risk, gone down to the source, and come out in control of a psychic energy which she has continued to tap throughout her painting career.

Life was stormy for the artist during the next ten years. Now married to Pollock, she lived with him in Springs, East Hampton, sustaining both him and herself in the face of his ever-increasing debilitation caused by alcoholism. Yet despite the painful precariousness of her situation Krasner produced enough work to fill two exhibitions. In 1951 she exhibited paintings at the Betty Parsons Gallery consisting of organic forms and sober tonalities which had evolved out of the "Little Image" works. Then in 1955 she showed a series of marvelous collages bursting with expansive plant and animal forms.

In 1956 Krasner underwent the trauma of Pollock's death in a car crash and a new kind of anthropomorphic imagery surfaced. Male-female confrontations became evident in her large, heavily pigmented forms. Eye-like shapes emerged, keeping an eternal vigil over these all too human antics. Color became brighter and richer as the series developed, while forms were fuller and larger, exploding with reproductive energy. Her paintings were entitled *Earth Green, Birth,* and *Embrace.*

In 1959 this more optimistic progression gave way to a descent into wild despair. Slashing, splintered strokes of raw umber and white replaced the more stable fecund forms, and from 1959 to 1963 the canvas became a battleground. In the middle sixties there was an easing off —color returned, red, green, orange, even blue and yellow, and nature images suggestive of birds and flowers began to coalesce once again. The change took place slowly but tensions appeared to abate. In works shown at the Marlborough Gallery in New York in 1968 desperation had dissolved, anthropomorphic elements were back, and the mood in such paintings as *Combat* and *Courtship* was even playful.

Another Marlborough showing in 1972 revealed a new serenity and confidence never before manifested. Krasner's paintings with titles such as *Majuscule, Rising Sun,* and *Invocation,* composed of stately, measured images, reveal the interior state of a woman who has at last come into her own.

After years of neglect by the art world, based on sexist prejudice, Lee Krasner has finally been accorded the recognition that her impressive, life-long achievement deserves. In November, 1973, she was given a major exhibition at the Whitney Museum of American art. Hopefully a full-scale retrospective will soon follow.

CINDY NEMSER   What led you into art?

LEE KRASNER   I had nothing in my environment or background that I can trace back to give me any indication of how I arrived at this word *art.* Nevertheless when I was ready to graduate from elementary school, I said I wanted to be an artist. I lived in Brooklyn at the time and there was only one high school in New York City where women could major in art and that was Washington Irving in Manhattan. I applied there and was turned down because they were too crowded and I lived in another borough. I decided to study law and to go to Girls' High School. Six months later, after I had flunked everything, I reapplied to Washington Irving and they admitted me. That is how I started my art career.

C.N.   Did your home environment have anything to do with your decision to be an artist?

L.K.   I come from a family of one brother and four sisters. My parents, my brother, and three of my sisters were born in Russia. So the household in which I grew up spoke several languages: Russian, Yiddish, Hebrew, and a smattering of English. Any member of the family could always break out in a language that I couldn't understand.

C.N.   Did your parents encourage you to make something of yourself?

L.K.   I think my parents had their hands full acclimatizing themselves and putting their children through school. They didn't encourage me but as long as I didn't present them with any particular problems, neither did they interfere. If I wanted to study art, it was alright with them.

C.N.   Did you think you were a rebel or a maverick as a child?

L.K.   No, not a rebel. But I was capable of rebellious acts. I was raised in an orthodox Jewish household and as a child I thought of myself as being very religious. I remember when I was twelve or thirteen I crashed into the living room just as my parents were having tea with a doctor who was a distant relative and announced that I was through with religion. Another incident took place at Girls' High School when we were being taught Christmas carols. Much to my own astonishment, I got up in the classroom and said, "I refuse to say 'Jesus Christ is my Lord.' He is not my Lord." Now you can imagine this caused quite a commotion.

C.N.   What was it like being an art student at Washington Irving?

L.K.   As you advanced you took more and more periods of art. As I was approaching graduation my teacher called me in and said, "I am going to pass you in art with sixty-five, not because you deserve it, but because you have done so well in all your other subjects." From Washington Irving I applied to Women's Art School, Cooper Union. I brought in work I had done in high school and was admitted.

C.N.   Did you run into any problems there?

L.K.   Yes. At Women's Art School, Cooper Union, you had to study drawing from antique casts with a Mr. Hinton. The school was divided into three alcoves. The first was drawing casts of hands and feet, the second was the torso, and the third was the full figure. Then you were promoted to Life. Mr. Hinton didn't like my work, and had a great deal of difficulty with me. Finally, he said that he would promote me to Life drawing not because I deserved it but because he couldn't do anything with me. I was there a short time and then I decided to go to the National Academy of Design.

C.N.   Why did you decide to go to the Academy?

L.K.   I remember Mr. Dykaar, a sculptor for whom I posed occasionally to earn some money, gave me a proper lecture one day saying that if I really was serious about art I would go to a serious school like the Academy. So I applied and was accepted on the basis of the work I did at Cooper. Ironically I was demoted to the antique. And lo and behold, in walked Mr. Hinton, as he was teaching at both schools. He looked at me and I looked at him and this time there wasn't anything he could do about getting rid of me as it took a full committee at the Academy to promote you. I spent that whole summer out in Huntington, Long Island, where my family lived then, with a mirror nailed to a tree doing a self-portrait. I submitted it in the fall to the committee so that I could get promoted to Life and I made it, but only "on probation." Then my new instructor accused me of playing a dirty trick by pretending to have painted the picture outdoors when I had really done it inside. No amount of explanation helped.

C.N. It is interesting that you chose to do a self-portrait at that time.

L.K. As a matter of fact in that period I did a series of self-portraits. Not because I was fascinated with my image but because I was the one subject that would stand still at my convenience.

C.N. What was your work like then?

L.K. The regular Academy. One Saturday a group of us from the school went to see an exhibition at the Museum of Modern Art and I saw my first live Matisses and Picassos. When we came back on Monday we automatically pulled the model stand in the middle of the room, pulled down the red and green draperies that were eternally in the background, told the model to wear the clothes rather than take them off, and decided to do what we saw in front of us. At the next criticism the instructor was so irritated with what he saw that though he was a mild-tempered man he picked up somebody's brushes and hurled them across the room saying, "I can't teach you people anything," and left.

C.N. How long were you there?

L.K. For about three years and then I went out to paint on my own.

C.N. How did you support yourself?

L.K. I decided I would teach in the New York City high school system. So I went to CCNY to get my pedagogic credits. I worked as a waitress at Sam Johnson's, a Bohemian Village hangout, through this period and there I met, among others, Harold Rosenberg, Parker Tyler, and Lionel Abel. They would come in evenings and discuss "the higher things in life." I was quietly in the background for a while and then I began to know them and I identified myself. But it was a short period while I was getting my pedagogy points at CCNY. Then I decided that the last thing I ever wanted to do was to teach. I wanted to have no part of it and by that time the WPA had opened up and I applied, was accepted, and was relegated to the mural. I also joined the Artists' Union and became an active member. I painted cityscapes from roof-tops. At the time I was on the WPA I started to work at the Hans Hofmann School.

C.N.   How did you find Hofmann as a teacher?

L.K.   He would come up to me, look at my work, and do a critique half in English and half in German, but certainly nothing I could under-stand. When he left the room I would call George McNeil, who was then the monitor, over and I would ask, "What did this man say to me?" So I really had George McNeil's version of what he thought Hofmann had said to me. Hofmann was teaching Cubism and that was pretty exciting. Matisse and Picasso were my highlights. It was as though I was swinging between them. First I started to work with color and then there was a heavy swing toward the linear.

C.N.   Yes, these oils on paper dated 1937–38 are filled with freely placed areas of color and though they may be abstracting from ex-terior objects they appear to be totally non-objective. Your Picasso-esque paintings, like the one reproduced in Sidney Janis's book *Ab-stract and Surrealist Art,* are also more abstract than any painting Picasso ever did.

L.K.   While I was doing this kind of work I became a member of the American Abstract Artists, a group that was formed for the sole pur-pose of exhibiting, although we did meet to have discussions on art as well. One winter during the period that I was a member, Mondrian and Léger were invited to participate in our exhibitions and they accepted. Mondrian asked me to accompany him to one of these exhibitions in which each artist was represented by three or four paintings. We started to go around the gallery and I had to identify the work of each artist for him and he made a short comment as we moved from one to another. When we got to the Léger, he walked by with no comment. Pretty soon my paintings were coming up and I was getting plenty nervous. Then there we were and I had to say, "These are mine." His comment was, "You have a very strong inner rhythm. You must never lose it." Then we moved on. Mondrian had said something quite beautiful to me. Hofmann was also excited and enthusiastic about what I was doing at this time but his comment was, "This is so good that you would not know it was done by a woman." His was a double-edged compliment. But Mondrian's evaluation rides through beauti-fully.

C.N.   Yet at this period your art is nothing like Mondrian's.

L.K.   Without getting complicated let me recapitulate my art training in the following way: the Academy first, the break with the Academy when I hit the Hofmann School which is Cubist. The next real break follows when I see Pollock's work and once more another transition occurs.

C.N.   How did you come to meet Pollock?

L.K.   John Graham had invited me to be in an exhibition he was doing of French and American painting at the MacMillan Gallery. The artists in the show included Matisse, Picasso, Braque, Stuart Davis, Walt Kuhn, Willem de Kooning, John Graham, Jackson Pollock, and myself. I knew de Kooning but I didn't know Pollock and I thought I knew everyone who worked abstractly in New York City. Well it turned out that Pollock lived a block away from me. I was on Ninth Street between University and Broadway and he lived on Eighth Street between University and Broadway. I proceeded to go up and knock on his door and introduce myself saying, "We are in the same exhibition."

C.N.   Didn't you meet him before that at a loft party?

L.K.   Yes, but that was several years before and even if someone told me his name it didn't stay with me. It was only on re-meeting him that we both remembered the incident of the prior meeting. In any case, up I went. I didn't know how unusual it was to get into his studio. Only later did I learn that wasn't everyday traffic. My response to his work was wildly enthusiastic and he asked to come and see my work and was very generous. We attended the opening of the Graham exhibition together.

C.N.   What was it in Pollock's work that made you respond so profoundly?

L.K.   It was a force, a living force, the same sort of thing I responded to in Matisse, in Picasso, in Mondrian. Once more, I was hit that hard with what I saw.

C.N.   Were you impressed by Pollock's formal treatment of space?

L.K.   I don't respond to painting that way. It doesn't come to me whether it is formal or informal, thick or thin, square or round. All these are later or imposed upon my response.

C.N.   So then after you went to see his work and responded to it, it changed your way of working?

L.K.   I began feeling the need to break with what I was doing and to approach something else. It wasn't clear what I was moving into. I went into my own black-out period which lasted two or three years where the canvases would simply build up until they'd get like stone and it was always just a gray mess. The image wouldn't emerge, but I worked pretty regularly. I was fighting to find I knew not what, but I could no longer stay with what I had.

C.N.   You met Thomas Hart Benton during this period didn't you?

L.K.   Yes. I had never met Benton physically but I had seen photographs of him and I knew this was a big name in Pollock's life. I was living with Pollock then, and we lived on the top floor, five flights up. The bell rang one day and I stuck my head out, looked down, and saw this foreshortened face of Benton looking up at me. He hadn't seen Pollock in quite some time so they had a big warm hello and then I was introduced. Benton said, "I hear you are a painter too." Now this is during the point at which my canvases were building up into gray masses and no image came through. It is not a good state of affairs. But I said, "Yes, I paint." Benton said to me, "I would like to see what you are doing." And I said, "I would love to show it to you" (knowing damn well that I had nothing but those gray slabs in there). And I took him in and that is exactly what he looked at. He looked a little awkward, a little embarrassed, and Jackson said something and somehow or other we walked out of my studio. Now I did it very intentionally.

C.N.   That must have been very hard to do.

L.K.   I couldn't help it if Benton walked into my life at that moment and wanted to see what I was doing.

C.N.   You mentioned that you and Pollock had been living together for some years. Why did you decide to get married?

L.K.   Jackson and I were very clear about not wanting to be married. I think everyone assumed we were. Later on my feelings changed. I gave it a good deal of thought and then one day I confronted Jackson and I said, "Here is the way I feel about things. Either we get married and continue as we are or we separate. I want very much to continue living with you. You will have to make the decision." He said he wanted some time to think it over and a few days later he said to me, "I have made my decision. We get married." I asked, "When shall we go to City Hall and get our license?" And he said, "City Hall, that's a place to get a dog license. This has got to be a church wedding or else no wedding at all." We were married at the Marble Collegiate Church. We were told that we needed two witnesses and so we asked May Natalie Taback, Harold Rosenberg's wife, and Peggy Guggenheim, Jackson's dealer. When I called May up and asked her to come and witness our wedding, she said she would be delighted but when I called Peggy, her response was, "Aren't you married enough? I'm sorry I can't come I have a luncheon appointment." So we arrived at the church with just May and they called some man who was in the church to be the second witness. That is how the wedding took place.

C.N.   Obviously Peggy didn't like the idea of Jackson Pollock having a wife. Did she ever help you as an artist?

L.K.   Well Peggy was never kind to women. I didn't realize that because I was so fond of her. I can give you some examples of her attitude toward me. The first time Peggy came to Pollock's studio to see his work we were a little late for the appointment. Anticipating we might be late we left the doors open for her. My paintings were up as well as Jackson's. Peggy had arrived before we got there. She started to bawl Jackson out for not being there on time saying, "I came into the place, the doors were open, and I see a lot of paintings, L.K., L.K. I didn't come to look at L.K.'s paintings. Who is L.K.?" And she damn well knew at that point who L.K. was and that was really like a hard thrust. In 1945 when we moved to the Springs, Jackson's contract called for $150 a month. He asked for an increase because he said we couldn't live on that. She replied, "Tell Lee to go out and get a job." (At this point in time the wives of Barney Newman, Adolph Gottlieb, and Mark Rothko, among others, were all supporting their husbands as artists.) Pollock wouldn't accept that solution and she never dared mention it again.

C.N.   That is, unfortunately, a typical reaction of the woman who has some power and wants to make it in the man's world. Peggy is the woman dealer who only takes on men because she believes that if she pays attention to women the men won't take her seriously.

L.K.   I understand the syndrome, but it's still hard to feel charitable toward women who are part of it, especially when you bear the brunt of it.

C.N.   I am interested that you signed your works L.K. Did you use your initials because you didn't want it to been known that you were a woman?

L.K.   No. Some of my paintings are signed L.K. and some have my name. Even today I do the same thing. At that time I didn't think that my problems had to do with being a woman. Now there is a consciousness about that. I view it on a different level.

C.N.   Let's continue on with what was happening to you as a painter. You went through a stage of trying to find yourself again after you met Pollock and the image wouldn't emerge.

L.K.   In '46 what I call my "Little Image" began breaking through this gray matter of mine. I felt fantastic relief that something was beginning to happen after all this time when there was nothing, nothing, nothing.

C.N.   These paintings are quite small aren't they?

L.K.   Yes. This one is about twenty-one inches by twenty-three inches and that one is twenty-two inches by twenty-two inches. That gives you, roughly, an idea of the size. Some are bigger, some are smaller.

C.N.   Did you do these paintings at an easel?

L.K.   No. The canvas is down on a floor or table and I am working out of a tiny can. In other words, I have to hold the paint so I can move it. But I wouldn't have been using Duco. My paint would always have been oil and I could get the consistency of a thick pouring quality in it by squeezing it into a can and cutting it with turp—the way I use paint today.

C.N.   Do you still work primarily in oil?

L.K.   Always oil or gouache. I tried a few things in acrylic, and I make no contact with the medium. I find it opaque, dense, dead as a door nail, and about as unsensuous as it can get. One of the qualities in oil that I respond to highly is the sensuousness of the paint.

C.N.   These paintings have no titles but they are characterized by a built-up surface and an all-over patterning. There is a play between the painterly and the linear—an interaction and tension between them. You have tapped a vital source and you know how to channel it. You have plumbed the depth, come out of it, and have used what you have learned in the process in a careful, knowing way. I think of these paintings as controlled chaos. This little blue and white painting with the squares is extraordinary. It has an ordered serial image, but each square is different, unique. They project out at the viewer and one is pulled into the center of each square. The use of paint becomes a vital force.

L.K.   I am fascinated by what you say and I would love you to go on in depth and see what you could bring out about these paintings both in terms of my own evolution and in relation to what my contemporaries were doing. The only thing I can say with absolute assurance is that my "Little Image" work starts about 1946 and ends in 1949.

C.N.   Well it seems that both you and Pollock were into the exploration of the inner self, the unconscious or whatever one wants to call it, but certainly you are very different in your approach. Your heavy crusty sufaces are much denser than his thinner, looser applications and your field never thins out at the edges as his does. Besides, the scale of your paintings is entirely different. The investigation of your relationship to Pollock is closely allied with the attitudes of the art world toward women artists. There is the idea that women artists are not innovative and are only capable of imitating male art. It's possible for some man to be influenced or activated by another man without being called a follower, but if a woman is in contact with a man—well she is his disciple forever.

L.K.   The cliché is that Lee is overshadowed by her husband and that's easy and we don't have to think about it. It is outrageous. The people who use this excuse, and they still use it today, are talking about their own shortcomings.

C.N.   It would be important to look at these "Little Image" paintings in relation to what your contemporaries were doing. For instance, Bradley Walker Tomlin.

L.K.   Tomlin admired a great many of my "Little Image" paintings. He saw them hanging in our guest bedroom as he was our house guest a good deal. He used to tell me how beautiful they were and his warm response to these paintings of mine I remember very well.

C.N.   Tomlin actually began to do his pictographic imagery in '49 after you did these paintings. We have to set history straight because nowhere is it written the Tomlin was influenced by Lee Krasner. In this other painting owned by Mr. and Mrs. Vanasse, there is a hieroglyphic-like motif which makes one think of ancient symbols of the past.

L.K.   Well, I think it does suggest hieroglyphics of some sort. It is a preoccupation of mine from way back and every once in a while it comes into my work again. For instance, in my 1968 show at the Marlborough I have a painting called *Kufic,* an ancient form of Arabic writing. Every once in a while I fall back to what I call my mysterious writings. I have no idea what this is about but it runs through periods of my work.

C.N.   Yes, you did two mosaic table tops in '47 and '48 in which the design resembles some form of ancient sign writing with circles, stars, and crosses. I also notice in the "Little Image" paintings that you tend to merge the geometric with the organic.

L.K.   I merge what I call the organic with what I call the abstract, which is what you are calling the geometric. As I see both scales, I need to merge these two into the ever-present. What they symbolized I have never stopped to decide. You might want to read it as matter and spirit and the need to merge as against the need to separate. Or it can be read as male and female.

C.N.   It must have been hard for you to have been married to an artist like Pollock who was getting so much attention and then to have people seeing you, a serious painter in your own right, as the wife who was supposed to stay in the background. You must have been torn between wanting him to succeed and reaching out to discover your own identity.

L.K.   If you remember my family background, I didn't get much encouragement. This was another tough nut to crack. It was self-imposed and I'm aware of that. Since no one asked me to live with Pollock, and since I wanted my independence as well, I damn well have to deal with it.

C.N.   Many people have told me that you gave Pollock a great deal of your time and attention.

L.K.   Of course and continue to. Right up until today Pollock takes a lot of my time.

C.N.   How much did it take out of you?

L.K.   I wouldn't know. And while you ask, "How much did it take out of me as a creative artist?" I ask simultaneously, "What did it give?" It is a two-way affair at all times. I would give anything to have someone giving me what I was able to give Pollock.

C.N.   Since you didn't have an exhibition of your paintings, was there a response to them?

L.K.   There was reponse. I didn't feel as though I were isolated. John B. Meyers admired my "Little Image" paintings and I can remember Clement Greenberg saying about an early one, "That's hot. It's cooking." I considered it a compliment. John Little, Jim Brooks, Linda Lindeberg, and Tomlin were others who saw the works and admired them. There wasn't time to do anything about the fact that I wasn't getting public recognition and showing. I was painting, Pollock was breaking through. We had our hands full. I couldn't take time off and say, "Look here. Why am I not being seen?" I didn't function that way.

C.N.   You also didn't have the support you needed. At that time there was no women's liberation movement.

L.K.   That's right. I couldn't run out and do a one-woman job on the sexist aspects of the art world, continue my painting, and stay in the role I was in as Mrs. Pollock. I just couldn't do that much. What I considered important was that I was able to work and other things would have to take their turn. You have to brush a lot of stuff out of the way or you get lost in the jungle. Now rightly or wrongly I made my decisions.

C.N.   Do you think it was easier for women like Frankenthaler, Mitchell, and Hartigan?

L.K.   They are the next generation and it is another scene—another story. You forget that in my generation Paris was still the leading school of painting and this situation was being changed by a tiny handful of artists to a scene called New York, America, which never before had a leading role in the art world. That didn't happen just by reading a newspaper. Now the next generation comes in and they may think it is rough for them but it is pie compared to what we went through. We broke the ground.

C.N.   It was still rough for women then but *you* had to fight for everything—being an American artist and a woman artist at the same time.

L.K.   And as Mrs. Pollock it intensified that problem. Let's put it this way: Pollock being the figure he was in the art world it was a rough role seen from any view.

C.N.   How about the running of your household? Was that all on your shoulders?

L.K.   No. Jackson shared a lot of it. Certainly I took the bulk of it but I did not have a husband who had to be waited on at all times. He perhaps favored the outdoor work and I had to do the indoor. But I think we shared. And if I needed special assistance, I asked for it, and as a rule, I got it.

C.N.   How did Pollock react when you asked him to come up and look at your work? Did he act as if he were doing you a favor?

L.K.   No. It wasn't like that. It was like, "Not now, later." But he is the one who would pull me out of a state when I would say, "the work has changed and I can't stand it. It's just like so and so's work." Then he would come and look and say, "You're crazy. It is nothing like so and so's work. Just continue painting and stop hanging yourself up." We had that kind of rapport.

C.N.   Then Jackson wasn't afraid of your being successful? He didn't see you as a competitor?

L.K.   On the contrary, he asked Betty Parsons to come and see my work and she gave me my first New York solo show in 1951.

C.N.   But you never did get to show the "Little Image" paintings in New York.

L.K.   Not in New York, though some of them were shown in a bookshop in East Hampton. By the time Betty scheduled my New York show, the work had broken into a totally different image and I showed what I was doing then.

C.N.   When you say your work had broken what do you mean?

L.K.   Just like when I had a gray-out for a period of time and then the "Little Image" emerged. It went along until about '49 and once more the work started to change. I can't tell why this happens. This process has continued right up until today. I go for a certain length of time and the image breaks again. By the time Betty came and looked at my work it was a far cry from what is now known as the "Little Image."

C.N.   What was your show at Betty Parsons like?

L.K.   You could say they started to blow up and the use of the pigment was very thin compared to what I was doing before. For me it was only holding the vertical, though some of them move horizontally as well. In a letter from Pollock to Ossorio, in 1951, he says, "Lee is doing some of her best painting. It has a freshness and bigness that she didn't get before."

C.N.   How was the show received?

L.K.   Not much happened. Stewart Preston reviewed it for the *New York Times*. I remember one line in his review which struck me as astonishing. He said it was a call to order.

C.N.   I find it strange that he should describe these works as a call to order because in relation to the "Little Image" works they are a breaking out, although there is still an orderliness about the painting.

L.K.   He was also speaking about the whole scene when he said it was a call to order. But I don't know what he had in mind.

C.N.   Where can I see these paintings?

L.K.   With the exception of two works, one of which is owned by the Museum of Modern Art, I reworked the rest into collage.

C.N.   Why did you decide to collage all the paintings after you had the show?

L.K.   I was collaging and I guess I felt that nothing much had happened with these canvases. It was a few years later and suddenly I got into them and started reworking. As a matter of fact it is dangerous for me to have any of my early work around because I tend to always want to go back into it at some point—so the less around the better. In this case they were around and I thought, well, nothing has happened. I got into one of them and that worked and I kept going and I collaged almost all the paintings.

C.N.   What led you into collage in the first place?

L.K.   My studio was hung with a series of black and white drawings I had done. I hated them and started to pull them off the wall and tear them and throw them on the floor and pretty soon the whole floor was covered with them. Then another morning I walked in and saw a lot of things there that began to interest me. I began picking up torn pieces of my own drawings and re-glueing them. Then I started cutting up some of my oil paintings. I got something going there and I start pulling out a lot of raw canvas and slashing it as well. That's how I started my collaging and the tail end of it was the collaging of the paintings in the Betty Parsons show. I showed these collages in '55 at the Stable Gallery.

C.N.   You didn't show again for four years?

L.K.   I didn't start the collage until about '53.

C.N.   You don't believe a painter has to have a show every year?

L.K.   When you are working and you are very excited about your work and there is no outside pressure (your livelihood is not dependent on it, your anxiety about your career and your image of yourself, your own insecurity aren't bugging you), then why interrupt yourself? It seems to me that you should set your own terms as to when you will show.

C.N.   How is it that you moved from the Betty Parsons Gallery to the Stable Gallery?

L.K.   It's very simple. When Jackson left the Parsons Gallery in '51 because Betty was not able to sell enough paintings, Betty asked me to leave too. That was a very severe shock to me. When I spoke to her about it, she said, very honestly, "It has nothing to do with your painting. I still respect you as an artist but it is impossible for me to look at you and not think of Jackson and it is an association that I cannot have in here." It took me almost a year to recover from that shock before I could work again.

C.N.   It was as if, all of a sudden, the outside world had closed in on you?

L.K.   Yes. She was the outside world and a sympathetic aspect of it. The world was announcing that which I was most apprehensive about. I probably knew it was there but I had never had to meet it head-on. I was kicked out of the gallery because I was Mrs. Jackson Pollock.

C.N.   Getting back to the collages, are they related to the paintings at Parsons?

L.K.   They also have that verticality. Verticality comes back in my work again and again but it comes back in forms that are not exactly as pure. If we use that word vertical with the meaning it has now taken on—the *vertical* doesn't interest me. It is too pure, and purity given to me in that form makes me nervous.

C.N.   Were the collages of '53 and '54 all involved with verticality?

L.K.   No. Like my "Little Image" paintings they break into several series, some are vertical and some are not.

C.N.   The collages are so intense and full of life. Yet at that particular point you are going through a very difficult period in your personal life —in 1955?

L.K.   In '55, yes. I entered analysis and Pollock re-entered analysis. It became a difficult year but that was when I was having my show. I was not working toward it then.

C.N.   You showed four years of work in this collage exhibition. It was quite an achievement. In the catalogue of your Whitechapel Retrospective in 1965, Bryan Robertson states that Clement Greenberg described your collage show of '55 as a "major addition to the American art scene of that era."

L.K.   Pollock was pleased with the show. Eleanor Ward who gave me the show remembers his pride and pleasure in it.

C.N.   It seems to me you are becoming more and more organic and closer to nature images. You are concentrating on the world of living, growing things. As if you were moving from one level of consciousness to a higher one.

L.K.   Well I don't believe that. I think for every level you go higher, you slip down one or two levels and then come back up again. When I say slip back, I don't mean that detrimentally. I think it is like the swing of a pendulum rather than better or back, assuming that back means going down. If you think of it in terms of time, in relation to past, present, and future, and think of them all as a oneness, you will find that you swing the pendulum constantly to be with now. Part of it becomes past and the other is projection but it has got to become one to be now. I think there is an order but it isn't good, better, best.

C.N.   You do believe in personal development?

L.K.   I think you can change—that has been my experience—that I am committed to.

C.N.   What happened after you had the collage show?

L.K.   In July '56 there was another break in the work. There is a painting called *Prophecy* which I did just before I left for Europe. Every time the work broke it sent me into a tailspin because I couldn't tell what was happening. I asked Jackson to come and look at this painting and he did and said I needn't be nervous about it. He thought it was a good painting and the only thing that he objected to was this image in the upper right hand which I had scratched in with the back of a brush. It made a kind of an eye form. He advised me to take it out. I said that I didn't agree with him and left it in, as you can see.

C.N.   You reacted to your own painting as if it came from some unknown place.

L.K.   It's not the source that shocked me, it's the change that I had to get used to and accept. It frightened me.

C.N.   I remember reading that after Henri Rousseau painted his jungle scenes he became so frightened he had to run out of the house.

L.K.   I didn't run out of the house but it frightened me, particularly because it happened just before I left for Europe. Jackson looked at it, said what he said, and I went off to Europe. Jackson was killed in the automobile accident while I was there and when I came back I had to confront myself with this painting before I was able to start again. I went through a rough period in that confrontation.

C.N.   It's a very powerful painting with rather monstrous forms. It's primeval. It drags up something from the unconscious.

L.K.   I felt that at the time and it frightened me. It took me quite some time to adjust to it.

C.N.   Were you involved with Jungian concepts or Jungian imagery at all at that time?

L.K.   No, in that sense, no. I hadn't had Jungian analysis, but I had read material by Jung and I knew Jackson had worked with Jungian analysis. I was somewhat sympathetic, but it was a fringe interest. I had had one year of analysis at the time I painted *Prophecy.* It was a splinter group from the Sullivan school and if one must separate Jung and Freud, this would be in the direction of Freud. So when you say I was dragging something up, and obviously I was, very much so, it frightened me. It was coming through a source, but I didn't know what that source was.

C.N.   Then comes a series of paintings in the spirit of *Prophecy.*

L.K.   *Prophecy* was painted before Jackson died and these were the first to appear afterwards. As you can see the eye is really coming through now. That's why I wanted to mention it in relation to *Prophecy.*

C.N.   There seems in these paintings to be a representation of the essential male-female confrontation, even in the titles, *Three in Two, Embrace, Birth.*

L.K.   Remember what happened to me in my personal life at this point. There are certain factual things that cannot be denied—the date of the painting, the kind of paintings that preceded it, the kind of paintings that happen later. But again I don't see how you can separate these things out.

C.N. Now recognizable images appear again. Did you do many of these paintings?

L.K. Just a handful and they are all murky and dense grays.

C.N. Some critics have said that this series is the beginning of Lee Krasner as an independent painter. They feel that only after Pollock's death were you able to be yourself.

L.K. Where have I not been Lee Krasner prior to that? I don't understand that point of view. It is an outside point of view and I am not in touch with it.

C.N. It implies that you couldn't be free or yourself until you moved out from the orbit of Pollock's influence.

L.K. Hogwash is my answer to that kind of thinking. Esthetically I am very much Lee Krasner. I am undergoing emotional, psychological, and artistic changes but I hold Lee Krasner right through.

C.N. These are all extremely personal paintings. It has been said that women are more revealing of themselves, more open than men.

L.K. I don't believe that—not for a second. To the contrary, women have veiled themselves, so now they are taking a couple of the veils off, but they are not necessarily more open.

C.N. What kind of work came after this group?

L.K. There is an opening up and the color is more pure, such as in a painting like *Listen* or *Earth Green*. That series was exhibited at the Martha Jackson Gallery in '58.

C.N. Your color is very bright and strong and distinctive, but it tends to put me off a bit at first.

L.K. In what sense?

C.N. Do you know the paintings of the Mannerists—El Rosso, Bronzino, Pontormo? Their color has been described as rather acid. Your color makes me think of those painters. It is as if you are making it more difficult—your color disturbs the viewer.

L.K. You're absolutely correct because once I get going that way, when the thing goes into this kind of color, it begins to get at me. I am doing in color, whatever it is, what I am doing in imagery because I think color can be used in this sense. It bugs me and I bug it. I can just try to get through with it and look at it and say, "Okay, now let's analyze."

C.N. Do you favor certain colors?

L.K. I would say, for a big division, red and green, or variations of red and variations of green. I have been preoccupied with these two colors for many, many years.

C.N. In this new series you are into brighter color but there is still that monstrous, underworld imagery.

L.K. I wouldn't call it monstrous or underworld. You use the word *monstrous* as though it were relegated to a realm other than man. I would call it basic, insofar as I am drawing from sources that are basic.

C.N. After the Martha Jackson show you did a large mosaic mural?

L.K. B.H. Friedman, then vice president of Uris Brothers, had seen that '47 mosaic table at the house and commissioned Ronald Stein and myself to do the mosaic mural at 2 Broadway. It is a variation of blacks, reds, greens, and a couple of blues, and a touch of yellow here and there—the warmer and cooler blacks were very exciting to work with. The mural in the front of the building is eighty-six feet by twelve feet and the one in the rear is fifteen feet by fifteen feet. The scale is really something. It was quite a feat. I thought I was going to be able to handle the material myself but since I had to work with the mosaic union, traditional Italian mosaicists, and I was not a union member, I was not allowed to touch the material. They were accustomed to having someone hand in a sketch which they executed. I refused to work in this manner. Moreover I did not want the material cut in the traditional manner. I wanted to smash it with a hammer. I had them ship it in as it comes out of the kiln which is in pancake form about twelve inches in diameter. Since I was not allowed to pick up the hammer or smash it or give them an idea of how I wanted to juxtapose these pieces in putting them back, the whole thing was quite complicated. What happened was the day I came in a few of the workman arrived with brand-new sets of gloves and a new hammer. They stood there and the head of the shop asked, "What do we do?" I said, "Take the hammer and smash the pieces of tile." About five or six times the hammer came down but it didn't crack the tile because they were afraid to apply enough strength. Finally I did get them to smash with heavier intensity and then with lighter intensity to get a bigger variety of broken pieces. When I got that far it was time to go out for lunch and when we came back they all had hammers and were all smashing away like a real Chaplin movie. Because they were breaking their own tradition of, who knows how many years, they just went all berserk. Willy-nilly the thing got under way. We were in the middle of installing it and I was leaving for Mexico for a Christmas holiday when I got a call that the building was on fire and that the fire department had washed out thirty-two feet where the cement hadn't adhered. We had to wash all of this and salvage whatever we could and send for whatever new material we needed as quickly as possible. This left little time for my holiday. When Barney Newman saw the mosaic finished he said, "Well Lee, it was baptized by fire and water."

C.N. I think it is an extraordinary work because here we have a piece of public art that is beautiful, original, and tradition-breaking. It reaches out to people and works perfectly with the building. In 1959 your work changes again and you go into a black and white period.

L.K. Not black and white but umber and off-white. As a matter of fact, Clement Greenberg, who was then director of French and Company, had scheduled a show of my work in New York in November 1959. He left for Europe that summer and when he came back in September, he came out to see me. When we got to the studio, there were many of these umber and white canvases on the wall. His reaction to this work was such that we had a big blow-up and I canceled my show immediately.

C.N. What did Greenberg say to you?

L.K. Let's put it this way. I didn't like his response to my new painting, and when I asked him on what basis he scheduled a show, he said, "On the basis of what I thought you would do." "As of this minute, my show is canceled," was my response. Now I daresay if this show had come about my "career" would have moved in a different direction, but it went the way it went.

C.N. Your decision took courage.

L.K. I know that's been said, but I can't imagine acting differently. So this series started and ended with a show at the Howard Wise Gallery, the first in '60 and the second in '62.

C.N. Let's talk about the paintings in the first show. The titles are fantastic: *Charred Landscape, Fecundity, Uncaged, White Rage.*

L.K. There is an interesting story attached to *White Rage.* Howard Wise made a policy of buying one painting from each artist. He decided he'd buy *White Rage,* but on one condition: that I would change the title. I said no. So he didn't buy it. Later on the painting went into a show at the University of Alabama, and after the students took a vote on every painting: this is the one they bought. And the title remained *White Rage.*

C.N.   That is ironic, you never thought the title would take on that meaning.

L.K.   No, never. I was talking about the white rage meaning the height of rage, like white heat.

C.N.   These paintings indicate that you were going through a somber stage, wrestling with something very deep and oppressive.

L.K.   Right. Once more I was undergoing some transitions. You can see it in the work itself. In this show I had an eighteen-foot canvas which was entitled *The Eye Is the First Circle.* So the eye is back again.

C.N.   There is an intensity and ferocity in those splinter-like strokes which I notice you have used many times before. They have a feathery quality and at the same time a tremendously explosive force.

L.K.   It is a thrust of a sort with the brush throwing off the paint.

C.N.   *Polar Stampede,* which was done at this time, seems to express an opposition of forces in its movement and also in the opposition of black and white—the absolute polarization.

L.K.   Yes, a stampede is something that you don't watch or take in casually.

C.N.   In *Along the Way* there is a subsiding of turbulence. The painting is calmer, the lines aren't so sharply drawn nor the oppositions so punctuated. *Along the Way* is toward the end of the series and after that comes *Primal Resurgence* in 1961.

L.K.   And that is, for me, really going down to root sources. It is in my '62 show at Wise. The '60 show is more of an explosion, all umber and white, while the other begins to have a little bit of color—only a touch, I would say.

C.N.   Here is one of those '61 paintings called *Assault on the Solar Plexus* from the second show.

L.K.   For me that is an embarrassingly realistic title. I experienced it. I had had the blow-up with Greenberg, my mother died shortly before, the Pollock estate was pulled out of the Sidney Janis Gallery and frozen. I didn't know how to deal with Pollock. It was a rough life. I think my painting is so autobiographical if anyone can take the trouble to read it.

C.N.   Each of your series is a total entity in itself, an expression of something that is happening to you at a different stage of your life.

L.K.   Different levels, different stages as an artist. I have never understood the artist who has stayed with one image. To me that is totally incomprehensible.

C.N.   But you are coming out of conflict by 1961 and your forms are getting larger and more separate. Color begins to come back—cobalt and pink. That painting in the '62 show called *Cobalt Night* is much more serene. You are seeking to emerge from the tangled imagery of the '60 paintings. In works such as *Night Bloom* there is that splattery stroke again, but it is used in a calmer way. It now creates the image of flowering and opening out. At this point, images suggesting birds turn up in your works, for example, *Night Birds.* Did birds mean anything special to you?

L.K.   Most of it occurs a great deal without my consciously knowing it. In other words, it is there and I see it and recognize it. So all right, I get a bird image. I get a floral image. But I don't go around consciously thinking these images up. They come through. So in that sense, it's archetypal.

C.N.   After the Howard Wise shows your work takes a different turn again—another break occurs. These paintings have titles like *August Petal* and *Flowering Limb* and they have an all-over patterning. The forms have become small clusters of images embedded within the defining lines. I get a feeling of lightness and playfulness in these paintings. You were taking yourself out of the conflict and the works are freer and more relaxed. In *Camouflage,* you have really gone underground.

L.K.   Right, protect yourself a little. *Camouflage* is intense yellows—the series is a variation of yellows, a color most difficult for me. Don't ask me why colors are difficult. I don't know why but yellow rarely ever appears in my paintings. It is one color that I haven't been able to live with peacefully until now.

C.N.   Yet though the overall tone of this series is light and playful, there is still the more somber work, like *Icarus.* Were you afraid?

L.K.   Of getting too close to the sun? I didn't do it, the painting was telling me that.

C.N.   When did you show next?

L.K.   In 1965 Bryan Robertson, then director of the Whitechapel in London, gave me a retrospective exhibition and the show, under the sponsorship of the British Arts Council, was seen in many museums throughout England. This exhibition is the sort of experience that should be allowed to every living artist. I have to confront myself with my own work from time to time, and it is impossible for me to put up a ten-year cycle of my work any place and look at it unless a museum puts it up. It should be a natural process every ten years so that the artist and the interested public can have a look at it.

C.N.   You had a major exhibition at the Whitney Museum in November, 1973 in which a goodly portion of your work was shown but I think it was truly unfortunate that the show was not conceived of as a retrospective. Your work has developed with such a variety and yet such continuity that only a fully documented chronological presentation can give it full justice. But getting back to our chronology, how about the personal part of your life from '56 to '65? How about the problem of handling the Pollock estate?

L.K.   I daresay that a great deal of my so-called position or lack of position, whichever you want to call it, in the official art world is based on the association with Pollock. It is almost impossible to deal with me without relating it to Pollock. There is no question in my mind that because I stepped on many toes in handling the Pollock estate as I saw fit I offended a great many people and so my name became a bit of an irritant as a painter.

C.N.   How did you step on toes?

L.K.   I just did what I saw fit to do which was offensive to many people who would have preferred that I do what *they* would have preferred. If you do it your *own* way as against *their* way, you are difficult.

C.N.   Is it true that certain people expected you to allow them to administer the estate?

L.K.   Yes. Well it didn't go that way.

C.N.   Did that create a prejudice against you?

L.K.   Yes, on a double front as the administrator of the estate and as a woman. It is offensive enough to have said "Hands off," but from a female it is inexcusable.

C.N.   You were also in a position to move from strength weren't you? To be candid, didn't it help you having the Pollock estate to get into the Marlborough Gallery?

L.K.   I will tell you how it came about. I was with Howard Wise at the time that I placed the Pollock estate with Marlborough Fine Arts in London. When I went over there for the opening of the Pollock exhibition in 1962, Mr. Lloyd of the Marlborough Gallery asked me to lunch. He had expressed interest in my work on more than one occasion (he had been out to see me at Springs and also had seen the Howard Wise show when he was in New York) and he said he would like me to join the gallery. I thought about it, thanked him kindly but told him my answer was no. He look astonished. I imagine he was not accustomed to inviting someone to join his gallery and have them refuse. He asked, "Is it because I have the Pollock estate?" I said, "Yes." He waited a moment or two and then said, "Has it occurred to you that it might be to your advantage to join the gallery because I have the Pollock estate?" I said, "Indeed it has. I have given it a good deal of thought. I am very flattered that you want me to join but my answer is definitely 'no.' " And that was that.

C.N.   When did you join the Marlborough Gallery?

L.K.   In '65 my show went on at the Whitechapel in London. I met Mr. Lloyd at my exhibition and in the cab on our way to lunch he said, "Miss Krasner, for the second time, I invite you to join my gallery." This time my reply was, "I accept your offer."

C.N.   When did your next solo show take place?

L.K.   In 1966, after I joined the Marlborough Gallery, a retrospective was arranged for me at the University of Alabama in 1967. My next New York show was in 1968 at the Marlborough Gallery in New York.

C.N.   In that show you exhibited work from '63 on but I noticed in paintings such as *Bird Parisol* of '64 another change is occurring. There are larger forms again and more canvas space showing. The images have an expansive quality about them. They seem to spring or extend off the boundaries of the canvas that holds them down.

L.K.   I do not mean extended to mean esthetic definition of space. For me, it is a matter of whether the canvas allows me to breathe or not —if the canvas soars into space or if it is earthbound. When it is earthbound it irritates me enormously. I would like to soar in a canvas.

C.N.   These paintings all have that characteristic oval form which often, earlier in your work, showed up as an eye. Now it has become much larger. Canvases such as *Combat, Gaia, Confrontation,* and *Courtship* are full of vital rhythmic movement. There is a sense of spilling forth which suggests sexual energy.

L.K.   I know what you mean. I think it is narrowing to define and explain only in terms of one set of formal values. I maintain that steadily through my work.

C.N.   Now, coming up to your new paintings of '71 and '72, one sees that the central image has grown even more and is taking up more and more canvas space. It is also becoming more clearly defined. These are extremely expansive, stately forms. You have reintroduced your characteristic vertical motif and isolated and combined it with the more oval images. Do these paintings have titles?

L.K.   Well the fact of the matter is, I have difficulty with titles. On rare occasions a title comes to me automatically; often friends suggest titles, particularly Richard Howard and Sandford Friedman. There is a fascinating story about the titling of some of the paintings I did with my left hand at the time I had broken my right wrist. I am not ambidextrous. Little Frances, the six-year-old daughter of the woman that cleaned for me, titled them. She didn't know what the word "studio" meant nor had she ever seen a tube of paint. She looked at one of the paintings and said, "That is a limb and it is flowering." She turned to another canvas and said, "That's a lady and she's happy." I couldn't see a lady, let alone a happy one, and I asked, "Why do you say she's happy?" She walked up to the canvas and pointed to the area, "Don't you see she's dancing?" Turning to another canvas with a kind of disdainful gesture of her hand, she said, "That's nothing but a bunch of eyes in the weeds." So I titled it *Eyes in the Weeds.* After all, I painted these pictures, but her reading of them gave me an insight that both fascinated and alarmed me.

C.N.   So you are very careful of the titling. You don't just attach any title. It's almost as if the very nature of making something forces you to put a name on it even if you don't wish to.

L.K.   Yes. I select it so it is I who force a response and this is what is so annoying about it—that I have to do that.

C.N.   Because now I can't read the painting without making associations with the title.

L.K.   Exactly. Now you have to read it in a certain way or go pretty strongly against the whole concept.

C.N.   Well the titles that I notice you have picked for these recent works such as *Majuscule, Invocation, Rising Green, Sun Dial* certainly are appropriate. These paintings have a strong sense of totality. They are emblematic and can each be read as a complete *gestalt* rather than images of parts, and though there is less freedom in the brushstroke and the handling is more congealed, the forms are not closed in on themselves. They are expansive yet contained—again there is your characteristic merging of opposites. They are the work of a person with a strong sense of confidence and quiet authority. Your rhythm has slowed down and has a measured, more majestic quality. Martha Graham comes to mind. These are very stately, slow-moving paintings.

L.K.   The new work is moving at a very slow pace using my own scale of how I work. There is no way I can force or push it. There is no way I can change the tempo. I tend to get impatient so I have to fight my own temperament at times.

C.N.   The pace of these works is very different from the way you did the series of gouache works.

L.K.   I had two gouache shows in '69, one at Marlborough and one at

Reese Palley in San Francisco. Oh, I loved doing them. I was just mad for doing them and they went at quite a clip. Just moved like magic. Some were done in one or two colors, others more, and I used that beautiful handmade Douglas Howell paper which took years of collecting. Once I got moving I went through it. It was just sheer delight.

C.N.   Have you always done works on paper?

L.K.   Quite a lot all the way through. I've done drawings, watercolors, mixed media, a good deal of gouaches. I think every once in a while I feel the need to break my medium. But there are limits. I have no feeling for sculpture whatsoever, so I am restricted to the two-dimensional surface, but it can be lithography or drawing. If I have been doing a very large painting I like to drop into something in small scale. It is a challenge to go into this size. It is just to hold my own interest, and then each media has its own conditions. I will be having a works-on-paper show at the Corcoran next year [1975] and an additional exhibition there as well. I would be curious to round up a lot of the stuff I've done through a period of time. I would like to start way back with what I did at the National Academy.

C.N.   Obviously, for you, working in a small or large format is equally important.

L.K.   I don't think scale has to do with the physical aspects of the work. I think you can have giant physical size with no statement on it so that it is an absurd blow-up of nothingness. And vice versa, you can have a very tiny painting which is monumental in scale. Too often there is confusion as to what's known as scale in painting. Footage doesn't mean scale.

C.N.   Recently you did a series of lithographs.

L.K.   Yes—working directly on stone and I got very excited about it on the basis of some accidents that occurred while I was in the shop during the printing. I used these accidents and got really excited about them. I'm against turning in a sketch or a study and letting the shop handle it. If I don't get involved there is nothing in it for me. That is the point. I have no understanding of detachment. For example, the what I call "Look Ma No Hands" school of painting, that kind of non-participation, is the antithesis of what I mean by creativity.

C.N.   It is as if art is not supposed to have feeling or any sign of the person who did it—to be somehow removed and antiseptic. The "Look Ma No Hands" school has been touted as the most effective way of making art these days hasn't it?

L.K.   A bully is a bully is a bully and I don't like bullies!

Self-Portrait, 1931–32.

Untitled, 1938.

Untitled (Little Image), 1949.

Stretched Yellow, 1955.

Prophecy, 1956.

The Seasons, 1957.

Polar Stampede, 1960.

Majuscule, 1971.

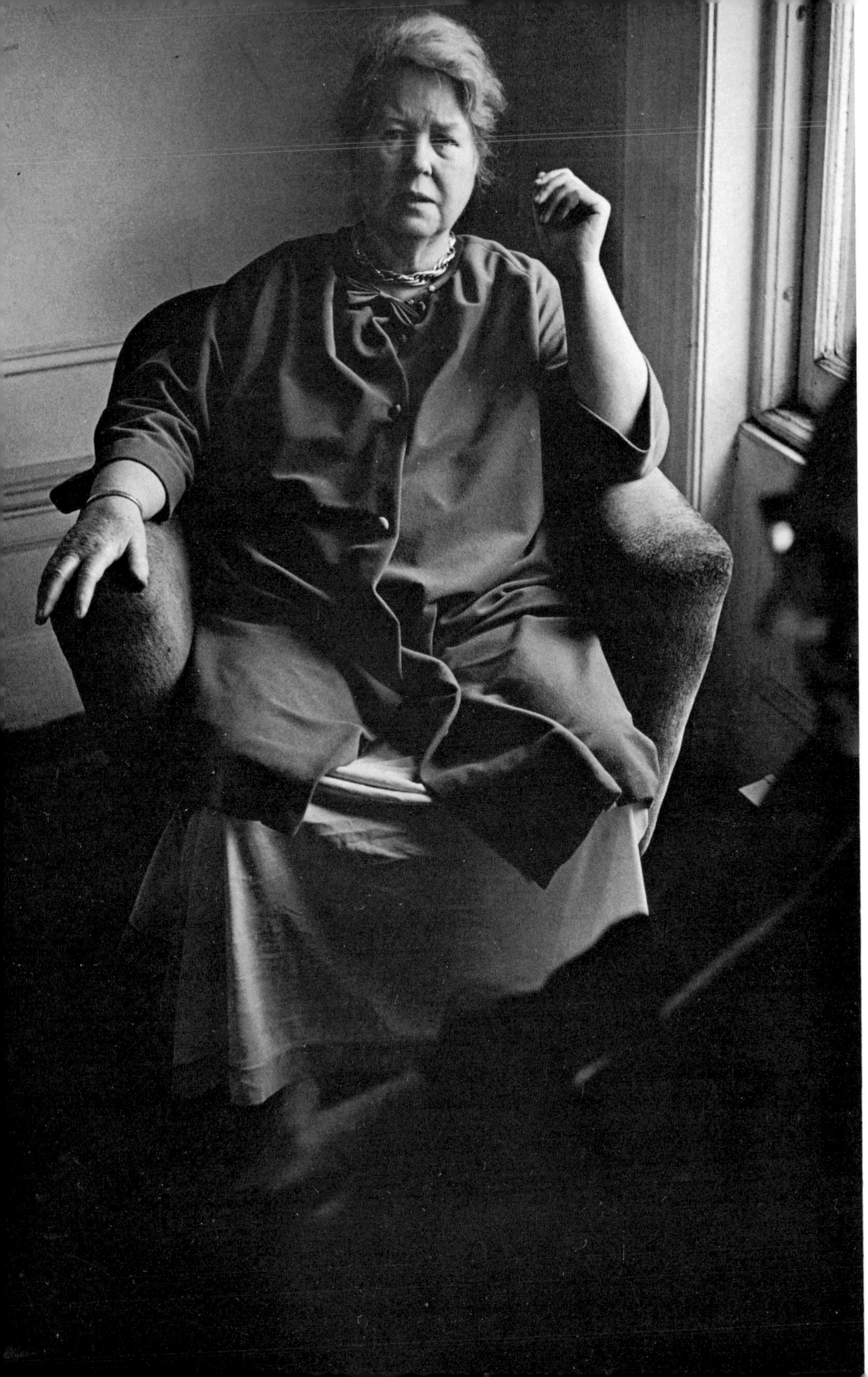

Alice Neel.

ALICE NEEL was born in Colwin, Pennsylvania, in 1900 and is the descendant on her mother's side of a signer of the Declaration of Independence. It is obvious some of that rebel's blood still flows in her veins. After graduating from the Philadelphia School of Design (which is today Moore College), she met and married an aristocratic Cuban artist and went off with him to Cuba to paint and live the Bohemian life. The pair returned to New York in the late twenties with a daughter, to starve in Greenwich Village. The child died of diphtheria, another daughter was born, and Alice Neel's husband embarked for Paris leaving the artist in New York and the little girl in Cuba. Bereft of husband and child, Neel had a nervous breakdown and was unable to work for a year. After recovering, she returned to Greenwich Village, and became involved with a rough and ready, but intellectually minded, sailor who tore up her clothing and canvases in a fit of jealous rage over her developing friendship with John, a Harvard man. Alice escaped them all by fleeing to Spanish Harlem with José, a Puerto Rican guitar player, with whom she had a son, Richard. This liaison lasted five years. The painter then formed an attachment with Sam, a "mad" Russian intellectual who was the father of her second son, Hartley.

During this entire period, Neel painted continuously and was on the Works Progress Administration, supporting herself and her children. Today Richard is a lawyer and Hartley is a doctor.

Neel's portraits are simultaneously documents of her own life and of the era in which she lived. She calls herself a collector of souls. Indeed, she digs down and then renders on canvas the essential being of those she choses to portray. Writers, artists, militant movement leaders, bums, men and women from every walk of life, clothed and nude, make their appearance in her burgeoning portrait gallery.

Economy of means is Neel's tradmark. Working in an expressionist manner, the artist reveals with strong touches of heavily stroked-on paint and wilful distortions of forceful line the interior functionings of the men and women before her. Often Neel is able to capture the total essence of her subject before filling in the entire canvas. When this occurs she will just sketch in the rest of the body and its supporting props and leave the background unpainted. These canvases may be unfinished, in the technical sense of the word, but aesthetically they are complete. Masterfully drawn and composed, all that needs to be said has been movingly stated.

Alice has been accused of seeking out the neurotic and grotesque in her subjects; these elements do often turn up in her work. Nevertheless there are noble, self-realized individuals, people with generosity and well-being written on their faces in her collection too. Can Alice Neel be blamed if these visages appear much less frequently than those that are riddled with anxiety, frustration, and cruelty? The artist's aim is not to idealize the human condition; rather she seeks to portray it accurately.

An artist with a highly original and daring vision, Neel ventured into controversial areas long before it was safe or fashionable to do so. Naked, pregnant women, unidealized male nudes with fully exposed genitals, defiant Black, Puerto Rican, and female faces have been part of her *oeuvre* ever since she began to consign her personal vision to canvas. From her first days as a painter, Alice Neel has dared to "tell it like it is."

ALICE NEEL   I was born in Merion Square, Pennsylvania. My family was Main Line and I grew up in a little town, Colwin, Pennsylvania—a benighted little town.

CINDY NEMSER   Did you study art formally?

A.N.   Yes. It took a great deal of courage. I entered the Philadelphia School of Design for Women which today is Moore College of Art. Now the reason I went there was, well, boys were very attractive and I thought if you really wanted to paint you had to concentrate and not think of anything else. And the good thing about it was that the Pennsylvania Academy of Art, in those days, was teaching Impressionism: all the lights were yellow and all the shadows blue. But at the School of Design there was a certain freedom and you could more or less paint as you wanted.

C.N.   Were all your teachers women?

A.N.   Oh no, but there was a very good drawing teacher named Paula Bellano who at the same time that she taught drawing taught anatomical construction. All the other teachers were just negligible. In fact, if they'd do something on my work, the minute they'd get out of sight I'd take it out. Also at the School of Design they had a great collection of facsimiles of the great sculpture of the world. I don't know what has happened to that collection. The collection I saw at the Victoria and Albert Museum didn't hold a candle to it. The old building where the school was was just grand. The ceilings were fifteen feet high. It had been the home of the late Edwin DeForest and it said on a plaque "The greatest tragedian of his day."

C.N.   It's interesting that the teacher who made the most impression on you was a woman.

A.N.   Because she was the best teacher. I don't think the quality of being a good teacher or a good artist has anything to do with sex. I think it's objective; you either are or you aren't.

C.N.   What was the curriculum like at the time?

A.N.   You got a degree in fine arts and it was also necessary to take a course in the history of art. The funny thing there was that the girls who were good painters were very stupid usually. They couldn't add or spell or anything. I could add and spell and I used to worry about it. I used to try deliberately not to be able to add or spell.

C.N.   How did your family feel about you being an artist?

A.N.   Well, the truth is I deceived them. They didn't interfere with it because they knew how much I wanted it, but at first I told them I was going to be an illustrator. Of course I soon realized that that was not for me and I was trying to do things that were completely impractical —just to be a good painter was impractical. I thought you had to give up a lot for art, and you did. It required complete concentration. It also required that whatever money you had had to be put into art materials. I had my own secret life in art school.

C.N.   Evidently you felt your family wouldn't approve.

A.N.   Well, of course, I knew they wouldn't. But how could they? Art, especially in those days—it was the late 1920's—was certainly not like it is today. You just can't think of it as we do today where it's hot from the easel to the front of something. Art wasn't important as it is now with all the universities going mad for it. And there was just no art in that town where I grew up. There were objects that could have been made into art, and the materials or events were there, but there were no artists.

C.N.   What happened when you graduated from the School of Design?

A.N.   I went to the Chester Springs summer art school and met a Cuban there. He came from a big, wealthy family and was very bad at mathematics so his father made him take a business course, but he really loved art and was always painting. As soon as he finished his business course he took this art course. At the end of that summer I married him and we went to Cuba and both painted. We completely lived the *vie Bohémienne*. I stayed in Cuba for a year and I had a show there.

C.N.   How did you like living in Cuba?

A.N.   It was backward and the women were very conservative. Not that they were stupid. It was just the rules. They even thought it was dreadful if a woman was in the streets too much. "Siempre en la calle" was considered a very derogatory remark about a woman. After a year we both came to New York.

C.N.   What happened then?

A.N.   We began to starve to death [laughter]. We had both left out the fact that you had to eat and live somewhere and he got very little from his family. We thought we'd make out as artists, which was just absurd; even now it may take some time; then it took even more.

C.N.   Usually artists today are backed by middle-class parents who help them.

A.N.   Of course. I once read that Marisol said she felt very sorry for artists who were poor. As a matter of fact, a lot of artists have been poor.

C.N.   Where did you live in New York?

A.N.   We had a big furnished room on West Eighty-first Street. I liked New York. I liked Havana too, for that matter. Both of these places were more exciting than that little town.

C.N.   What was the subject of your paintings then?

A.N.   I did a lot of watercolors—street scenes in New York.

C.N.   You painted the life around you?

A.N.   That's exactly it! The people and the life around me. That's my thing really!

C.N.   Even though you liked the life it must have been hard for you without money.

A.N.   I had a baby in Havana and this baby got ill with diphtheria and died here in New York. This, for me, was a frightful, tragic thing. In fact, out of this tragedy came the picture painted in 1930, the one I call *The Futility of Effort*. I made an earlier sketch of this work when the baby died in 1928, but I didn't paint it until 1930. It's symbolic really.

C.N.   Yes. Just one small figure with a calligraphic line hovering about it, a tiny life-line which is incredibly expressive. There is such hopelessness in the way that little figure in the bed droops.

A.N.   I read in the paper about a baby that had climbed down to the bottom of the bed and choked to death in the framework of the bed. This painting was a combination of my own tragedy and that event. It was reproduced by the WPA. They had an art magazine that came out every month. After I was on the WPA for a while and everybody was getting politically instructed, I'd go to see murals of Orozco and Rivera, and I began to think it was frightful of me to be so passive.

C.N.   There's a stylistic relation in this work to the painting of the Belgian artist Ensor and also to the Nabis and the artists who were around Gauguin.

A.N.   But I didn't know Ensor existed then. I was young and while we had the history of art at the School of Design, it wasn't all that thorough a course. It was from those university prints which really don't handle all the modern artists. No, no. This was painted right out of my experience. You know, I think it was a very revolutionary painting in this country. I don't think that anyone was doing anything like that. It was an experience felt and painted.

C.N.   In Europe the Expressionists worked out of their experiences. You were doing the same thing here by yourself. Certainly this is a personal painting. It's so sad—that line which just hangs down.

A.N.   That's the futility. What I like about it is its economical quality. It connects with my later work—with the portrait of Andy Warhol—in its hypersensitive economy. It gets down to the raw essentials. You know it's very hard to maintain a theory in the face of life that comes crashing about you.

C.N.   That economy came out of your experience.

A.N.   It's also effective in the depiction of grief. Even Picasso only used gray and white when he did the *Guernica.* Color is just too cheerful and happy for this sort of situation.

C.N.   What happened after your baby died?

A.N.   After that we got an apartment on Sedgwick Avenue along the Harlem River and I got pregnant again and had another girl. Here is a painting I did of the Well-Baby Clinic at the Fifth Avenue Hospital in 1930 where she was born. I did that from memory.

C.N.   Look at all the people—the infants all over the beds and the mother with the bare breasts and the bared teeth.

A.N.   [Laughter] Even that dreadful wretched mother being so happy over that baby that looks like a bit of hamburger—really awful, isn't it?

C.N.   You must have had all sorts of ambivalent feelings about being a mother and having a child.

A.N.   I think I did, although at that time I wasn't aware of it.

C.N.   You could hardly call that saintly motherhood.

A.N.   Oh no [laughter]. It's not idealistic at all, but it may be more the way it is really. The walls and the nurse and everything are so perfect and immaculate and the sprawling scrappy kind of people are so opposed to it. The walls look so hard and neat and the people so mangy and wretched.

C.N.   So now you had another child.

A.N.   Yes, and we were all just starving to death in New York. Well, my husband's rich family said they would send us to Europe and he thought that would be just great. He went down to Cuba with my daughter but by then the depression was having its results and they changed their minds and wouldn't do it. So his friends took up a collection for him and sent him off to Paris by himself. They told him he was being a petty bourgeois having a family. He wrote to me at first and said "I'll send for you in a couple of months," but I knew perfectly well that he just didn't know how to make money and he'd never be able to send for me. So I began painting like mad. I went to my school friend Ethel Ashton who had a studio on Washington Square in Philadelphia and painted all day long. Art was my one occupation. I actually have quite a few things from that time. Remember that pregnant woman with a man in the railway car? I painted that in the summer that Carlos left.

C.N.   The man is so content with himself.

A.N.   Yes, he looks so satisfied with himself and she looks wretched [laughter]. Well, that's the way it is [laughter]! I also did this nude then and the boat that used to go from Manhattan to Coney Island. They resemble the hospital painting in a way.

C.N.   You outline a great deal in these works, as you still do.

A.N.   At that time I would think theoretically. I was after the minimum you had to leave so that the painting would not just be a copy of something but a communication. That Coney Island boat exemplifies this because it's very simple and it's also a little mad, don't you think?

C.N.   Yes. And you are using color again in a very wild way. That green on the cheek of the person in the boat and that red mouth. It almost has a cartoon quality.

A.N.   Remember my show in 1970 with the painting of the transvestite Jackie Curtis and Rita Red? Now of course it's nothing like this, but there is some slight family resemblance.

C.N.   It's interesting that in this Coney Island boat painting you didn't finish off the color in the jacket, and you've begun to do that again.

A.N.   Yes. Because I thought you don't have to slavishly put the whole thing down. If you suggest it to the person, the person knows. Of course these paintings were never shown.

C.N.   This one of the woman in the fashionable-looking jacket is very striking.

A.N.   Yes. I remember the day I painted it was a hot day in Philadelphia. You see she has only one eye. It was so many years later that Larry Rivers made such an obvious point of having one eye in his paintings.

C.N.   She's painted in an elegant way. You are a little more charitable to her.

A.N.   Do you think I'm uncharitable?

C.N.   I think you go right to the essence of the person and show whatever you see there.

A.N.   She looks a bit prissy though.

C.N.   What year was all this taking place?

A.N.   That was in 1930 and then I had a horrible nervous breakdown. I was in and out of the hospital for a whole year. It was frightful. I was deserted and my child Isabetta was in Havana. My husband took her down with him and was going to come back in a month. I didn't see her for years—not until I painted this picture of her in 1934 when she was six. It was once shown at the Graham Gallery and Michael Benedickt said the early paintings showed great formal structure. This is a nice painting, but think how many years ago I painted it. It was painted in 1934 and it was first shown in 1966—and the others have not been shown at all. You have to have a retrospective to show old stuff because when you have a new show it has to be the new stuff.

C.N.   When you were painting were you showing your work at all then?

A.N.   No. I had no outlet. I just painted.

C.N.   Who took care of you while you were in the hospital?

A.N.   My family and, yes, then this Cuban husband came back from Europe, but I was just too far out to be able to get well. It took a whole year.

C.N.   Did you paint during that year?

A.N.   No, of course not. I didn't do anything but fall apart and go to pieces.

C.N. When did you begin to paint again?

A.N. In about 1931, when the whole thing was over. Then I came myself to New York and got an apartment on Cornelia Street right off Fourth and Sixth Avenue. I lived with a sailor, a rather interesting chap who played the guitar and sang and was rather nice except that he liked dope. He had a coffee can full of opium. I didn't dare smoke opium since I had just had this nervous breakdown, but they smoked opium at my apartment. This chap and Kenneth Fearing became so elegant and refined under the influence of opium. That was about 1933, the year I painted Joe Gould. He was one of the beats of the thirties.

C.N. You wrote Joe Gould's name on his portrait.

A.N. Yes, because I knew I wouldn't show it for years. I thought it was very creative—the fact that he had three sets of genitalia rather than one. Joe Gould was never circumcised so the one on the left side was the way he was and in the one on the right side he pushed the foreskin back and so it was just as if he were circumcised. But it's still Joe Gould, still an intimate portrait of Joe Gould. Don't you think it's basically intellectual?

C.N. He looks rather devilish—smiling that way.

A.N. There's a book about him. It's called *Joe Gould's Secret.* Joe Gould was working on an oral history of the universe but he used no typewriter. He wrote it with a pen. In fact when his mother died he bought several radios and smashed them. He was completely against the twentieth century. Recently Harvard has bought ten or eleven of Joe Gould's manuscripts of the oral history of the universe.

C.N. Why did you give him all those penises?

A.N. Because I don't think he ever had any sex life, but I felt that such exhibitionism as he had practiced really stemmed from there. And of course he just loved posing like that. In fact he wanted to wave out the window and that was an Italian neighborhood and I would have been ruined. But it's still on an intellectual level in some way, altogether there's a creature there.

C.N. It's interesting how you've used the patterning of forms and the color.

A.N. Don't the forms look like something ancient come back? Poor Joe. I used to call his portrait *Variations and on an Old Theme,* or *The Source of Russian Architecture.* At the time I painted him I painted a lot of other broken ruins. I also painted a great portrait of Sam Putnam, a famous American intellectual and translator, and the same man who owns the Joe Gould portrait owns the Sam Putnam. He's a Unitarian minister of all things.

C.N.   Do you think there's any kind of anti-male feeling in this painting?

A.N.   No. I never was like that. I was never that subjective. I feel when you are that kind of a person you're definitely limited because you can have any kind of experience but that can't turn you against the thing itself. That would be stupid. In fact that's one thing that's wrong with some women liberationists. Although I'm for women's liberation, sometimes it's taken on a petty level of some woman resenting not men but some specific man that she just didn't get along with. Now maybe she's right, but that's not what the approach should be. However both this painting and the one of my father lying in his coffin do show a certain attitude.

C.N.   In the Gould painting you cut the great masculine image down to size.

A.N.   And look what trouble Hemingway had in keeping it up. And do you know that the man who took the part of Superman, the great He-man, committed suicide just like Hemingway? Yes, Joe was pitiable, but that doesn't mean all men are. I don't think women and men should go after each other in that small way. I don't think women should take any crap, any insults, any putting down; they should fight all of it. But I don't think we should fight each other because we are all creatures in a way, aren't we? Both men and women are wretched and often it's a matter of how much money you have rather than what your sex is.

C.N.   The sexual aspect does often take precedence.

A.N.   Well, I suppose sex really is the greatest act of aggression in the world. But women want it, so they will have to adjust to the acceptance of aggression. It is aggression, but it's the law of life. But they don't have to accept other insults.

C.N.   Women are now beginning to be aggressive too about their sexual needs.

A.N.   I think it would be much nicer if we could act natural. Even though I am for women's lib now, and I am, for me the whole business of sex was rather difficult. I could never have been the aggressor. But all those insults, all that putting down—you know what they are? They're just a waste of time and costly to society. Not only that— women who are put down plot and become manipulative. I remember a man who was working at the Whitney Museum came over and said to me at the time I was painting Joe, "Why it seems as if you live in a matriarchy." I had that other painting there of the two nudes, *Nadya and Nona,* and a few others. I didn't know exactly what he meant.

C.N.   So at the time Joe Gould was considered scandalous.

A.N.   Yes, but by the time it was shown in my Philadelphia retrospective in 1971 so much had happened. *Joe Gould* was almost passé. But if it had been shown in 1933, it would have really been a shocker.

C.N.   Yes, for a woman to have painted a painting like that. There's the painting of the two female nudes you mentioned just now. You come back to that theme throughout your work.

A.N.   It does show women as being victims, doesn't it? This woman, while she does look a little like a prostitute, also looks a bit put-upon.

C.N.   There is also a symbolic feeling in this painting.

A.N.   Yes, that moon image. You know women's menstrual cycle was supposed to be connected with the moon.

C.N.   At one time it was said that your paintings of women could only have been painted by a woman. Do you feel that way?

A.N.   No. On the art project some Puerto Rican chap used to say of me, "Oh, Alice Neel—the woman who paints like a man." I always painted like a woman, but I don't paint like a woman is supposed to paint. Thank God, art doesn't bother about things like that. But you see humanity does because they are always thinking of their little careers. But art itself doesn't.

C.N.   I wouldn't know the sex of the artist who painted these nudes by looking at this picture. Yet I would say it was a very sensitive treatment of women and the person who executed it had a great empathy with these women and a great compassion for them. Between these nudes there is a kind of sympathy. They are two human beings and aren't treated as objects in the way most nude models are.

A.N.   Oh no. They were people I knew.

C.N.   These early thirties' paintings are rather dark, but the portrait of your little girl has brighter, more liberated color.

A.N.   I got on the PWAP [Public Works of Art Projects] that preceded the WPA and that gave me an income. It wasn't a very big income but it gave me enough to live and paint on. In the beginning of the project artists were not even picked for need. I got on it. I got a letter from the Whitney. I used to show on the Square. In fact, one day a man came over to me and asked, "Whose paintings are you watching?" I said, "My own." He said, "Oh no, you never painted those pictures." You see I always looked very sissy and I was rather pretty. So I had a completely double life. I was myself, but for social reasons I was that other person. In one way it was very useful. It made all the boys crazy about me. I never did believe in fixing up like an artist—that was "arty." If you ever look at Pablo Casals, he certainly doesn't look like much—just a little fat man. He doesn't give a damn or bother to fix himself up at all.

C.N.   You just wanted to be yourself.

A.N.   I'm not sure I was ever myself. I was myself but myself in our social systems. The place where I had freedom was when I painted. When I painted I was completely and utterly myself. For that reason it was extremely important to me. It was more than a profession. It was even a therapy, for there I just told it as it was. You see it takes a lot of courage in life to tell it how it is—of course not so much now as then.

C.N.   You were constricted by life?

A.N.   Yes. For one thing it was so hard to make money with art because art was not considered a profession, although some people did make it into one, but I didn't think they were always the best artists. I used to say the thing in this country was to be like a box of wheaties —to turn out a product so that everyone knew you by that product. Of course I never did that. My work is biographical in a way, and it changed with the times, not really in essence but to a certain extent outwardly.

C.N.   You reflect where you are and what's happening.

A.N.   The *zeitgeist*. Do you know the paintings that were being done in those days? There was that frightful landscape painter John Stewart Curry who used to show at the Whitney. Well, compared with that tepid stuff my paintings are wild and revolutionary.

C.N.   The paintings that were seen in the thirties were those of the social realists and the regionalists, weren't they?

A.N.   Well, in the thirties, just like any other time, it wasn't the best artists that were the most known. On the art projects the ones that were supervisors were the most mediocre. Just look in that book that Gertrude Stein wrote about Alice B. Toklas. She said there was official art and then there was art. Now, of course, everything is blended and there are no separations.

C.N.   Did you go on living with the sailor for a long time?

A.N.   I met a well-to-do liberal, a Harvard man named John who had a travel bureau and the sailor got jealous and cut up all my work and my clothing. He destroyed about sixty paintings and three hundred drawings. He used a curved Turkish knife. I just got out of the house in time or I would have been murdered. It was frightful. I was thrown into the world and then I began to hate both of them and I met José, a Puerto Rican singer. He was a nightclub entertainer who had a beautiful voice and played the guitar very well. Do you know what he was? He was a substitute for my Cuban husband although he was completely different. He was a nice person who also had a spiritual streak.

C.N.   And you went to live with him?

A.N.   First in the Village. Then I got sick of the Village. I thought it was degenerating. I moved up to Spanish Harlem with him. You know what I thought I'd find there? More truth; there was more truth in Spanish Harlem. And in a sense, there is more truth in the ghettos now than there is in all these festival places.

C.N.   In the Village you have basically the middle class or children of the middle class.

A.N.   Yes, Bohemians. So I went up to Spanish Harlem.

C.N.   Did you like it up there?

A.N.   Well, you know there is a certain level where there just isn't any art, especially for a woman. It was difficult. At one point I lived with a whole family. I never had any common sense in my life and everything always seemed feasible to me. But I did like Spanish Harlem and finally I found a tremendous apartment there, cheap like the lofts downtown used to be, with eleven windows.

C.N.   You painted *The Spanish Family* there. That dignified mother and her three children. That's another rendition of the family theme that goes through your work.

A.N.   Yes. And her husband is the TB case in this other painting which is very much like a crucifixion. It even had the purple and somber colors. I was on the WPA all these years and they got out a guide book in 1940 and it said the highest incidence of TB was in Harlem.

C.N.   He's very emaciated in your portrait.

A.N.   They took out his ribs and collapsed his lung. He's all bandaged up because he had all sorts of infections. He looks like Jesus Christ, but while galleries love Jesus Christ they don't love anyone else on a cross [laughter].

C.N.   His wife and children in the other look so strong and dignified.

A.N.   She was very bright and had lots of courage.

C.N.   How long did you live with José?

A.N.   Five years.

C.N.   What happened to him?

A.N.   Well, you know how Spanish men are? He was always *enamorado*—always chasing the girls. This didn't bother me so much because I wanted freedom to paint, but when I had a baby with him, my son Richard, it seemed worse.

C.N.   Did he support you?

A.N.   I was on the WPA all this time and I used to hand in a picture every six weeks, twenty-four inches by thirty inches. I did all the street scenes you saw and many other works and of course José made money too.

C.N.   It's extraordinary that you found time to work having to care for a little child.

A.N.   Oh, listen. I used to work at night when the baby was sleeping. I was more an artist than anything.

C.N.   So you feel women artists can't afford to take ten years off to have children?

A.N.   No. If you do, you lose your art. If you decide you are going to have children and give up painting during the time you have them, you give it up forever. Or if you don't, you just become a dilettante. It must be a continuous thing. Oh, you may stop for a few months, but I don't think you can decide to stop for years and do a different thing. You get divorced from your art. After all, art in our society was never natural as, say, in African society. That's why those things that they did were so great. It comes from the fabric of the society. Ours was always a bit ivory-tower—separated from real life. Theirs was real life and somewhere up above it—real art. With Pop art they have tried to get it back, but what has it become? It's advertising. But that may be because this country is advertising. Africans are nudes sitting on the ground, but Americans—we are the "Five and Ten." Hilton Kramer wrote a review of a primitive show saying that whatever these Africans are about we aren't able to understand it. But some of us have understood it. The painter Albert Pinkham Ryder would have understood it, or, for that matter, Blake and Picasso understood it. Now we are overbilged and all the bilge is coming out from the kind of life we've had. This superficial life is turning out all these horrors—in the prisons, in the schools. Life just isn't that superficial.

C.N.   You are saying we can't live with just materialism alone.

A.N.   They're doing it now in the art scene. They're living with science and materialism. It's spiraling up to a fantastic point, materialism, super-materialism. You can't leave mankind out. The time I went to Europe for the first time in 1965 when I left New York they had just shown Giacometti at the Museum of Modern Art. Then when I got to London I saw Giacometti's show again at the Tate Gallery. Then when I got to Florence I saw Michelangelo's work—the David—and I wondered what had happened to mankind in those centuries. With all those advances what had happened? We had become an alienated wretch, an emaciated dog wondering somewhere in a square. Isn't it sad? I defended human beings from the beginning because the Bible says man is the essence of all things and they are only finding this out now in relation to science and technology. Technology is ruining the ecology. It's getting out of the size that man can live with comfortably. Anyway, in the end, what is the thing if it isn't humanity? You wouldn't have anything. Now we are confronted with that possibility —not anything at all. That's nihilism. That's desperation. That's a lot of the thinking of the art world today.

C.N.   Coming back to your life. You spent five years with the Puerto Rican singer, and then what happened when you separated?

A.N.   I kept on living in Spanish Harlem and I kept on painting. Then I met a Russian who was born in England and grew up in Paris who had a terrific intellect but was rather a wild, mad creature. He was very cultured. Just knew more than anyone else I ever met in my life. This was great for me because, after all, in Spanish Harlem, wonderful as it was, there is a big cultural difference. Sam was entirely different from anyone I knew where I had grown up as well—and glamorous for that reason. He knew a number of languages and was one of the editors of *Experimental Cinema* in the thirties, along with Harry Allen Potemkin, and when Eisenstein came over here they took him around. He was just a brilliant fellow. You saw the paintings I did of him?

C.N.   Yes. I particularly like the one of him with his beautiful hawk-like nose. He was very aristocratic.

A.N.   He was, but he was also mad. He resented my little baby although I think in the beginning he was attracted to me because of the baby.

C.N.   That was your first son, Richard. What about the baby you had with him?

A.N.   Of course he loved that baby who is my son Hartley who is a doctor. Hartley went to Dartmouth and then to Tufts and is now a radiologist and a resident at Massachusetts General.

C.N.   Everybody admires you tremendously for putting your sons through school.

A.N.   They were just bright. Of course I wanted Hartley to be a ballet dancer and Richard to be a concert pianist. Richard plays very well and sings in the Canterbury chorus and Hartley had a scholarship to the American School of Ballet for about four years. Then one day he said to me, "You know there are some strange chaps there." And so I didn't dare send him there anymore [laughter]. That's the way life is. Life in *Amerika.*

C.N. So your sons decided they wanted to be respectable professionals. Richard is a lawyer and Hartley is a doctor. It's Richard's wife Nancy you have been painting so frequently, isn't it?

A.N. Yes, although I have one of Hartley's wife with a parrot on her arm. But Nancy lives close to me.

C.N. And you often paint her pregnant or with her children as in the recent paintings you've done of her and the twins.

A.N. Yes, the twins are just five months old and there is a portrait of her nursing them. They are girls but they look like gladiators [laughter]. Nancy is a New England girl and she's wonderful, completely unconventional. Thank God.

C.N. Let's go back to the forties and Spanish Harlem. What other works did you paint then?

A.N. I did one of a boy named Georgiarsi. I met him on the street and I had a boxer dog and he wanted to come up and play with it. His face is the face of Puerto Rico. To begin with he went to school and he was very proud and wouldn't let them know that he didn't know how to read and write. I'm sure his mother was illiterate. Later on he taught himself from ads and signs. But you saw those two portraits in the hall —one with a knife. He had a rubber knife and used to pretend to cut my throat. This was just fun and games. He once said to me, "I don't like to play." He was a desperate little character, but why shouldn't he have been desperate? When I lived in Spanish Harlem there were no Spanish teachers in those schools and Spanish culture was completely suppressed.

C.N. Your colors are so somber at this time.

A.N. After all, it was a depressed area, although I never thought of it like that. The truth is even before I left there the colors got brighter. I did this portrait of Edward Avedisian the artist before I left there, and even in the other portrait of Georgiarsi the pink background is brighter.

C.N. When did you do the portrait of Harold Cruz?

A.N. 1950. He was an orderly at Harlem Hospital and he came and posed. I don't think he was a writer then. In fact he was a communist and he used to worry about it. The cultural head of the party told him it was reactionary to like Debussy, but he told me he really did like him. I remember saying to Cruz, "What the heck. Go ahead and like Debussy."

C.N.   He has such a sadness about him, a resigned quality, and his hands are so sympathetic and graceful.

A.N.   He's written a great book since then. He wrote of the plight of the Black intellectual. I have all these historic people but somehow the gallery world doesn't include that. They used to accuse me in the thirties of being too literary, but isn't that nonsense. Who made that exact line? Whistler even called his paintings musical terms—nocturnes. I think all the arts are related. I have to show you this painting of Hugh Hurd. He's a Black actor who was in *The Death of Bessie Smith.* It was painted in '64 or '65.

C.N.   Were you still living in Spanish Harlem?

A.N.   No, right where I live now.

C.N.   The expression on Hurd's face is different from that of Harold Cruz's. Finally there is evidence of resentment.

A.N.   Yes. This must have been '64 because I remember saying Hurd looked like a panther about to spring and that was before the Black Panthers. Did you see that one of Abdul Rhamon, the Black Nationalist, with the sun in the corner? I felt that was the rising sun of the Negro cause.

C.N.   Why did you eventually leave Spanish Harlem?

A.N.   I was just put out. I never would have left. They divided the whole house in half and rented each half for much more. You know who lives there now? Mostly poor Negroes. The whole family works to pay the rent. My same landlord brought me over here to Broadway and 107th Street and showed this apartment to me and I took it because it was so big. And then Hartley and Richard were both going to Columbia at that time. It was nice here because they could both walk over.

C.N.   When did you start to show at the Graham Gallery?

A.N.   In 1963. I had a reproduction in *Art News* in the summer of '62 and then in the fall I had a big article by Hubert Crehan. I met Crehan and I have a portrait of him. He came up to see me and he said, "My God, this is so good—so wonderful." In fact I converted him from being a follower of Clifford Still to being a follower of me.

C.N.   You did some of your greatest paintings in the sixties.

A.N.   The return of the figure show was at the Museum of Modern Art and the Kornblee Gallery put on a show of artists they thought should have been included. I had recently met Jack Kroll and he loved my work. So he put four of my paintings in that show. Tom Hess went to the show. He never had heard of me but he photographed my portrait of Edward Avedisian and included it in an article about the return of the figure in *Art News*. Later Tom Hess and Harold Rosenberg came to the house and then they gave me the Longview Purchase Prize for that portrait of that millionaire, Stewart Mott. In fact, there was an article in 1966 about me doing two pictures of one person. I did two of Stewart Mott and also two of Mimi Gross and Red Grooms and one of them received the National Academy of Design Award. I did one of Stewart more finished and one less finished. I did one version up to a certain point and then I copied it and carried it further in the second one, but they both turned out good. I thought the first one was perfect as it was but I had the desire to finish it more. I could still do that today. I did two because I see them two ways. Maybe I'm schizophrenic.

C.N.   Here's the portrait you did of the Negro draftee.

A.N.   He has a marvelous head. I thought it would be interesting to leave a work in progress so I just sketched the body in.

C.N.   Some people have criticized your ability to draw.

A.N.   Oh, they're crazy; they're mad. I'm a master, don't you think? Recently Hub Crehan did a syndicated article about my Philadelphia show. He said idiosyncratic drawing. Now I would admit that it may be idiosyncratic drawing—that it is not straight matter-of-fact draw-ing—but look at the hands and feet in that painting of Persilla Johnson of Short Hills, done in 1966. She was very brilliant and went to Smith. But in real life she was rather lost. Her brilliance was all of a literary nature. She was out of this world.

C.N.   The shape of her hand parallels the shape of the leaves in the planter near her and the leaves look like they are reaching out to clutch at her.

A.N.   They are predatory too.

C.N.   And so is her hand. And here is this wonderful portrait of your daughter-in-law Nancy with her first baby. The eyes are compelling.

A.N.   Yes. Nancy—mother and child—and she looks a little terrified. Here's Jenny, Hartley's wife, and here is Julie Alkitis. She is the model in the painting of the pregnant woman with her husband who is clothed that you reproduced in *Artsmagazine*.

C.N.   I thought of her as a woman exposed in her most vulnerable state.

A.N.   If you think of it without being conventional there were tribes that used to make all images of the women pregnant and the men with erections. When you think of it, it's just part of life. But now everybody is approaching everything. I'm sure in the show *Hair* they went much further—nudes running right down into the audience.

C.N.   In the Living Theatre performances they really did strip down.

A.N.   Oh yes. I have a great portrait of Julian Beck.

C.N.   It's fascinating how you have painted all these outstanding people all your life. In the *Village Voice* they referred to you as the court painter to the underground art world.

A.N.   You mean Andy Warhol. Well, I'll show you a portrait of a chap I painted who used to be on the Bowery. It's one of my very good portraits but hard for my gallery, which is a little bourgeois, to take.

C.N.   How did you come to paint all these well-known people?

A.N.   It's been mostly accidental. Sometimes it's been because people thought I would do it so well. And usually the subjects can't afford to buy their portraits.

C.N.   Yes. You've done so many portraits and so few have been bought.

A.N.   Well, you see I never wanted to work for hire because I don't want to do what's going to please some subject. If they are pleased I love to sell, but I don't want to have to turn out a product.

C.N.   How many shows have you had at the Graham Gallery?

A.N.   '63, '66, '68, '70, '73, five. They just never sold anything. Maybe I'm hard to take. You see they could never take my work at all until 1960. I never got any publicity at all until 1963. It's true I had a show at the Pinacotheka Gallery in 1944 and a couple at the ACA in '50 and '51 but I just painted the kind of pictures that people never bought. It was just something they couldn't take and suddenly in 1960 they could take it more. I think people developed more.

C.N.   What do you think of the developments in abstract painting of the sixties, like the work of Frank Stella?

A.N.   I think it's interesting and very nice to look at, but it's not all of life and in the end it's decorative, although because it's so geometric it may be more than decorative. I like it. But I don't see why they have to cross out other things, but they do. They have fads. Then I thought when they started liking the figure again at the end of the sixties that I'd be right in there because I'd done the figure for so long. I thought I was the best one doing it. But I was wrong. They had that big realist show at the Whitney, and . . .

C.N.   They didn't include you.

A.N.   And they were beginners compared to me. It's true the Whitney now has the *Andy Warhol* but then they had nothing of mine. I never had a thing hung in the Whitney. It's true that I didn't push myself enough—ever.* I could never go around pushing; it's repulsive to me. I'll tell you what; it's sad to live on the shelf.

C.N.   In these great portraits of the sixties and early seventies I feel that you get right into the essence of the person you are painting.

A.N.   I do. The persons themselves dictate to a certain extent the way they are done. If they are very liberated people I, in turn, feel very liberated and can paint them in a more liberated way. But look at the Dorothy Pearlstein. Isn't she a fairly conservative person? And really her portrait is quite finished—and deliberately so.

C.N.   The details of her dress echo the sitter's personality—the fur on the coat and the patterned stockings.

A.N.   I love that face, though. She seems to me like those very serious Spanish women. She's very bright and kind and I like her.

C.N.   I love your portrait of Henry Geldzhaler. What interests me is how you handle his face and hands.

A.N.   Well, his hands bend more than most hands.

C.N.   They are so small and staccato. They look like little whips that would like to flick you aside.

A.N.   He was very nice to me. We had tea every time and he would take a nap after the painting session.

C.N.   What did Geldzhaler think of his portrait?

A.N.   He came back to the gallery four times and stayed an hour each time.

C.N.   Maybe he found it disturbing?

A.N.   I don't know. There's a bit of satire in it, maybe, but no more than in the man himself. I think he looks more powerful here than he looks in life. I really painted what I thought was there besides what shows. Is he very powerful?

C.N.   As curator of modern art at the Metropolitan Museum he has a lot to say. You've made his head so much larger than the rest of his body.

A.N.   Well [laughter], you know, I don't control these things. I think I could, but I let myself go and that's what happened.

*In February 1974 Alice finally had a small retrospective at the Whitney Museum.

C.N. I think in your greatest portraits you completely become that person.

A.N. I do. Oh listen. Sometimes I feel awful after I paint. Do you know why? Because I go back to an untenanted house. I go back to a place where there isn't anything. I leave myself and go out to that person and when I come back there's a desert. Oh I feel awful for a while—for maybe a half hour. You know what it is for me? It's an esthetic trip like an LSD trip. But though I participate a lot I do not leave my self completely because you have to be in control of the situation or no painting comes out at all.

C.N. I also feel that your portraits have a great universality in them. It is as if the person is himself and yet he represents a large segment of humanity.

A.N. Of course, of course. My son Hartley represented all the youth of that day. In this portrait of him in 1966 he was twenty-five and threatened with Viet Nam and with everything else that threatened the youth of that day.

C.N. He has this puzzled sadness with his body slumping as if it were all too much for him. He becomes Everyman in that condition. All your great portraits are touched with this quality. There is the one of the transvestites Jackie Curtis and Rita Red.

A.N. It should be Rio Red because he's male but Jackie gave him that name. He just adores Jackie so and although Jackie is a career person he's still very, very kind. He wrote me a little poem. It's beautiful. The night of the opening of my show at Moore College the head of the college was delighted to be photographed with Jackie and Rita in front of their painting.

C.N. It's interesting how people with respectable façades are drawn to the unconventional.

A.N. Of course, they want to be diverted. They don't want to have that dull fare all their lives. It can be dull in a school, don't you think? [laughter] Do you like *The Gruen Family* portrait?

C.N. That's the critic John Gruen and his wife, the painter Jane Wilson.

A.N. He looks like a gypsy father. You know this painting should be called *The Gruen Family* or *Six Patent Leather Shoes*. Wait, here's someone we forgot—Walter Gutman. You know I saw him in the Martha Jackson Gallery and then I didn't paint him until two years later, but I saw right then what I wanted to paint.

C.N. What was it?

A.N.   He was standing with that hat that looks like he sits on it every night or every day. I think he's rich—stock market. He gave me his book *You Only Have To Get Rich Once.* But he was born rich. He financed *Pull My Daisy.* I was in that. That's a big portrait of him. You know what? He looks like a bull, doesn't he? He looks like the bull and the bears. In the Philadelphia show he looked magnificent because you could get the menace of him walking out of the canvas.

C.N.   How was it painting Andy Warhol after he got that scar?

A.N.   Oh, he's a very nice person. He posed beautifully. And here's a portrait of my son Richard.

C.N.   He's the lawyer.

A.N.   He has cordovan shoes. He has the cordovan badge of captivity. You know, like the Red Badge of Courage. When John Canaday saw this portrait he said, "Who is that? It's a great painting," and I said, "It's my son and he's a lawyer." Then I talked about his shoes and I said, "He's just captured," and Canaday said, "There are worse fates," and I said, "You know, given life as we have it, his fate is perfectly all right." Yet still I hate to see my sons lose their freedom.

C.N.   I imagine your sons are very proud of you.

A.N.   Yes. And they're much nicer to me than most sons are to their mothers. Here is Linus Pauling. He's a chemist and won two Nobel Prizes and I went to Big Sur to do that.

C.N.   He doesn't look captured or pathetic.

A.N.   He isn't. He had a great mind and he's free and does the best he can for humanity.

C.N.   His body and head are in proportion.

A.N.   He is noble and kind and unpretentious—just associates with people. Well, all these fancy reactions to portraits. I painted a man who was a poet and he fell in love with this girl. They were living together and she just loved this portrait and was dying to buy it. Then they quarelled and then she wouldn't even look at the portrait. The portrait was like a totem. It wasn't a portrait any more. It was him.

C.N.   I've notice you have never painted any self-portraits.

A.N.   I'm suicidal. I hate myself [laughter], I never did my own type.

C.N.   I think that portrait of Harold Rosenberg's daughter with her fishnet stockings is extraordinary.

A.N.   She was a force. I was quite mesmerized. She overpowered me. Did we talk about the portrait of my father? Well he died in 1946. I painted him from memory the day after the funeral—lying in a coffin

—not for morbid reasons but so I would remember what he looked like. He retained a lot of what he was. He had a certain nobility of character and was very calm and gentle.

C.N.   What about the Kate Millett portrait you did for the cover of *Time* magazine?

A.N.   That was a surprise for me. It was done from a photograph. I had never done anything commercially but they said she was just too hardpressed. I did it from photographs but the truth is it's better from photographs than if I'd done it from life, although from life it would have been more accurate because she looks smaller and more doubled in. She looks more heroic on *Time*. When I met her at the Art Students League I said to her, "Why didn't you pose for me? After all you believe in women's liberation. I'm a woman." She said, "Because the Daughters of Bilitus of which I am a member do not believe in having a leader." So I thought of all the way back to the thirties when Clifford Odets had a play called *Waiting for Lefty* and revolutionary theory was you don't have any leader because if you have a leader he may get killed and then no one will know what to do. But I said to her, "You couldn't possibly fight American publicity. Once you wrote that book you were done for. No matter what you wanted to do, there you were —in the saddle." In fact in Norman Mailer's *Prisoner of Sex*, Kate Millett is his main protagonist; he goes after her the most. Of course the greatest insult he gives her is that she is so much of the university.

C.N.   Do you think that's true?

A.N.   Well, the colleges are trying to absorb so much of the arts. I don't think they ever can completely because there's something about putting art into a curriculum. It doesn't serve. The most that can be done to teach is to create an atmosphere where whatever form of art they're doing is the most important. If it is important and other people are working all around you, then the whole atmosphere is conducive. They could at least have that atmosphere. Instead they fall into the atmosphere of credits and marks. I think this is a result of our excessive concentration on individualism. Mr. Rockefeller is always talking about it. He can have a lot of it—he can afford to—but because of it we are apt to forget we are related to other creatures. Yet, come to think of it, even though it's good to be related, if one is forced to, it becomes a sideshow. Women's oppression has been universal, but I couldn't read Betty Friedan because of all those statistics and because I was such a snob. I couldn't identify with the housewife in Queens. I didn't have her aids—her washing machine, her security. I didn't have any of that. But I realize, at the same time, that was snobbish of me.

C.N. How did you feel about being on that panel with other women artists—with Louise Nevelson, Pat Mainarid, and Faith Ringgold?

A.N. Well, Faith Ringgold said that her greatest enemy was the Black man. Now it might be true, if you separated all things, that the worst thing is to be pushed into a completely feminine position, but if she would just look a little further socially she would see there're even reasons for that. I also contradicted her on another panel at the Art Students League when she said all Black and Puerto Rican women should stop having children. I said to her, "Why don't you say they should force Nixon to have nurseries? Why do you say they should stop propagating their own race? The only way they're going to get anything is to have enough numbers to fight for it."

C.N. What about Louise Nevelson?

A.N. I think her work is very impressive and her show at the Whitney looked great. Louise is not against women. She's perfectly willing to cooperate, but when a woman makes a complete success like that she's absolved from having to be for women. She's the exception. (Although it isn't right to say you don't have to be for women because if you are a woman and have a brain you would be anyway.) Lucy Lippard, the critic, is in the same position. She's been to a lot of women's lib things but she has a favored position. What is it they call it? The pecking order? Dreadful. I hate that phrase. But you know you can't always blame the men for taking everything because life is hard and when some advantage is given you on a silver platter you just take it. It's the same with some women. By special intelligence or by talent they get a favored position. Not that I think that you just work from your position and that's enough. You do things too.

C.N. Getting back to the portraits you did in the fifties and sixties, here's the one of Edward Avedisian you mentioned before.

A.N. I met Edward Avedisian and Robert Smithson together. But Edward doesn't look as if he trusts me in this portrait. Do you see that foot? Doesn't it look as if it is ready to kick you any moment?

C.N. What about Robert Smithson?

A.N. Oh, he was very nice to me in those days. I went down to his studio and do you know what he was doing? He was doing things in crepe paper and Christs covered with blood. So I said to him, "If you can use all that blood, why can't I use a little more on the cheek of your portrait?" Because he had made me take it out. This was before he had any success at all.

C.N. Here's the Ivan Karp portrait.

A.N.   There's a dreamer in Ivan. Don't you know those bits of old architecture, those romantic things he does. I've accentuated that, although he looks a bit Napoleonic too, don't you think? This is Mamie Bradley, the mother of Emmett Till—that Negro boy they murdered down South. I went up to a meeting in Harlem and I think I was the only white person there. Here's an early portrait of José. Isn't he beautiful? He has a guitar. I used to love it because he'd buy those ties on Forty-second Street.

C.N.   Here are some of the landscapes you did in the forties.

A.N.   You know who liked them? Clement Greenberg. In 1944, you know what he said about this landscape painting? "Whoever looking at you would think you were schizophrenic?" Later on in the sixties I told Greenberg I'd like to paint his daughter Sarah. Then his wife brought the little girl all dressed up in rose velvet with a big lace collar. You see, it looks like one of those paintings of the infantas that Hoving showed in his "Age of Kings." Later that year Clement saw the portrait at the Graham Gallery but he didn't even sign the book nor ever tell me what he thought of it. Still, from his exclusive abstract stance this is perhaps to be expected. As for me, I believe in "let all flowers bloom" —once a tenet of Mao Tse Tung. I do not believe any movement should monopolize the market.

Here's a portrait of James Farmer that Jack Kroll mentioned in *Newsweek*. He was marching in Mississippi. You can see he's very conservative in some ways still, but in the gallery they said I made him look too angry—that he looked more Madison Avenue than I made him. But he's not Madison Avenue at heart. He was marching in Mississippi. He bought a portrait I did of his two children. Would you like to see the Baron Eric Von Eckerstrom? I did him in the nineteenth-century manner because that's the way he is. Isn't he grand and utterly decadent and he looks like a piglet around the ears. Here's a portrait of the Baron's aunt—she had all the money. When the Museum of Modern Art came, her portrait was among the pictures they chose from. I wish they'd taken it instead of the little boy they took. I thought they reduced me down to nothing. Here's a portrait of a man whose wife committed suicide. He's a famous professor at Princeton. I never would have gotten him to sit if she hadn't committed suicide. He was so disturbed and at loose ends. Doesn't he look miserable? And listen, he's a very advanced guy. He has a big class on political economy and once the *Nation* had a whole number devoted to his opinions. Here's William Seitz, the museum curator. I did him when I first moved into this house. He came to New York to see me. Listen, you know why I put that hand like that? It's an uncommitted hand. This hand is the traveler. Do you know what he'd say to me? We don't form any opinions, we just reach out there. I said to him, "Look, the minute you hang things on your sacred walls you are making a judgment." He was very nice to me, though, and came all the way from out of town to see my last show. I think he was instrumental in the Museum of Modern Art's buying the one painting, but he never did any more than that. I'll show you the two Seitzes together—this is Irma Seitz. Neither of them knows how good their pictures are. I guess they didn't like the portraits very much. Look, here is a portrait of a woman I picked up on the street. She's mad, and you know what she is? She's a religious fanatic. I followed her into a bank and there I captured her. I said, "Will you pose for me?" And she said, "If God will let me!" But then she called me and posed.

C.N.   Here is the portrait of your old friend John, the Harvard man.

A.N.   Yes, he still comes around to take me to dinner at the Harvard Club. He hates that portrait because he thinks I made him look like a working man.

C.N.   He looks Bohemian actually.

A.N.   Well he has a streak of it. Going all the way back to the thirties here is the childbirth I did of the woman in the bed next to me when I had Richard, Goldie Goldwasser. I telescoped the whole thing together. Maybe I should have put a little red baby there too. What you see is empathy. You're not aware of your shoulders when you are in labor so I left the shoulders out. I did the painting when I came back from the hospital. She had already had the child. I'll show you a portrait of Hub Crehan.

C.N.   He looks like a cab driver.

A.N.   I know he does but he's really an artist. You know why I made those glasses like that? Because he's always drunk and also he looks tragic to me. That mouth looks as if he could cry. For the last twenty-five years he's drunk at least a quart of hard liquor every day. He had very narrow hips and a tremendous thorax. He's even bigger than in the painting. William Seitz and his wife came here one night and brought with them the editor of a magazine in San Francisco who doesn't believe in knowing anything because he wants to be ignorant. So he told me I paint portraits in the grand manner. Anyway Hub came here with his little children and got roaring drunk. I was afraid for Bill Seitz because Bill was writing the forward to the catalog for the Hans Hofmann show and Hub Crehan said, "I'm sick of Hans Hofmann. What did Hans and his pigs knuckles ever teach anybody?" Bill just looked at him and figured Hub could make mincemeat out of him.

C.N.   That's how women are intimidated. They don't dare to argue back for the same reasons Seitz wouldn't stand up to Hub Crehan.

A.N.   What do you think overpowers women if they misbehave? The cave men just beat them up. That's right. Oh my God, if I had only been able to knock some of my braves down, my whole life would have been simpler—much simpler. If you have a weapon, you use it. But Crehan was a nice fellow.

C.N.   Here's a portrait of him and his child.

A.N.   That's Sasha his daughter. This is a father and child instead of mother and child. Why not father and child for once?

Well Baby Clinic, 1929.

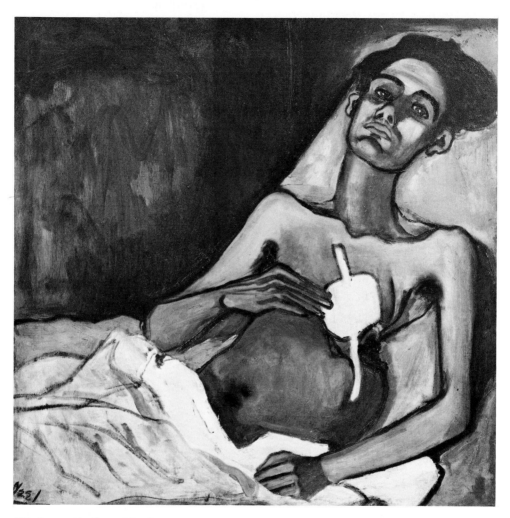

TB Case, Harlem, 1940.

Harold Cruz, 1950.

Hugh Hurd, 1964.

Georgie Arce, 1955.

Hub Crehan, 1962.

Hartley, 1965.

Henry Geldzahler, 1967.

Jackie Curtis and Rita Red, 1970.

Julie and Algis, 1967.

Nancy and the Twins, 1971.

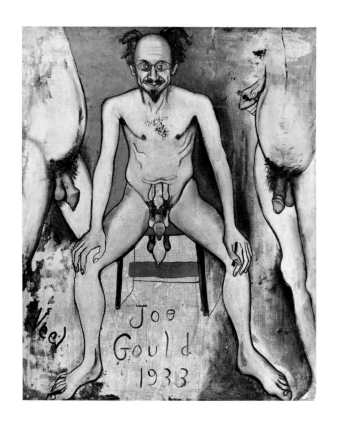

Joe Gould, 1933.

John Perreault, 1972.

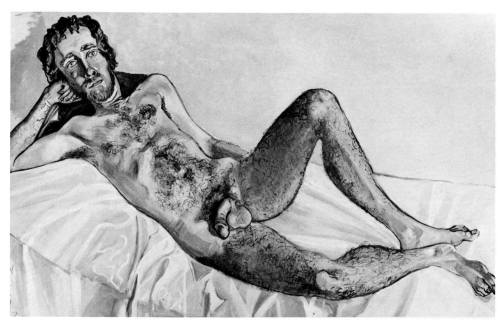

The Gruen Family, 1970.

Grace Hartigan, 1971.

RACE HARTIGAN, the blond, beautiful, and vivacious painter, created a sensation in New York in 1952 when her painting *Persian Jacket* was purchased by the Museum of Modern Art. One of the first women artists to earn an international reputation, Hartigan was a member of that small band of New York Abstract Expressionist artists who helped to move the art world center from Paris to New York.

Hartigan was born in Newark, New Jersey, in 1922 of Irish-English stock. Although her parents could not afford to send her to college, the artist attended the Newark College of Engineering at night and mastered mechanical drawing. She worked as a draftsman and also studied with painter Isaac Lane Muse in the forties. During this period Hartigan, who had married at the age of seventeen, had a son whom she raised singlehandedly while her husband was in the army.

Arriving in New York in 1946, Hartigan soon made contact with the first generation of Abstract Expressionists—de Kooning, Kline, Pollock, Gottlieb, and Rothko. She lived the same difficult, poverty-stricken life as the men and, according to the the artist, was accepted whole-heartedly into their ranks.

Her first break occurred in 1950 when the dealer Samuel Kootz exhibited her work in a New Talent exhibition selected by the critic Clement Greenberg and the art historian Meyer Shapiro. In 1951 she had her first one-woman show in the newly formed Tibor DeNagy Gallery. Hartigan's paintings of the early fifties were deeply influenced by de Kooning and Pollock. Presented in an all-over format, these passionately painted canvases lovingly explore the sensuous potential of the painterly medium.

After designing the stage sets for a production of *Red Riding Hood* by poet Kenneth Koch and collaborating with poet Frank O'Hara in a series of *Poem Paintings* which combined words with heavily brushed-on abstract images, Hartigan, in 1952, abdicated from her totally abstract position. Sensing that she had been working with borrowed forms, the artist attempted to find her own roots by re-examining the works of Rubens, Velásquez, Goya, and on through Matisse and Picasso. This exploration lasted until 1958. During this period the painter produced some of her most outstanding works—the *Persian Jacket* (1952), the imposing *Grand Street Brides* (1954), and the dynamic *City Life* (1956). In these works the artist combined the shallow frontal space of the Cubist painters with the dynamic excitement of the Abstract Expressionist brush stroke to create a new and uniquely realistic vision of her own external surroundings on New York's Lower East Side. Toward the end of this investigation, Hartigan's conception of the outer world became more and more fragmented with only snatches or wisps of recognizable matter thrown into her combustive painterly patterns. In 1958 she totally abandoned the exterior world and withdrew once more to complete abstraction. Although recognizable images have been abolished in such intense paintings as *Essex and Hester Red* (1958), *Since Rousseau* (1963), *William of Orange* (1964), and *Barbi* (1964), nevertheless the organic linear elements and the pulsating sensations rendered by the sensitive application of the paint stroke continue to suggest that these are· very personal responses to an immediate environment. These undecipherable linear shapes, painterly slashes, and drips all refer, if indirectly, to a visceral reaction to an external reality.

Unable to exclude the outside world indefinitely, in the mid-sixties Hartigan once again found the facts of her everyday existence creeping into her imagery. By then she had married Dr. Winston Price and moved to Baltimore, where she lives today in a gracious suburban setting surrounded by all kinds of lush vegetation, and at the same time rents a studio in a rough downtown Baltimore area that is very like her earlier East Side situation in New York. *The Year of the Cicada* (1970), in which plant forms and furnishings crowd out human concerns, reflects the suburban side of Hartigan's present life, while *Autumn Shop Window* with its deliberately strident orange and green tonalities, its price-tagged displays, its reflections and incorporations of street activity, all laid out in a shallow frontal space, presents an effective pictorial vision of the more staccato flow of life in the inner city.

During the Pop Art craze, Hartigan and the other Expressionist painters of the New York School found themselves temporarily out of favor. Many left New York needing a more congenial environment in which to continue their own personal forms of development. Hartigan, too, dropped out of public favor for a time but she has never ceased to explore the nature of her own reality nor hesitated to present it, eschewing all fashionable imperatives, from her own point of view.

CINDY NEMSER   I am interested in your experience as a woman artist.

GRACE HARTIGAN   I can't talk anonymously about being a woman artist. All I can talk about is my own experience. To be truthful I didn't much think about being a woman. I thought about how difficult it was to paint.

C.N.   When you had your first solo show you did call yourself George, rather than Grace?

G.H.   I will never be able to correct that misunderstanding. It had absolutely nothing to do with the feeling that I was going to be discriminated against as a woman. It had to do with a romantic identification with George Sand and George Eliot. George Eliot is a great writer. I don't think of George Sand as a great writer but she certainly was a great force historically. I wanted to identify myself with these two great women.

C.N.   Then weren't you looking for female role models?

G.H.   You could say that that was what I was doing. I was identifying. I respected Georgia O'Keeffe but I didn't feel that the kind of life I had in New York was similar to her kind of life there or in New Mexico where she had, by then, moved. I really didn't identify with her. A couple of years after I had done the identification part, it just didn't seem to make any sense any more. So I dropped it.

C.N.   Weren't there other women artists around then?

G.H.   The only women around who were deeply involved with painting were Lee Krasner and Elaine de Kooning, the wives of the two great painters Pollock and de Kooning. It wasn't until a few years later that I met Helen Frankenthaler and Joan Mitchell.

C.N.   It is interesting that you mentioned Lee Krasner. I have done extensive research on the work she did from 1946 to 1949 which she called her "Little Image" paintings. They are extraordinary yet there is no mention of these works in the writings about the art of that time.

G.H.   I met both of the Pollocks in 1948. I thought that Lee's paintings were fascinating and remarkable but his had such scope and power. She had just begun painting again. It was after a period of several years during which Jackson was so competitive that he couldn't bear another personality painting around him. I thought of them equally as artists but she was working against a barrier of ego. It took her a long time before Jackson would let her move, really move, as an artist. She deliberately submerged her personality to his genius, if I can use that word.

C.N.   She said that her "Little Image" paintings started in '46. Until then, from '43 to '46, she had this break where an image wouldn't emerge.

G.H.   She worked very little. When I met them out in Springs, Jackson had this huge barn and Lee had just a tiny little bedroom in the farmhouse. The farmhouse wasn't heated so she couldn't work in the winter. Jackson couldn't work in the winter either because his barn wasn't heated. But it wasn't as though she was allowed a real studio. That was their thing. I have never been like that.

C.N.   Lee felt that at the time she and her contemporaries were creating a new art and transferring the art scene to New York from Paris. In the midst of all this it was impossible for her to make a stand for herself.

G.H.   She couldn't do it and stay married to Pollock. That is one of the bitternesses Lee has. She could have done it if she had split.

C.N.   What was it like for you in New York in the forties and fifties?

G.H.   I was poor as was everybody else. I had no private income. I worked as hard as everybody else and shared the life.

C.N.   Were you part of the famous Artist's Club of the fifties?

G.H.   I went to the Club all the time and to the Cedar Bar and that whole realm. Once the men saw how serious my work was they respected it. They were also touched by the fact that I was so poor. They weren't used to young women going into that life. I lived like the men.

C.N.   Was that important—to live like the men?

G.H.   I had no choice. What else was I to do unless I wanted to go on working as a draftsman? But I had no feeling of discrimination or of being set apart.

C.N.   I have heard people say that you were very tough during that time.

G.H.   I was probably quite defensive. I am still pretty tough. I don't want to take any guff from anybody. But then never in my life did I consider a woman to be a fading waterlily. I always thought I was a person. Fortunately my mother and father never treated me like a flower. They always asked me, "Who are you? What are you going to do with your life?" I was going to be a detective when I was ten. I was the oldest and the smartest and my parents never thought I was just going to be a housewife like my mother. But they couldn't send me to college because they didn't have the money.

C.N.   I grew up in the fifties and I just drifted into teaching elementary school because my mother said it was a good occupation for a woman. It was a secure job and I could teach and have a family at the same time. My parents had gone through the depression.

G.H.   So did mine. My parents (my father had just died) were very middle-class suburban New Jersey people. But somehow, they never treated me as if I was going to be anything but difficult and different. They knew it—as if they had a changling on their hands. I think they treated my two younger sisters differently—in a more stereotyped way. They were to fill in with a little job until they got married and raised families. That is exactly what they did.

C.N.   Your parents' attitude toward you made a tremendous difference.

G.H.   Yes, but I created that attitude by the kind of personality I had from the time I was two years old. They adjusted to the personality of this weird creature. They didn't try to force me into anything that seemed silly.

C.N.   What brought you into art?

G.H.   It's just a series of ridiculousnesses, but if you want to know I will tell you. I married as soon as I left high school to the first young man that I met who knew about poetry and literature. I was not interested in painting at all. I was seventeen and he was nineteen. Nine months and two weeks later I had a baby and all during that time this young man was saying, "Who are you? What are you going to do?" He was like my parents. Realistically, I answered, "I can't be a composer, it's too late." He said, "I know you are going to create something." I said, "I've written." (I did write a great deal but we agreed that it wasn't very good.) He said, "How about being a painter?" I said, "I can't paint." He said, "Oh, come on." So while I was pregnant we decided to go to evening classes. The minute I picked up a pencil just to draw a vase I started to sweat. I began to suffer while he was pretty good. He made a drawing and there I was crying and sweating with this pencil in my hand. I got hooked in some way. I chose, of all mediums, watercolor. All during the time I was pregnant and then after the baby was born I drew, all on my own without any teaching, in the evenings and weekends. Then my husband went into the army and I went into the College of Engineering nights and got a job as a mechanical draftsman. This was in Newark, New Jersey. At work I met a draftsman who asked me if I was interested in painting. I said, "I am trying." He said, "Do you like modern art?" I said, "I don't know what that is." He said, "I have a teacher and I go two nights a week. Would you like to see what he does?" I said, "Show me what it is like," and he brought in a book of Matisse. I really got hooked. I thought that looked wonderful and real easy. I said, "Okay, I will go to that teacher." I was nineteen when I went to Isaac Muse in Newark and studied for about three years. I painted weekends and then, gradually, it took over. In the drafting room where I worked I had a very understanding boss and he fired me so I could get unemployment compensation. I think that was in '47. That was the first time that I had the whole year just to paint.

C.N. It must have been very hard.

G.H. It was terrible because I had no facilities. I was a terrifically good draftsman but I had no art facilities because I hadn't done it when I was a child. Nothing was given to me in that realm. I was a very clumsy artist.

C.N. In a way that was good. Sometimes people with too much facility get caught up in it and they can't get away from it.

G.H. Well, it is not very comforting when you are going through it. But after you have gone through it, won the facility after years of hard work, and are able to say what you feel and think, then it is a sweet triumph.

C.N. How did you take care of your child while you were mastering your art?

G.H. That was extremely difficult. I had to juggle that. It was grand-parents helping out, then nursery school. Jeff, my son, bitterly opposed my painting. He would stay after school and would come in at five o'clock, look at me and say, "I know, you have been painting again." When he got to be twelve and his father had remarried, I sent him to California. I have never seen him since. It is a very bitter relationship.

C.N. I'm sorry.

G.H. I went through a lot about it but it was inevitable because I couldn't have kept him on the Lower East Side. I had hardly enough money to support myself and the studio. I lived on something like thirty dollars a week and it was a terrible environment for a sensitive, waspy-type boy.

C.N. If a man is in this situation it is incorporated into the art myth. Think of Gauguin, abandoning his wife and children and going off. In the end society excused him as the great artist who did what he had to do.

G.H. If a woman does it, she is a lousy mother.

C.N. I have an eight-year-old daughter and I am fortunate that my husband has been able to take on a lot of the responsibility.

G.H. If you are a woman alone and divorced it is just impossible. When Jeff was twelve, there had been enough women in his life. I thought the best thing for him was to be with his father. He stayed there in California and now he and his father are in business together. They are very close friends. So for him it was a very good thing. It was just very hard for me. Very, very hard.

C.N. When did you come to New York?

G.H.   In the mid-forties. I was in my middle twenties. Ike Muse with whom I was studying had moved his studio to New York in 1946. We had fallen in love and were living together so I moved to New York with him. He was about twenty years older than I was. Through him I got to know Milton Avery and through Avery I met Gottlieb and Rothko. They talked about Jackson Pollock who had just moved out to Springs. By then I had left Ike and was living on the Lower East Side near Morty Feldman, John Cage, and Sonia Secular. She was a very interesting and tragic artist who showed at Betty Parsons. I think she killed herself. She was a friend of Pollock's and talked to me about him. I had just started to see his work. It was very confusing. You can't imagine what it is like to see, for the first time, something that has never before existed. I was amazed, mesmerized by it. Sonia said, "Why don't you call Pollock up and tell him. He has just moved to the country and is very lonely. No young artist has ever said he is any good, practically no one has."

C.N.   That was in '48?

G.H.   Yes. So I called him. Pollock said that he was just overwhelmed that young people liked his work. He invited me out to see him. I was going with a young painter named Harry Jackson and we hitch-hiked out to see him. In 1949, Harry and I went to Mexico but we continued to see Lee and Jackson all the time from '48 through '51.

C.N.   When did you begin to show?

G.H.   I showed in Kootz's New Talent Show in 1950. It was the first time Franz Kline, Bob Goodnough, and Al Leslie showed. Then I had my own first show at Tibor DeNagy's first gallery in 1951. It was a very small space located off Third Avenue. That was where Helen Frankenthaler, Goodnough, Leslie, and Larry Rivers had their first shows.

C.N.   That New Talent Show was a historic exhibition.

G.H.   It was incredible. It surprised Kootz as much as it did anybody. Motherwell couldn't have a show so there was an open date. Kootz asked Clem Greenberg and Meyer Shapiro, the art historian, to dig up some young artists for him to exhibit. They did. Some of us were brought to their attention through our participation in Studio 35, an informal art school, which was started before the Club. It had empty walls and some of the young people among us, including Franz Kline, asked if we could put some paintings there. We wanted the opinion of people like Pollock (although Pollock and de Kooning did come to my studio). The people who ran Studio 35 agreed and one day Meyer Shapiro and Clement Greenberg wandered in, saw the show, made mental notes, and picked out some of the people for the New Talent Show.

C.N.   How were you developing as an artist then?

G.H.   I was in my late twenties. After studying the School of Paris, a pastiche of Picasso, Braque, and Matisse, I was having the first break-through into something that I felt was my own. I don't think the paint-ings from that time are terribly good but there is one in the other room from 1950 that I think has a full voice to it.

C.N.   Were those first paintings very abstract?

G.H.   Yes. But after I met Pollock and de Kooning I was torn between Pollock's more automatic approach and de Kooning's tremendously developed intellect. I wavered. My first show in 1951 shows both influ-ences, but I never removed my touch from the canvas the way Pollock did with the drip. I stayed with the brush but I went into the all-over concept, the continuum, no beginning, no end, no central image, no background. All the revolutionary ideas that were then in the air.

C.N.   But you had this very sensuous touch—a love of the paint and the stroke.

G.H.   If you are insinuating that is because I am a woman . . .

C.N.   No, not at all.

G.H.   I don't know that there is any more sensuous a touch than Roth-ko's for instance.

C.N.   Also de Kooning.

G.H.   Excuse me for being defensive.

C.N.   You have every right. It has become a stereotype to associate women with the sensuous.

G.H.   Exactly. That is what I am absolutely against. I would like to see the point where we can use words without these prejudiced sexual connotations.

C.N.   And we can. Robert Goldwater writing of the New York School in the fifties makes a point of saying that the works of the Abstract Expressionists are very painterly, very much in love with the medium.

G.H.   Yes, we were in love with paint. I was very much influenced by Pollock and de Kooning from 1948 or '49 until 1952. Then I had a bout of conscience. I thought I was a robber, that I had taken from people, older than I, who had struggled tremendously for years to find this breakthrough. I thought I didn't deserve it. I started to paint through art history and I spent almost all of 1952 painting from the masters— Rubens, Velásquez, Goya. I didn't do exact copies, rather I worked freehand, trying to understand where I really came from. There was no world out there demanding that I do this. But I had to go through with it. That cost me a great deal, particularly in terms of my friendship with Pollock. De Kooning and Gorky were more understanding because they understood a young artist wanting to find roots somewhere. Pollock thought it was an abdication of an advanced position and that I was reactionary. He was quite unpleasant about it. Franz Kline was pretty nasty about it too but he liked me a lot, so it was back and forth. Rothko didn't think much of it. I lost friends for that year. The people that understood were the people who were always there, like Larry Rivers. He has always been into history—remember his *Washington Crossing the Delaware.* That year Larry and I got to be very friendly. Then about 1954 I came bang up against Abstract Expressionism again. By then I had found that my best work had some roots in the visual world. I just had to throw in something of the life around me, even if it was just fragments, little memories, little snatches, little wisps of a corner, a piece of fruit, a vendor going by, something. I felt I had to throw it in to the junk and scramble it around. That lasted from say '52 until about '58 or '59. Then I lost my belief in the outer world and didn't find snatches to put in. There was another period of total abstraction lasting until the mid-sixties.

C.N.   What about the street scenes that you did?

C.H.   I love those paintings but I consider those to be coming head-on into Abstract Expressionism again. By throwing a mango in, throwing a vendor in, throwing an awning in, there was still a little something from the world around me.

C.N.   Did you do some paintings of women? You did a painting of a bridal shop.

G.H.   My studio in New York was on the Lower East Side. It was two blocks away from Grand Street where there is one bridal shop after another. I am very interested in masks and charades. It can be women or it can be something else—the face the world puts on to sell itself to the world. I have always been interested in empty ritual. I thought of the bridal thing as a court scene like Goya and Velásquez and I posed the bridal party in that same way. I had a photographer friend take pictures and I bought a bridal gown at a thrift shop and hung it in the studio. Every morning I would go out and stare at the windows and then come in and paint.

C.N.   It's interesting that you picked up on that particular ritual. It is one that women are trying to come to terms with today.

G.H.   I really hadn't thought of it. I was really thinking of Goya and

Velásquez, of that empty ritual of the court, all of the trappings, the gowns, the lace, and those strange mad stares that the king, the queen, and the princesses have on their faces—those awful blank looks, like . . .

C.N.   Like mannequins?

G.H.   Yes. Exactly. I got very interested. I did another painting that the Metropolitan has of mannequins in a window.

C.N.   Roland Barthes writes about today's mythologies. He traces the archetypal ideas behind contemporary phenomena. You too were picking up on a contemporary myth of our culture.

G.H.   It is interesting that you said that. Jack Tworkov was just here looking at my new painting and he thought I was inventing a new mythology. But if you are a painter you can't get too self-conscious about it. You can't say, "Here I am, I am creating a marvelous myth." It comes out of a combination of some inner need and some external experience. It is not a deliberate act; it is more an instinctive one.

C.N.   You did a painting called the *Persian Jacket* at that time. It is owned by the Museum of Modern Art.

G.H.   Yes. I sold every painting that I did between 1952 and 1959. I have almost nothing.

C.N.   The way you portrayed the women is very different from de Kooning's violent interpretation of his women.

G.H.   I disagree with you. The violence is in the paint. De Kooning's women are very loving. Since imagery became part of my work I became closer to de Kooning than to Pollock. I saw most of those women being created in Bill's studio and we were very good friends. When those first women—those fifties' women—were shown, I had a big argument with Jim Fitzsimmons who is now the editor of *Art International.* He said that they were destructive, that it was hatred, Kali the blood goddess. He pointed to one painting that had big palette knife strokes slithering across the chest and said, "Look, de Kooning is wounding her with blood." So I went to Bill and I said, "Jim Fitzsimmons said that you stabbed that woman and that is blood." Bill said, "Blood? I thought it was rubies."

C.N.   You know people are not always conscious of what they are doing. There are unconscious impulses behind an act.

G.H.   No one is going to convince me that Bill de Kooning does not love women. Look at this work of his [pointing to a de Kooning pastel]. I call it a pearl. You can't say that doesn't have a lyrical, loving line, tender pastels, and a marvelous electric look. I think it is filled with vitality.

C.N. She is covering her face in a protective gesture.

G.H. Maybe she is hiccoughing, maybe she is shy, maybe she dropped her fan.

C.N. What about the women de Kooning paints who are grimacing and gnashing their teeth?

G.H. You must understand that it is very hard to reinvent a face. I have done a lot of painting in which I use teeth and it has nothing to do with wanting to bite anybody; it has to do with the form. How often can you use a pretty little pursed lip if you are going to do a face. Teeth are very fascinating things to draw and they make a marvelous form within the area. To reinvent a face, to reinvent any part of the figure, is a formidable problem. You have to measure the psychological effect of these things with the formal problems involved.

C.N. There is a psychology test in which the subject is asked to draw a figure and if he or she accentuates the teeth it is interpreted as a sign of aggression.

G.H. I think it is a tremendous misunderstanding to take a highly intellectually developed artist with a great background and to equate his work with the unconscious work of the child. Bill de Kooning is a great artist and he is finding solutions to tremendous problems of the human image. It is very different from the child unconsciously reading something into the teeth.

C.N. They do the tests with adults too.

G.H. They do it with schizophrenics. My marvelous art form is being used as therapy.

C.N. Don't you think there is an interplay between the formal aspects of the artist's work and his or her personality?

G.H. Why you choose certain images is very interesting and very hard to know. Where did Miró get all his images? What do all those stars, moons, fish, and elongated figures mean? What is that double-image woman of Picasso's? All those images an artist chooses probably have a great deal to do with his or her personality, psychology, and so forth.

C.N. I think to interpret art strictly on a formal basis is ridiculous. But it is equally silly to ignore formal problems and only interpret them psychologically or sociologically.

G.H. One must balance it out. It is a tightrope that image-makers, and I think I am an image maker (I don't think that I am an abstract artist) must walk.

C.N. One must synthesize all these factors in making a work of art and even then it remains a mystery. There is no way you can really analyze it all.

G.H.   It is rather nice to think that there are some things that can't be analyzed into the ground. Certainly poetry, literature, and music can't be analyzed to the point where they are finished off.

C.N.   You were very involved with poets weren't you?

G.H.   Very much so. It was a very important part of my life and I miss it terribly.

C.N.   You did an exhibition with Frank O'Hara?

G.H.   It was in 1952, the same year that I was reinvestigating the art of the past. Frank and I became very good friends. We thought we would like to do something together. I didn't trust his handwriting so he gave me a suite of poems called *Oranges*. I took very large sheets of paper and on some of them I wrote an entire poem, on some I just wrote parts of a poem and then imaged back and forth. There were twelve oranges, and they were shown right after they were done, at the DeNagy Gallery. In the late fifties Frank collaborated with Larry Rivers on a series called *Stones*. Larry let Frank write and Larry did the images in between. We had a joint show of the things I had done earlier and the things that Larry Rivers did.

C.N.   Before I came to see you I went through the art index and I was surprised to see that very little has been written about you. Considering the great reputation you have as an innovative painter I was amazed that there wasn't even one complete article tracing the chronology of your work.

G.H.   That has a great deal to do with art politics and the art world. It also has a lot to do with the fact that I moved out of New York in 1960. At that time Pop Art came in and all of the Abstract Expressionists suffered tremendously from the impact of Pop Art. It didn't alter my painting or anyone else's but it was almost as though you were obliterated from the face of the earth as far as the public was concerned. I continued to exhibit at the Jackson Gallery, but no one wrote anything. Then Canaday devoted a whole Sunday *Times* column to killing me.

C.N.   That was awful. Of course he was always against Abstract Expressionism.

G.H.   Well he succeeded in making me feel like an idiot in terms of explaining my work publicly. I did make some very subjective remarks about it, but the work in my show was for young people. (I get along very well with young artists.) I thought they would be interested in knowing what was going on in my mind. I had no idea that it was going to reach the banality of Canaday's mind. Since then the world of art hasn't had much interest in what I am doing.

C.N.   The sixties was the decade of the trend. If you weren't involved in the latest trend then you weren't there as far as the art world was concerned.

G.H.   Exactly. I didn't exist.

C.N.   It was a terrible time, in my opinion, because it was so one-tracked, so limited. Anybody who was doing something that was different or exploring in another direction wasn't counted. I think things have changed again for the better. There are many different kinds of painting and sculpture going on now and a great deal of exploration. People are freer to pursue whatever they want.

G.H.   I have always done what I had to do. But it is very hard after having had attention, appreciation, and love. We do want love, and to have rejection, silence, and indifference was very difficult. But I have painted through it and I am still painting and we will see.

C.N.   After the sixties you went back into figuration?

G.H.   I painted in the realm of Abstract Expressionism from say 1958 or '59 until about the mid-sixties, but slowly images began to appear again. My studio in Baltimore is in a neighborhood that is very similar to the studio that I had in New York City on the Lower East Side. There is a lot of market activity. People shopping in the streets, vendors, shop windows—as a matter of fact, my landlord owns a bridal gown shop. That's a perfect circle.

C.N.   This painting here in the living room has some of that imagery in it.

G.H.   That is called *Autumn Shop Window.* There are price tags and objects that were in the window and now there is a dog walking by.

C.N.   And there are plants and fruit. It is like your surroundings in your home.

G.H.   It is a combination.

C.N.   I see that you love natural things.

G.H.   Yes. I like them especially in the city where they don't overwhelm you. In the country it is too much. A friend of mine once said that I should never paint in the country because I would fall apart. I get so lyrical that I am just limp. It is all so lovely. I want to celebrate it and celebrate it. I lose the edge. I like that tension. I need something a little harsh, a little grating to react against, to make beauty about. If all is beauty around you, all you can do is just sing songs to it. But if you have harshness—and all cities have harshness (believe me, downtown Baltimore is harsh in ways that I never saw in New York)—you have this counter-effect. It is a kind of power that sets me on edge to see if I can counterbalance it.

C.N.   I was reading Sophy Burnham's book *The Art Crowd* in which she says that contemporary American art grew up in the cities, particularly in New York, because it is so ugly; in San Francisco people don't need art because it is such a lovely city and they live such a pleasant life.

G.H.   That is a little simplistic because Paris is a very beautiful city and they made great art there.

C.N.   Come to think of it, though, the Cubists were living in squalor when they were starting out.

G.H.   Yes. They were living near Sacré Coeur. It was pretty slummy. They had a hard time just like the Abstract Expressionists. We didn't live in the great places of New York. We really scrounged.

C.N.   What made you leave New York?

G.H.   I felt that the pressures of the city had gotten to me. I was well known then—and the demands—all that kind of thing. It was too rough. It's exciting at first but then it gets very displeasing. I really had a very bad painting year in '59. I felt that I had lost contact with myself so I bought a house in Bridgehampton near where Pollock had lived and where de Kooning had moved. I had two floors in this crummy building on the Lower East Side in New York. I thought I would keep one floor just to come in occasionally when I had business in town. I was painting out there, and as I said, starting to fall apart in nature. It was all so wonderful; the expanses of the potato fields, the skies, the sea. All so gorgeous, that I was worried. I was happy there but I don't mind being miserable as long as I am painting well. Anyhow at that time I had a show in Washington. Winston Price, whom I had met, bought a large painting of the potato fields in Bridgehampton and said he didn't believe in just buying one painting of an artist. He wrote me a letter saying that he wanted to continue to buy my paintings, and to let him know the next time that I had some work. This was very reassuring. I wrote him a note when I had about four or five paintings and he came to see them. We fell in love and decided that we would marry. He was here in Baltimore. He is a research scientist with Hopkins. I had the problem of removing myself from New York and the

Long Island environment, where most of my friends went in the summer, to a strange city. The South was very difficult to contemplate and the adjustment was very, very hard.

C.N.   But you have been a real force here in Baltimore, haven't you?

G.H.   I don't know. I found after a few years of totally desperate solitude that I just couldn't bear it. I went to Eugene Leek who is a painter and President of the Maryland Institute and said, "I have never taught in my life but I have to have contact with someone. Do you have anything that I can do that won't take too much time?" I didn't want to spend more than a day a week because I was continuing to sell my work. I had to support the studio myself (Win supports the house). Leek said to me that he had just started a painting graduate program and would I like to see the graduate students once a week. I said that sounded fine. So I started to do that and some of my best friends now are the former graduate students. I sent these little eagles out into the world and it is wonderful. The young woman who gardens for me is a painter. She just graduated and she is staying around here for a year. There are about four other former graduate students who are in Baltimore painting. Some, about three or four, are in Washington. Lots of them have gone to Soho. So I have this realm. That is my only force. The mature artists in Baltimore couldn't care one way or another about the fact that I am here. But I think for the young artist it has been important. Certainly it has been important to me to be in touch with them.

C.N.   I heard that you had delivered a talk on Kenneth Sawyer the critic the other day.

G.H.   Well I didn't really know Ken. He was here when I was in New York and then when I came here he started to roam around the country picking up different jobs here and there. I knew him in New York only at the Cedar Bar when he would come in from Baltimore. He was like a kid pressing his nose up against the candy store window. Everything going on was fascinating to him: our fights, yellings, discussions, the crisis of "You're a louse because you are using an image," or "You are abdicating your responsibility because you don't do anything in the lower-left-hand corner." I couldn't understand why anyone from the outside would be so interested in this but Ken was very fascinated. They wanted me to talk about what was happening at that time and why Ken was so hooked on it. So I talked about Abstract Expressionism and not much about Ken.

C.N.   Your paintings are very much involved with the surface of the canvas, with bringing the painting right up to the front. Since your art crystallized is this a principle that you have adhered to?

G.H.   I would say that that is a fundamental formal concern of mine. I can see new possibilities of even making more of the painting surface but I can't see any regression, for me, into deeper space.

C.N.   You apply figurative aspects to that kind of space?

G.H.   Yes. It's very difficult because as soon as you make an image you set up a condition of regression, I mean of deeper space and forward space. The problem is to keep the tension of the surface and, at the same time, to image it. It is very, very hard but it makes it very interesting.

C.N.   I know that there are realists who wish to do that but as soon as they get into volumetric form immediately there is a recession in space. Possibly the painters who work from the photograph which is flat to begin with are dealing successfully with that problem.

G.H.   There are only two painters that I can think of who, in a very sly way, get around the deep space thing. One is Giacometti and the other is Francis Bacon. They managed to make images and to float them in a field of some sort. Sometimes, as in Giacometti, it is a field of nothing where the image just disperses itself into a void. Bacon made bars and barriers around the void. Those are the only two artists besides de Kooning, Miró, and Gorky who have managed to image and, at the same time, keep the surface.

C.N.   Is this a problem that you are working on right now?

G.H.   Yes. Very much so.

C.N.   Do you think that the controversy dealing with impasto versus stain painting still exists—the Clement Greenberg–Pollock faction as opposed to the Harold Rosenberg–de Kooning group?

G.H.   I think that the controversy isn't over a brush stroke as much as over a certain kind of spatial ideal. The image idea versus a field and staining idea. There is no way these two things can meet. In the paintings that I am working on now I am not using heavy paint. Actually the paint is stained. I am using rags, Japanese brushes, and a mitt that is made of lamb's wool that you slip your hand into and use as a brush. I am imaging and I am using drawing. The de Kooning and Gorky tradition is drawing and I am very much into drawing too. The Pollock line is drawing in a certain way also, but the people who have come out of that are almost denying line and drawing.

C.N.   Like Morris Louis?

G.H.   Yes. They fuse the field with floods of color. They are allied to Matisse. I love Matisse but somehow Gorky and de Kooning and others among us are involved more with Picasso and Cubism. It is really two different points of view.

C.N.   I know that Joan Mitchell was bitter about the way her painting was received by Greenberg and also by Helen Frankenthaler because of her heavy impasto. They seemed to feel that a heavy surface was a denial of spatiality.

G.H.   What does Joan care? Maybe she doesn't like Frankenthaler or Greenberg either.

C.N.   I think what she was objecting to was the imposition of one kind of attitude.

G.H.   But wouldn't she like to impose her attitudes? They just got lucky. Their attitude took over. If Joan had her way, her attitude would take over. I am a little more ironic about it than that. I just realize that that is the way it is. It is Greenberg, Frankenthaler, Nolan, and Louis and then on into Stella and Olitski. It is like a party line. But if I had my way it would be Gorky, de Kooning, and Hal Rosenberg.

C.N.   Why not have both?

G.H.   Greenberg has become a takeover force. Hal Rosenberg who is the champion on the other side is much more of an intellectual and not a power man. Harold is brilliantly articulate but he isn't going to go around barnstorming. He is not going to call the power play as Clem does. It isn't his temperament.

C.N.   Greenberg, on the other hand, is hardly writing any more. He has made his grand stand and now he is just out to hold the line. Rosenberg, though he continues to write, hasn't shown any interest or taken up any art movement since he made his action painting pronouncement.

G.H.   But he still keeps his interest in de Kooning and he was passionately involved with Phil Guston's new image paintings. Guston and I are very close. We write to each other, see each other, reinforce.

C.N.   Guston felt the need to reinstate the image and to deal with it in a social way.

G.H.   I haven't seen his most recent works, but he said that he has dropped that Klan look. He is doing more of what I am doing, picking fragments from the world. It's more a James Joycean thing.

C.N. That does reflect the culture as it exists now. We are so fragmented. It is hard to relate the urban existence to the organic, to nature.

G.H. The structures are broken down and one can only grab onto some fragments of what people call reality. So you grab a little, you pick a snatch here and there, you throw it in and try to make some kind of order, some kind of meaning. I think in that way Phil and I are very close in what we are doing.

C.N. Our whole culture is broken up into different parts. Scientists are doing one thing, mathematicians are doing another. Nobody really understands what the others are up to. And there is no way of getting the whole concept together, no way of putting your hands on everything.

G.H. I had a dream about moving down here. It was a Renaissance idea. I am an artist and my husband is a scientist. We would find artists, scientists, poets, writers, and put together a salon. Was I ever a dope! My husband is the only scientist that I have met, not only in Baltimore but in Washington, who has the slightest interest in painting. But he isn't interested in literature and poetry. All the other scientists are just interested in science. They are not even interested in politics. Whereas during my life in New York I knew Merce Cunningham, John Cage, and all the New York poets. It was a full creative life. I don't know what it is like in New York now, but here everything is in fragments. If you are a scientist that is where you are; if you are in politics, that is where you are. If you are a poet . . . but I haven't met a poet here. It is a fragmented life.

C.N. It reflects the general tone of society.

G.H. It is really a pity. Peabody is here; it is one of the greatest music schools in America. The Maryland Institute Graduate School is here and that is becoming one of the best schools in America for sculpture and painting. You would think those students would see each other, wouldn't you? Young composers and musicians seeing young sculptors and painters. No way. They never see each other.

C.N. But even during the Abstract Expressionist period there was no contact between science and art.

G.H. Well, we saw Bucky Fuller all the time because architecture was close to it. Science—no.

C.N. In Boston there is MIT with the Center for Advanced Visual Studies. They invite artists to come down and work with the scientists.

G.H.   That is a little self-conscious. Nope, it is all in little compartments.

C.N.   Our culture is compartmentalized. But wasn't the work of the Abstract Expressionists which denied the image so completely a withdrawal? Wasn't that a reaction against what was happening in the world of the fifties? Our country was becoming a huge monolithic power, based primarily on our technological advancement.

G.H.   I think that had a lot to do with it. But you have to think about Europe too and the Second World War. There was a very definite link with existentialism, Camus and Sartre. A kind of cynicism had set in all over Europe and it pervaded the thinking of the intellectuals in America. In New York life it was a strong force. Here we had gone through this holocaust and for what? What is there left? What was left was a private conscience, an individual searching his or her feelings, and making a move into an unknown. One could only move as honestly and closely toward oneself as possible. For the painters the unknown was a blank area or space. That was all there was. There was no structure, nothing interwoven. A lot of the music, dance, and poety also had this as an underlying philosophy. Then what happened was we reacted against Europe. We had a very strong sense of being American, of being pioneers again, creative pioneers.

C.N.   Taking off into the unknown.

G.H.   Right. It was like going to the unknown West. It's not just a coincidence that Jackson Pollock was a Westerner, a kind of pioneer person. Pollock and de Kooning were great friends and great foes. The greatest insult that Pollock could give to de Kooning was to say, "You are nothing but a goddamned European." Whereas Pollock was a hero like Daniel Boone and a real pioneer, a real American.

C.N.   But that was all a myth too.

G.H.   The myth was something that happened afterwards. Then it was little boys fighting—how can you put the other guy down.

C.N.   There was a lot of that *machismo* going on then, wasn't there? A lot of concern about being a tough guy and an individual.

G.H.   Sure. But it didn't just happen among the men. It happened with the women who were painting too. Take Joan Mitchell and Helen Frankenthaler. Joan Mitchell's two favorite criticisms of me were that I couldn't make up my mind because I would go between imagery and abstraction, and (this was a real dig) that I had the courage to make such ugly paintings. My answer was, "I make them as beautiful as I can. I just don't know how to make them beautifuler." Helen's argument with me was that I was using imagery and I should be abstract. My argument with her was that her paintings looked as though she had painted them between cocktail time and dinner. So you see it wasn't just the men. There was bitchery in this wonderful world that we were living in, but we needed each other. Your best friend would put a knife between your shoulder blades.

C.N. Could part of that bitchery have been due to the ambience of cutthroat competition created by the men?

G.H. I think that women are competitive too.

C.N. I agree but it was the men who set the tone because they were running the show. They created a super-hyped-up scene in which the object was to one-up the next guy. I think it was related to the terrible sense of impotency the artist had in terms of the entire culture.

G.H. Have you read Françoise Gilot's *Life With Picasso?* I like it, because even if a lot of it sounds corny, she got the essence of his ideas. Gilot tells a wonderful story about herself. One day she was painting and had locked the door to her room. Her son Claude knocked on the door and said, "Can I come in?" She said, "No, dear, I'm painting." He said, "I love you, momma," and she said, "I love you, dear," and went on painting. He said, "I love your painting, momma." She said, "Thank you dear," and went on painting. Finally he said, "I love it more than poppa's." She opened the door. So it is basically human. Don't blame it on the Abstract Expressionists.

C.N. I can go along with that. I have had experiences with women's groups and, in some cases, never have I met such a bunch of cutthroats. I was in a consciousness-raising group one summer which met once a week. It almost killed me. There were constant insinuations and put-downs and all in the name of sisterhood and being supportive. People were pretending to be my friends and wanting to help me while they were actually giving me the knife.

G.H. Right between the shoulder blades.

C.N. Yes and they were so very envious of any success or independence that I might have obtained.

G.H. I don't think this a disease that is caught from men. I think it is human.

C.N. I felt that they were very frustrated people, women who had dedicated themselves to their men.

G.H. I have never done that. I have had marvelous relationships with marvelous men but it has never been a situation where I have said,

"You are more important than I am so I will be your slave." That is why I have respect for Helen Frankenthaler and Joan Mitchell. Their work is the core of their life and it is mine too. Some people would say that it is not human for a woman or for a man to put their work before everything. But I don't see how you can create and not have the feeling that it is the most important, all-consuming thing.

C.N.   Excepting when you have to be cruel.

G.H.   If you have to, that is very bad. I have discussed my relationship with my son. That was very cruel, very harsh, and very difficult.

C.N.   Today's culture is still so constituted as to make it more difficult for women than men. Society could help women by taking on part of the responsibility for children. They could provide day care centers which would make it possible for women to function independently. They could create a very different environment from the one you and I grew up in.

G.H.   I can't truly conceive, at this moment, how it would be possible. I see some of my young women students as very gifted artists and I like launching them into the world. I have a special concern about the women. I don't see any characteristic about their art that makes it "women's art," but they are facing a special circumstance which does have to do fundamentally with the fact that they bear the children. If a woman gets a man who is a lover, a good friend, and is mutually supportive that is a very human and creative situation, but I don't know how society can solve the children part of it.

C.N.   We must completely overhaul the way we exist economically. Men as well as women should take responsibility for the upbringing of children. They should be given the time to do it and not have to work a conventional eight-hour day.

G.H.   This is your realm and I know that it is a great concern to you. I can only deal with the young women I know as a friend and as an artist. The personal part of their lives they must slug out themselves.

C.N.   That is unfortunately the way it has always been, but hopefully it will change because of the pressures that are being exerted. However it is not going to happen overnight. It is going to be a long hard haul. Nobody overturns society with just a little tap on the shoulder. It will take a large concerted effort and it means women getting together and exerting force on the power group. I must look forward to a better future because I am not satisfied with the way things are. I am doing what I can to change things in the art field.

G.H.   I am very glad that you are involved with this but I have to devote my energy and time to my work—selfishly and thoroughly.

There is no free time. If you are not in it, you are thinking of it. I may not be there in the studio but I am there in my mind. I am sustaining it until I get to work tomorrow morning. I can't be thinking about other things or writing letters or doing anything else. I am carrying this painting. I am pregnant with it. I can't drop it. I have to carry it through because it is about half way there. It's all-consuming.

C.N.   The most important thing that women can do is to create. It has always been said that there haven't been any great women artists.

G.H.   We have had great precedents for women novelists and women poets. We just have to have enough backlog for great women artists.

C.N.   There were women artists of the Renaissance who did marvelous work. In the sixteenth century many of them were apprentices to their fathers and also attended the academy. They had opportunities and they used them. You yourself have created a body of work which is like a signpost to the young women who will come after you.

G.H.   I'd like to think that, but I don't think about it too much because I think about the work that has to be done. I don't want to get self-conscious about it. You know you don't go into the studio and say, "Oh here I am this marvelous heroine, this wonderful woman doing my marvelous painting so all these marvelous women artists can come after me and do their marvelous painting." There you are alone in this huge space and you are not conscious of the fact that you have breasts and a vagina. You are inside yourself, looking at this damned piece of rag on the wall that you are supposed to make a world out of. That is all you are conscious of. I simply cannot believe that a man feels differently. I don't think a man goes striding into the studio thinking, "Here I am this marvelous man with this great power of the male figure and all these young men are going to be inspired by me." Inside yourself, you are looking at this terrifying unknown and trying to feel, to pull everything you can out of all your experience, to make something. I think a woman or a man creating feels very much the same way. I bring my experience, which is different from a man's, yes, and I put it where I can. But once that is done, I don't know if it's a woman's experience I'm looking at. If you take, for example, George Eliot and Thomas Hardy, if you didn't tell me who wrote which, I would be very hard put to know which was the woman's work and which was the man's. They are both great writers.

C.N.   I wrote an article about that subject in *Arts Magazine.* No one, not even the artist, can pinpoint every element that goes into a work of art. And then something mysterious happens between the process of input and output. An entire new entity is created out of so many different factors. Sex is just one of them. How would you be able to pick out sex as opposed to race, personal background, geographic location, overall culture, and so on? Isn't art really a synthesis of all these things?

G.H.   You live humanly and you have certain series of experiences. You use those experiences to express what you have to say.

C.N.   I believe that it all goes back to the individual. Each individual has another unique thing to say, is another voice. The total comes from the addition of many, many voices. You became part of that total when you delved into art history and with an Abstract Expressionist approach created a new reality out of it. You took universal subject matter, images of daily life, and presented it in a new way. You gave us another view of human life.

G.H.   You bring to the past the present.

C.N.   Exactly. That is why writers read the great classics. They are not going to imitate, they are not attempting to write like Dostoevsky, they are trying to find out about the essential so they will be able to go after it themselves.

G.H.   Yes. Everything is available but what has been created before has to be absorbed.

C.N.   That is the unique thing about painting in the twentieth century. One has all of this at one's fingertips.

G.H.   It can be confusing.

C.N.   But those paintings of your Old Master period were enormously successful and well received weren't they?

G.H.   There is a time when what you are creating and the environment you are creating it in come together. That is a very lucky coincidence. It has nothing to do with the values of the work. Perhaps the work I am doing now in the end will turn out to have a much deeper meaning even though, at this moment, it is not in tune with what the world wants, needs, and cares for. It is not going to alter the pattern of the work. It's just that in terms of the outer world the relationship isn't going so well.

C.N.   It's very hard to be ahead of one's time or in a different place.

G.H.   Ahead would be very kind of you to say, but I don't presume that. The world is in one place and I am in another and we are not meeting.

C.N.   But you are bound to have another meeting soon. There is now a great interest in looking back and seeing where we have been and what we have come to. We need to re-evaluate. Lee Krasner is going to have an exhibition at the Whitney Museum. So is Joan Mitchell. She too left New York but she continued to do what was necessary for her as an artist and now the art world is coming to her. Alice Neel is also going to have a show at the Whitney. I am sure that the same thing will happen with you. You have made your mark and have come forth as a strong personality and a strong painter with your own statement. You are part of history. That can never be wiped out.

G.H.   I can't be too self-conscious about it. It doesn't interest me to think of myself in a retrospective way. One doesn't want to be one's own history. I just think about the next painting.

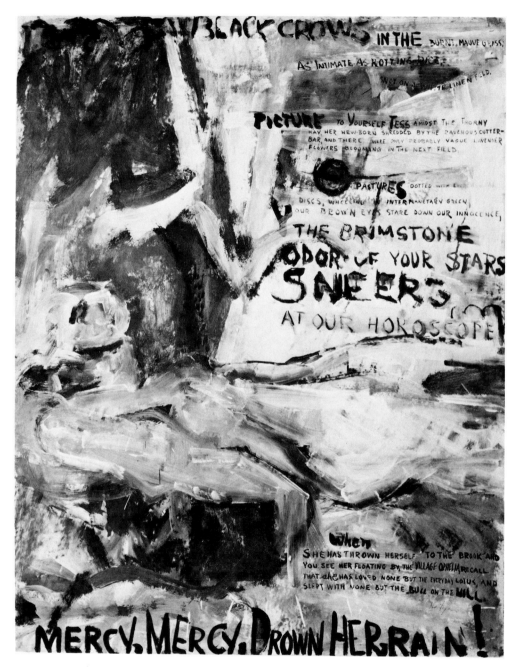

Black Crows, Poem Painting, 1952.

Grand Street Brides, 1954.

City Life, 1956.

Essex and Hester Red, 1958.

Barbi, 1964.

The Year of the Cicada, 1970.

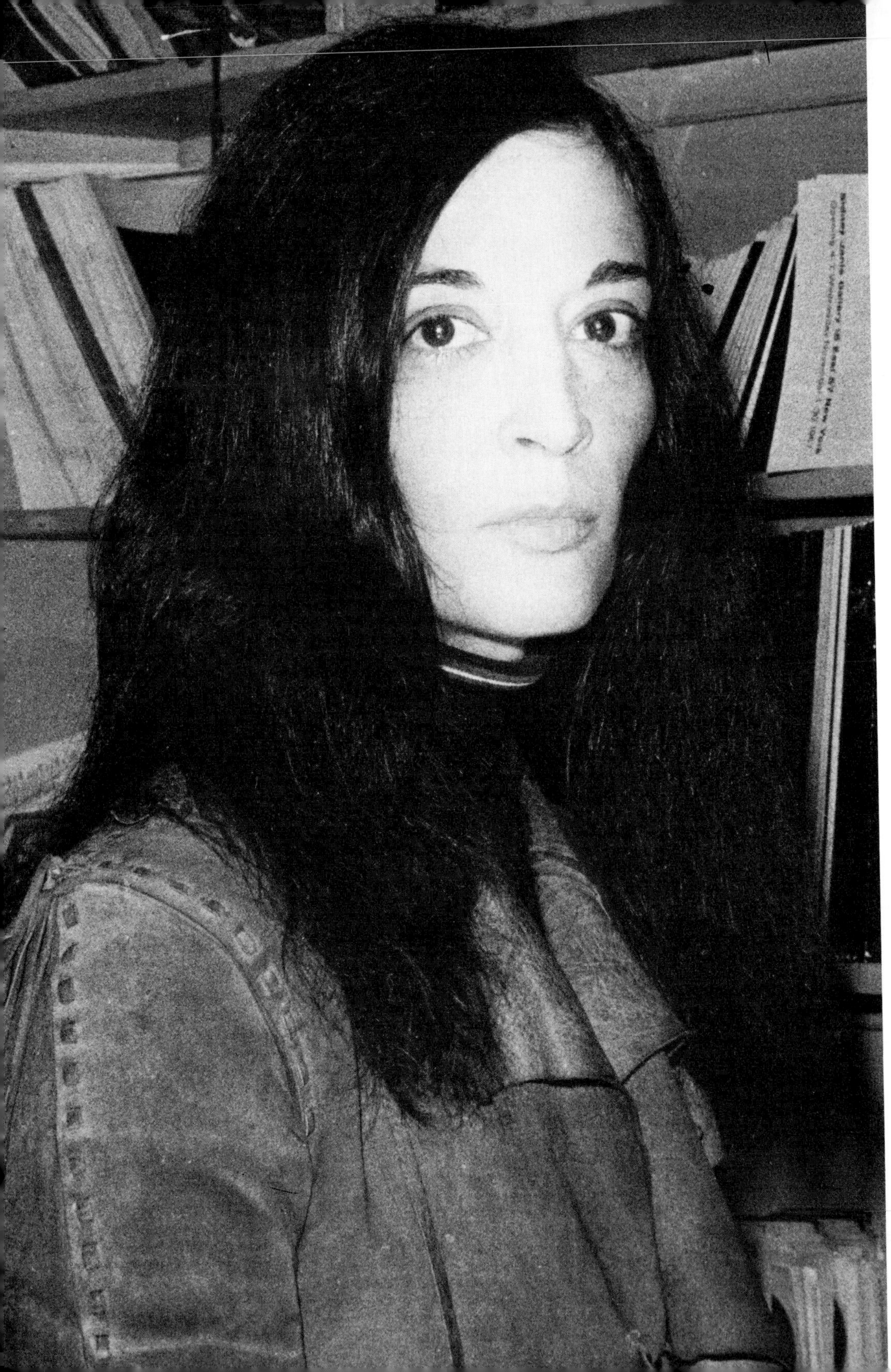

Marisol, 1973.

ARISOL ESCOBAR became famous during the 1960's for her brilliantly satiric collaged sculpture, her own personal beauty, and her long mysterious silences. Her assemblages, frequently incorporating female figures formed in her own image, were seen in important New York galleries while Marisol herself frequently turned up at chic New York social gatherings.

Born in 1930, the daughter of wealthy Venezuelans, Marisol was brought up in Paris, Venezuela, and California, always moving in sophisticated intellectual circles. The artist lost her mother early in life but was supported and encouraged financially and emotionally by her father.

Marisol came to New York in the fifties and became part of the beat generation that made Greenwich Village its haunt. Her art was influenced in the fifties by an exhibition of Pre-Columbian Mochica pottery jars shown at a New York gallery; by Mexican boxes with pictures painted inside, and by early American folk art.

In the sixties she used these primitive and folk approaches to create tableaux that reflected the political and social attitudes of the time. Her work dealt with all classes of people from the migrant workers in *Family from the Dust Bowl* to the socialites of the multifigured piece entitled *The Party* and the supreme aristocrats of the English *Royal Family.* Political leaders are special targets for her deft political and social analysis. The big man *LBJ himself* is represented holding three little women, his wife and daughters, in the palm of his hand. His over-life-sized proportions in contrast to the Lilliputian women is a visual revelation of male chauvinism long before the women's liberation movement had even formulated this phrase. Social celebrities such as Andy Warhol and John Wayne also form part of her scenario.

From the beginning Marisol has investigated the various social and political phenomena that surrounded her from a very personal point of view, and frequently the personages taking part in her various dramatic assemblages are none other than Marisol herself. Engaged in an endless quest for self-identification, the artist makes multiple casts, drawings, and prints of her face, her hands, and her entire body.

In her recent work she has withdrawn from the external world of social roles and political events into the mythic underworld life of the sea. Identifying with the shark, the barracuda, and other marine monsters, she has attached her own features to beautifully

Marisol

carved out, meticulously stained, mahogany fish bodies.

Marisol speaks in soft, girlish tones; her conversation is ingenuous, her smile infectious. Yet one never quite knows who the real Marisol is and what she really thinks. Perhaps that is her message: We must go on playing various roles until we can play no more.

CINDY NEMSER   Did you find it particularly difficult as a woman to pursue a career as an artist?

MARISOL   Well, I didn't have any difficulty.

C.N.   I read that your father encouraged you as a child.

M.   He liked that I was an artist and he supported me . . . I had an income through him.

C.N.   What about recognition from men artists? Back in the fifties when you were showing in the galleries on Tenth Street, were the men that you knew encouraging to you?

M.   Yes. When I was showing in a group, it would be some of the men friends I had there who would ask me to show. That was long ago. I was more a student then . . . I couldn't think of myself as an accomplished artist then. I was showing things in, maybe, one show. I never had a very big ego. But then at one point a friend of mine, a man, said that Leo Castelli was looking for a young artist, and so he brought him to my studio. Castelli gave me a show. It was very easy. That was in 1957.

C.N.   You weren't in Henry Geldzahler's show at the Metropolitan Museum. There was only one woman in that exhibition, but the male Pop artists were all in it.

M.   Maybe that was personal. Maybe Henry Geldzahler doesn't think my art is so good. I don't care. I am in museums all over the world.

C.N.   You studied with Hans Hofmann in the fifties. I've heard from lots of women artists that he was very prejudiced toward women. He would say to them: "You paint very well for a woman," or "you paint like a man." Did you ever get any of these reactions from him?

M.   No. Because I used to go to his class and he didn't hear. He would take off his hearing aid, and there was never any communication. I would go into class and I was very intimidated. I think I was one of the youngest people in the class. He would come up, and when we were drawing in charcoal, he would erase it and draw on your drawing again and erase it. That's the way he would teach—without saying anything. All was visual. He was very enthusiastic about his school and the students. The atmosphere was very encouraging. I used to go to the Art Students League, and that was like something European— from the nineteenth century.

C.N.   Did you look up to any women artists at that time and see them as people to pattern your career on?

M.   I admired the women in the old Artists' Club, like Elaine de Kooning, Joan Mitchell, and Grace Hartigan. But I couldn't talk to them. I was a student, and I thought they were much smarter than me. I couldn't communicate with them.

C.N.   Do you think they had a hard time as women artists then?

M.   Well, Helen Frankenthaler was like me. She had no money problems and was successful at a young age. That's why she doesn't like to be with other women artists and doesn't think they have problems. But Elaine de Kooning signed her name E. de Kooning and Grace Hartigan called herself George. Those women paved the way for me.

C.N.   In your sculpture you make many different kinds of women, although many of them have your own features. I'm standing here in 1973 and looking back into the sixties. It seems to me that, even then, you were a precursor of the women's movement in that you were looking for an identity—trying to explore different aspects of woman's identity.

M.   Yes. There comes a point where you start asking, "Who am I?" I was trying to find out through my sculpture. That's why I made all those masks and each one of them is different. Every time I would take a cast of my face it came out different. You have a million faces. It's like photography: it's spooky.

C.N.   I know. Whenever you see a photograph of yourself, you always look different. You try to figure out which photograph is really you.

M.   Well, sometimes—no, most of the time—the photographs look like the person who's taking them—the photographer. I don't know how that happens. Well, maybe that means that everybody really looks alike. It's so spooky.

C.N.   I read about that stunt you did in the fifties at the Artists' Club. Grace Glueck, in her article in the *New York Times Magazine* in 1965, described how you came with a Japanese-style mask painted white, and when you took off the mask, you had your face made up exactly like the mask. That was a marvelous thing to have done. Was it a kind of protective device?

M.   That was just for fun, because those lectures had become so boring.

C.N.   But if you probe deeper, weren't you perhaps protecting yourself through your art from people who could hurt you?

M.   I don't hide anything. I'm not embarrassed about anything.

C.N.   But you have this mystique that people talk about—this mystique of silence. People say, "Marisol never talks."

M.   Well, I think that's a way to wipe me out. They used to say I am mysterious and like a madonna, and that I don't say anything. I was thinking about it the other day. It is a way to wipe you out, isn't it?

C.N.   Well, you were a myth. All the fashion magazines wrote about you. Andy Warhol said you were the first glamorous girl artist. That is the kind of thing done to women to make them into the mysterious Other.

M.   I'm a very good artist, but I have to seem like a spook and not really like a person. I think Andy Warhol did it so I could get away with being an artist. Now, maybe I've become paranoid, but it seems to me that in the sixties the men did not feel threatened by me. They thought I was cute and spooky, but they didn't take my art so seriously. Now, they take my art more seriously, but they don't like me so much. But, maybe I'm paranoid.

C.N.   No, I don't think so. The whole idea of a woman making an achievement could be explained away by making her something un-real. Otherwise, she becomes very threatening. It's the same with Louise Nevelson. She was always presented (and presents herself) as the great eccentric. But she's also a very real, warm human being. Nowadays, however, there are too many women artists on the scene to allow one to get away with being a woman just because she is different.
   How did you feel about this mythmaking around you in the sixties?

M.   I went along with it, just for the experience. Maybe it was a way of doing my art. But I also enjoyed it, because I am very curious. I like to do lots of different things. So at one point I was like a beatnik; then at one point I wanted to be a society girl; then a diver, a skier. I'm very curious. But it is not that I really believe in all these things.

C.N.   But isn't that like wearing masks? Like roles one plays.

M.   No. It doesn't have to be such a role—just an experience from life.

C.N.   Do you think there is such a thing as female art? Do you think there's anything different that you would find in women's art, as op-posed to men's art?

M.   No. I can't tell the difference. If I go to a group show at a museum, I can't tell which one was made by a man or a woman. Do people really say there is a difference?

C.N.   Some people are saying that.

M.   I went to the big show at the Whitney a few months ago [the Biennial] and I wasn't even thinking about it in those terms. I was thinking about which piece I liked and which I didn't. Maybe men can make art bigger, because they are stronger? Like a sculptor?

C.N.   Even that would be hard to say. Take an artist like Barbara Hepworth, who makes large pieces. She says size has nothing to do with strength.

M.   Also, I've noticed that in the artist there is a little bit of a mix-up. The men are very feminine, and the women are more masculine.

C.N.   What we mean by masculine and feminine becomes a problem.

M.   Maybe the women are just more open to it. Yes, of course, it must be that they're more open about it. Because men and women both have the masculine and feminine.

C.N.   And because it's more sanctioned in our society for women to be masculine than for men to be feminine. But it's interesting that you just went on doing what you had to do. You mastered so many skills that people considered appropriate only for men. You work with a power drill and saws and all sorts of carpentry equipment which women aren't supposed to know about. You are very independent in the way you live.

M.   I never thought of myself as a woman artist. I don't think anybody did in the beginning. It's only because of women's liberation that they noticed it. I was just an artist like any other. I never had that problem of people putting me down because I was a woman.

C.N.   Except being taken up by the glamour industry.

M.   I encouraged it for a while. I went along with it. Why not wear a nice dress for a change? It's not like I work like that in my studio. Why not wear a nice dress and go to a party? They make me feel guilty about it now. Louise Nevelson wears her false eyelashes and her mink hat.

C.N.   Why should women artists have to conform to an image like the men artists do? Lots of men artists get themselves dressed up like workers to prove their masculinity. Why should women have to prove their masculinity?

M.   Even the workers in the street change their clothes on weekends. They get all dressed up and have a car. They don't go out all the time in dirty old pants.

C.N.   Only artists come to openings in dirty old pants. It's a funny bind women are in. If they appear "feminine" in nice clothes, they are not taken seriously; and if they don't appear in nice clothes, they are not considered women.

M. Yes. Then you might be a dyke.

C.N. And that's another way of putting you down. Any woman who doesn't conform isn't a "real" woman.

M. For a long time, when I was a student, I was against the bourgeois thing and I went around in dirty jeans for years. I was ugly in those days, and all through school and afterwards. Then I had that little change, and I enjoyed it. It was nice to get all dressed up in fancy clothes and have people say that I'm so beautiful.

C.N. Have you found now that women liberationists are hostile and make you feel guilty for that?

M. Yes. People come up to me and they talk about all those parties and getting all dressed up, as if I had done that all my life.

C.N. It was a media thing.

M. I think Andy Warhol started the whole thing. Part of it was to communicate, so people notice you and then they notice your work. Otherwise not so many people notice your work. I've changed my mind about that since [laughter], that was in the old days. Now I don't want anybody to know me again.

C.N. You just want them to know your work?

M. Yes. Because people get belligerent. It's scary. Yes, if there is one person who stands out, lots of people give you compliments and lots of people insult you. It's hard to take. When some people get really angry, it's frightening. The expression on their faces is as if you did something wrong.

I know these people who talk in a group about movie stars like Marlon Brando. They don't even know who this person is, but they start putting him down. Then they talk about all his personal little stories; they talk about something they think he might have done that's bad, and they don't even know him.

C.N. That's the problem of becoming a myth. It's hard to get through to the person who has become mythologized. And in a way you helped make the myth yourself. You went along with it.

M. Yes. But mostly for them. I don't feel like a myth. I spend most of my time in my studio. You know, it's something they have fun with more than I do. It's like going to visit these friends and they spend maybe half an hour talking about Marlon Brando and he doesn't know they're talking about him. He's just sitting in a chair somewhere—

brooding or reading a book. It really doesn't have much to do with him. I don't feel like a myth. Do people really think I'm a myth?

C.N.   I think so. It sells art and art magazines. People love it even if it doesn't have much to do with the person at all. I think myths are something that people need. If someone comes along and supplies the need, they use it.

M.   People are very romantic. They need to make up a story. Why?

C.N.   Because most people don't have much excitement in their every-day reality, and it's much more fun thinking of somebody else doing something or being something they are not. Then they don't have to face their own reality. They can project themselves on to someone else. I think Andy Warhol is one of the biggest mythmakers around.

M.   And he's a myth.

C.N.   Does he do it on purpose?

M.   Yes.

C.N.   That's very clever of him to recognize what people want and to supply them with it. But now you want to be demythologized?

M.   [laughter]

C.N.   Did you do Abstract Expressionist art at the beginning of your career?

M.   No, that was just drawings in school.

C.N.   Were your early independent works influenced by archaic or folk art?

M.   Yes, Early American Art. There was a little group with William King who bought some houses in Maine, and they had early American furniture in their homes and even objects like that. That's why I got involved with it. I was looking at all the things that people didn't take seriously before, instead of getting influenced by the Hofmann paint-ing. But I'm not really a folk artist—that's ridiculous. It's like saying that Picasso is an African artist.

C.N.   That kind of categorizing of your work might be considered patronizing—as if to imply you are not trained or sophisticated.

M.   Maybe that's an insult.

C.N.   Well, much of women's work has, throughout history, been rele-gated to the decorative and folk arts. We make a distinction between high art and folk and decorative art, and the latter comes out less important. It's as if the fine arts are basically Western male art, and everything else—the so-called decorative and folk art and art done in

Africa, Asia and South America—is not as good or sophisticated or knowledgable.

M. Oh yes. People in the West think their art is better. About three and a half years ago I went to Asia, and I couldn't believe the art they have there. People told me that art is here, is here, and I had never seen anything like that, even in Europe. I was influenced there. I went to Angkor Vat, and it was really a surprise. It shocked me.

C.N. Yes, they teach students the history of art as if it were only Western European art with very little attention to art of the East. It's an imperialistic attitude.

M. And it's detrimental.

C.N. So when someone talks about folk or South American art when they look at your work it's necessary to evaluate carefully their motives and attitudes.

M. Maybe I *was* influenced by Pre-Columbian art. I saw it here in this gallery, I think, for the first time. They had a show of Pre-Columbian art in the fifites. I think nobody had seen it here. The art looked as if it had lots of feeling.

C.N. I notice in your sculpture that you have so many different types. You range from a portrait of a *Family from the Dust Bowl* to the society women in *The Party*.

M. That was from meeting those kinds of society people. It was some kind of commentary on that experience.

C.N. In the past you've said that your art didn't make a commentary —that you were just interested in the forms you worked with and not the content.

M. No. My work had a lot of content. My idea was to work for everybody, because I saw that art had become such a highbrow thing—just for a few people. It's just that I think people see it, so why should I explain every detail? I remember when I did a group of politicians, a man came up and he said, "Well, is this political art?" And I said, "No, it has nothing to do with it."

C.N. Yet there's a difference between your art and such other Pop artists as Warhol, Lichtenstein, and Rosenquist. They took vulgar advertising images and made them into high art. However, that art wasn't for many people, because most people saw they were just advertising images and felt the artists were putting them on—making fun of them. But there's more sympathy for people in your art. You aren't throwing lowbrow images back into people's faces and telling them it's high art.

M. No. It's criticism—social criticism. I'm surprised that, up to this day, some people never understood what I was saying—like a close friend of mine. I always thought everybody knew it.

C.N. Don't you think a reason they didn't know was due to the way your art was treated and written about. People just talked about how the forms were put together—the aesthetic approach. Often they never discussed content at all.

M. People don't think. Because finally, I remember I took a piece to South America, and they wouldn't show it. They said the government wouldn't like it. There they notice.

C.N. Yes. In dictatorships like Russia or in South America anything that is different from the government's way of thinking is dangerous and can't be exhibited. Here, we suppress in a different way. We show everything, but we make believe it has no content. If there's a political meaning, we ignore it. For instance, you did a sculpture of the Kennedys in 1962, but it was treated like an abstract piece even though it made a political statement.

M. Yes.

C.N. The same thing happens with Andy Warhol's work. He paints Marilyn Monroe and Jackie Kennedy, images that are icons for our day, and people write of them as flat surfaces that just happen to have configurations on them. They dehydrate the work of all its vital juices. That was typical of the attitude of the sixties—as if people were only interested in keeping things superficial and not probing too deeply into the underlying meaning of what was going on. Did you find that the people you knew were serious or just interested in having a good time?

M. The artists or the other people?

C.N. The whole art crowd.

M. Because I had to work very hard, making all those pieces, most of the time I was working. The people who were having fun were the people outside. People kept telling me, "Oh those parties," and I spent most of my time working.

C.N. But everybody said you went to those parties. Grace Glueck quotes you as saying your chief recreation is going to parties. That you were a party girl—the toast of New York. A great deal was made of your appearance, your beauty, your chic. It's part of the glamor thing, as if you weren't a serious person and the social commentary in your work didn't have to be seen.

M. I don't know how many parties there could be, maybe one every two months. I can't remember how many parties I went to. But about the parties and the clothes—it was to relax. Because it's very depressing to be so profound all day. I had been like that before; ever since I was a child, I was putting everything down. If you are profound, everything is bad. It's very depressing.

C.N.   And the only way you can get out of it is to . . .

M.   Be superficial. Because if you really think about it, it's like a horror, this whole world here. So with some of my things I was thinking about that. They would have humor—something to laugh at. At the same time, I think they were very strong put-downs. I used to get scared of my own work sometimes, working late at night. It has those two things at the same time.

C.N.   There are a lot of facets to your work of the sixties. It's very complex. You could do a portrait sculpture of a Dustbowl family and then a party of chic women or portraits of political heads of state.

M.   That party of elegant women, that's a criticism. I mean I wasn't making some beautiful women having a good time. That's a criticism. I didn't like talking to women, then. They would tell me I had to get dressed up like a model and get a man to pay the bills. Models were very popular in the art world of the sixties. I remember that interview you speak of that I had with Grace Glueck. She was so cold, so detached, and she made me sound so detached. I don't think she liked me.

C.N.   In terms of the women's liberation movement, the sculpture you did is very telling about the way women live in our society. In 1972, Judy Chicago and Miriam Schapiro encouraged their students to fill an entire house with images of how many women in our culture spend their lives. It's an exposé and a put-down at the same time. It shows the kinds of fantasies and frustrations some women are subject to. Such pieces as your *Babies,* and *Bride and Groom* and *The Party* seem, to me, related to what women are attempting to do now—to examine their entire existence and to separate fact from fantasy.

M.   Yes, but I see the *Babies* differently. For me, that meant America. This huge baby monster taking over. I even had the flag here—stripes. And people think it's a child.

C.N.   You did that in 1962. You really understood what was happening in this country.

M.   I just don't think that's something that happened in the sixties. I'd been here for twenty years and used to hang around the beatniks, and those people all thought that way. It's not something that happened because a few students thought of it in 1968.

C.N.   The fifties were a terrible time for intellectuals and liberals. It was the time of McCarthy trials, and people were afraid not to conform. It was a time of retreating and going underground. Pollock and Krasner and Newman and Still must have been aware of what was happening.

M.   In the fifties when I came to this country, the students were really unaware. I didn't want to go to college because it was so dead there. Only a few people were protesting. They were the beatniks. I used to hang around with them in the Village, and everyone thought they were a bunch of kooks. Art wasn't popular in those days, and there were only a few galleries in which you could show. My work was priced at $250. Art became popular in the sixties.

Then the whole atmosphere was very exciting in this country because of Kennedy and Jackie Kennedy. I was very enthusiastic. It couldn't have been that many years, because I had a show in 1962 and there was nothing then. Then maybe in 1964. It was just for three years, because then I went to the Far East. It must have been three years—and people remember it as if it were a lifetime, partying and all kinds of things.

C.N.   It's interesting that in the late sixties, in this country, we have the emergence of all the liberation movements; the Black movement really emerges and students began to rebel and demonstrate around 1968.

M.   That's when I left. I started getting very depressed, and then I went to the Far East.

C.N.   Why?

M.   Curiosity. I had never been there and I always wanted to go, but I was scared to go alone. I went, and it was fine.

C.N.   Did going to the East change your feelings about many things?

M.   Yes. It was so nice for me to find so many thousands of people who had feelings. Here, I only know a few. Then all of a sudden I went to India and everybody looks like an artist there. They have bright eyes and they're intelligent. There, and also in Thailand and Cambodia. Everybody is beautiful. I was very depressed, because I thought this Western culture was the only thing that existed, and it made me very happy to know that I can go somewhere else.

I was away a year, and when I came back I was so depressed I couldn't live here. I didn't know what to do. I couldn't even do my work well anymore, because I had seen so many beautiful things there. Then I went to South America and Central America for a year. I didn't like Venezuela. I liked Guatemala. When I came back here, so much time had gone by and then, all of a sudden, I feel different again. People keep telling me that it's changed here. I think it's always been the same. People think about money all the time. I'm not commercial.

C.N.   Yet, we've had so much upheaval here, and people say they want to be different—to be more in touch with themselves. Do you think that's all talk?

M.   The general population—it's hard to tell. Because all this excitement that we were talking about was just a little group—a few artists, and maybe three hundred people hanging around. That's not the whole of America.

C.N.   It seems to me that the period from '64 to '67, which we talked about, was the end of something. It was the end of a time when things could be swept under the rug. All sorts of fermentation was taking place, all the seeds for the rebellions, the demonstrations, the reactions against the war were growing in this country. But the art world acted as if it wasn't happening. It was in the art, but nobody saw it, nobody wanted to see it. The people at the top were having an exciting good time, but the rest of society was getting angry and eventually they exploded. You must have felt this, since you became depressed and left about the time everything erupted. These new fish images you are doing now emerged after you left, didn't they?

M.   I think that's from going to the Far East. When I came back I felt like doing something very pure, just for the sake of it. In some cases I worked on one piece for six months. I wanted to do something very beautiful.

C.N.   Yet the faces, your face which is joined to the body of many of the fish, looks as if it is in great pain, experiencing terrible anguish—like a baroque sculpture of the seventeenth century. Some of the fish are predators. They are frightening and dangerous creatures.

M.   Most of the fish are evil fish. There are barracuda and tiger fish. I haven't analyzed what I am doing this time. At one point I thought that I was making weapons, because I had these skinny long pieces, and they were aiming out of the window like missiles.

C.N.   They have that kind of sleekness about them, but these pieces are very far from the kind of work you did in the sixties.

M.   I am not working for the general public any more.

C.N.   Why is that?

M.   I lost interest. I don't want to reach them. I've lost interest in them. They look ugly to me. Yes . . . Suddenly I made a portrait of Nixon, and it was like a nightmare thinking about this person. I would go into the subway, and everybody had that face—the very tight lips and sort of grayish complexion. I really would have nightmares at night. So I can't think about those people or represent them. I want to make something very beautiful.

C.N.   But in a sense these are very frightening things you've made.

M.   Oh, awful.

C.N.   There's the pain and anguish of someone who's suffering, on the faces of the fish, which is your face. They are surreal-nightmare visions. They are monsters from the sea. Was doing them like making a descent?

M.   I think it's that I was sort of disturbed. When I was on an island, some people taught me how to go scuba diving. When I first went down I went to the bottom and I was resting. I didn't get up and my teacher, who understood me so well, told me, "Go down to the bottom of the sea and take a rest."

C.N.   Melville in *Moby Dick* talks about the sea as the bed of creation. It's the nether world and the source.

M.   I didn't have all those ideas. It's not premeditated. It just happened. Everybody else in the world is frightened about going under water. But I wasn't. I just went down there and felt very comfortable. I don't know what it means yet, but it's not premeditated.

C.N.   The ocean has a great attraction. It's all-encompassing and always in motion, and yet it never changes. It's eternity.

M.   It changes all the time. Every ten minutes you see something. If you are out in a boat for a long time it's very interesting, and underwater there are all kinds of things going on—monsters. But I don't see it as an evil.

Lots of men go down there and want to kill everything. They think it's a threat. You can also think about it as very peaceful, and you don't have to bother any animal down there. They don't bother you. But lots of people jump in, and they think it's a challenge, and they want to kill everything. I think it's the way of the thought of the West.

C.N.   But you chose to sculpt the predator fish, the shark, and tiger fish. Isn't that a comment on evil?

M.   I think it is unconscious. The shark and the barracuda are the most beautiful. They scare you, and so they must have impressed me.

C.N.   They're beautiful as long as you remain detached, but if you get involved with the danger inherent in those fish it's hard to concentrate on their beauty. It's interesting that you combine your own face with the body of the fish, as if you are not making a distinction between humans and animals. Were you looking for oneness?

M. I don't know what that means.

C.N. It's the idea that everything is part of everything else. That the plants and animals and human beings are all from the same living stuff. We human beings, in the West, tend to think of ourselves as a superior race. We might be better off if, like the Indians, we did not separate ourselves from other living creatures but respected equally all forms of life. You've merged plant and animal in these fish which are made of wood.

M. Mahogany.

C.N. It's a beautiful wood and you've left the grain showing. How did you get the color in some of them?

M. Some of them have a dye, and they have many coats of varnish. Some have thirty coats.

C.N. Where do you think art is going at this time? Are you hopeful or pessimistic? Some people are saying art is finished.

M. They are always saying that, all the time. For some reason today there are not so many good artists, but then there never were. You see lots of bad things around, but then even before—when we had Abstract Expressionists—there were lots of bad paintings around. Nowadays, they've only saved the good ones, so we think everybody was so talented. In those days they were saying, "It's all over, what can you do after this?"

C.N. And now we've had Minimal art and Conceptual art and people who work on their bodies and are so obsessed with themselves.

M. They used to do these things in the early sixties—those Happenings. Now they call them Performances. I imagine from all that thinking something will come out. We always come up with something.

C.N. Are you interested in film or video?

M. No. I couldn't make a movie. I haven't that kind of a mind. I can't even take a photograph, because I can't see what's coming out. It's so abstract. You have to imagine the future.

C.N. You like the idea of having something emerge under your own hand.

M. Yes. I have to look at it.

C.N. I notice you've been doing prints and that you put your own self, your own body, into it.

M.   I was never interested in prints. People talked me into it. They talked me into making them. I felt, for a long time, that if people asked me to do something I should do it. I hardly ever said no, until recently. I used to get so excited about the idea that I could do something for somebody, until I found out that lots of people were just taking advantage of me. In the past, l tried to make whatever they asked of me good.

C.N.   What do you plan to do when your show is over? Will you stay in New York?

M.   Yes. I'm living in Soho. It's easy here. You just go out and talk to anybody. It's not like I have to call somebody on the telephone and make a date. It's a nice atmosphere here. It's friendly.

C.N.   Yes. This is relatively new.

M.   Yes, for a long time there wasn't anything like that. Except before, with the Abstract Expressionists, it was the same. Everybody would meet in the bar, and you didn't have to telephone anybody. And then, for a while, it was lonely—come to think of it—in the sixties. It was lonely. People think it was so friendly, and there was really no place to go. I really didn't go to that many places, like Andy Warhol. People used to give these enormous parties with maybe five hundred people, and you would go there and get drunk. It was very lively, with lots of dancing but there wasn't any small group. You never really knew anybody.

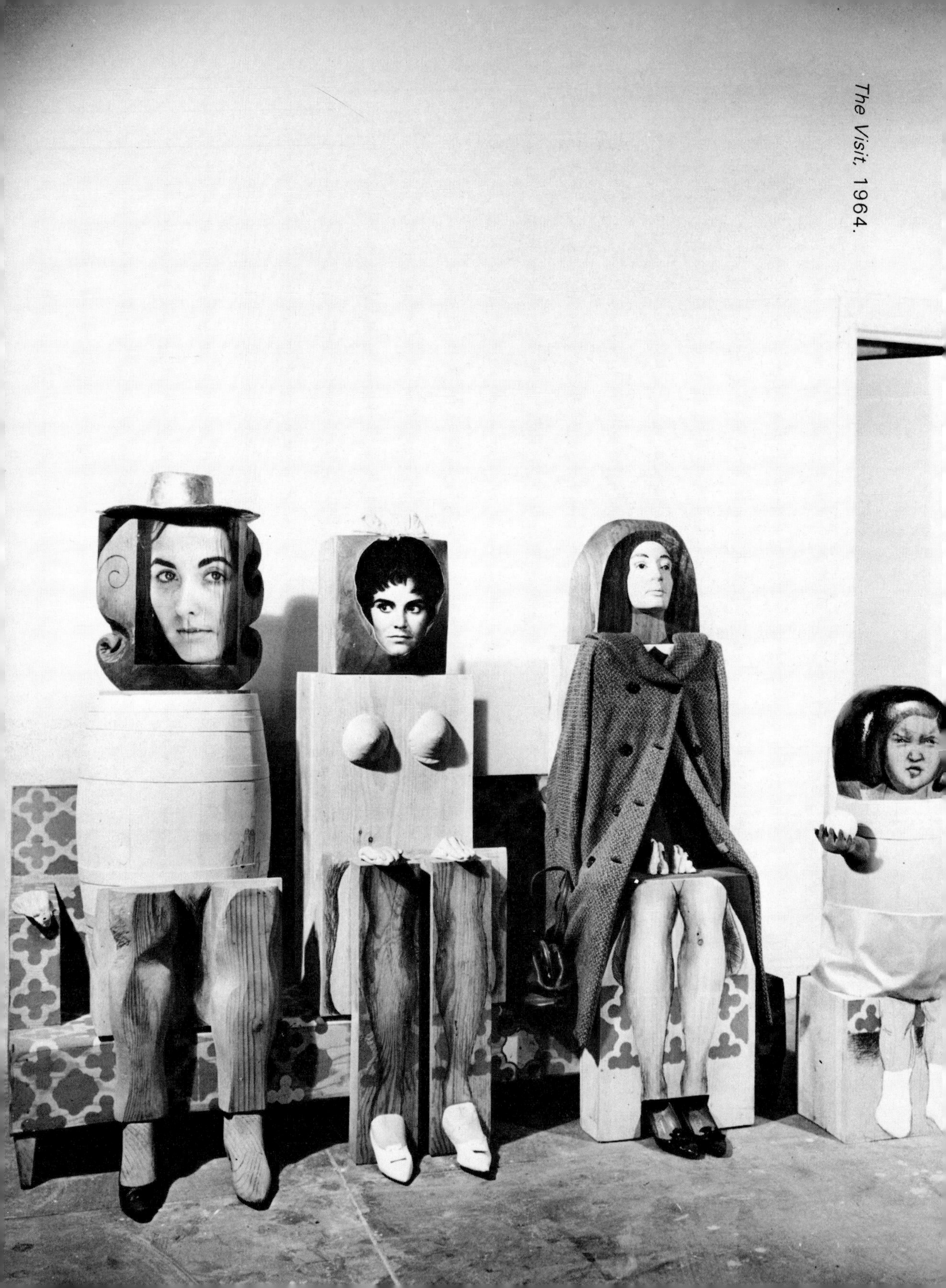

The Visit, 1964.

Women Leaning (detail), 1965–66.

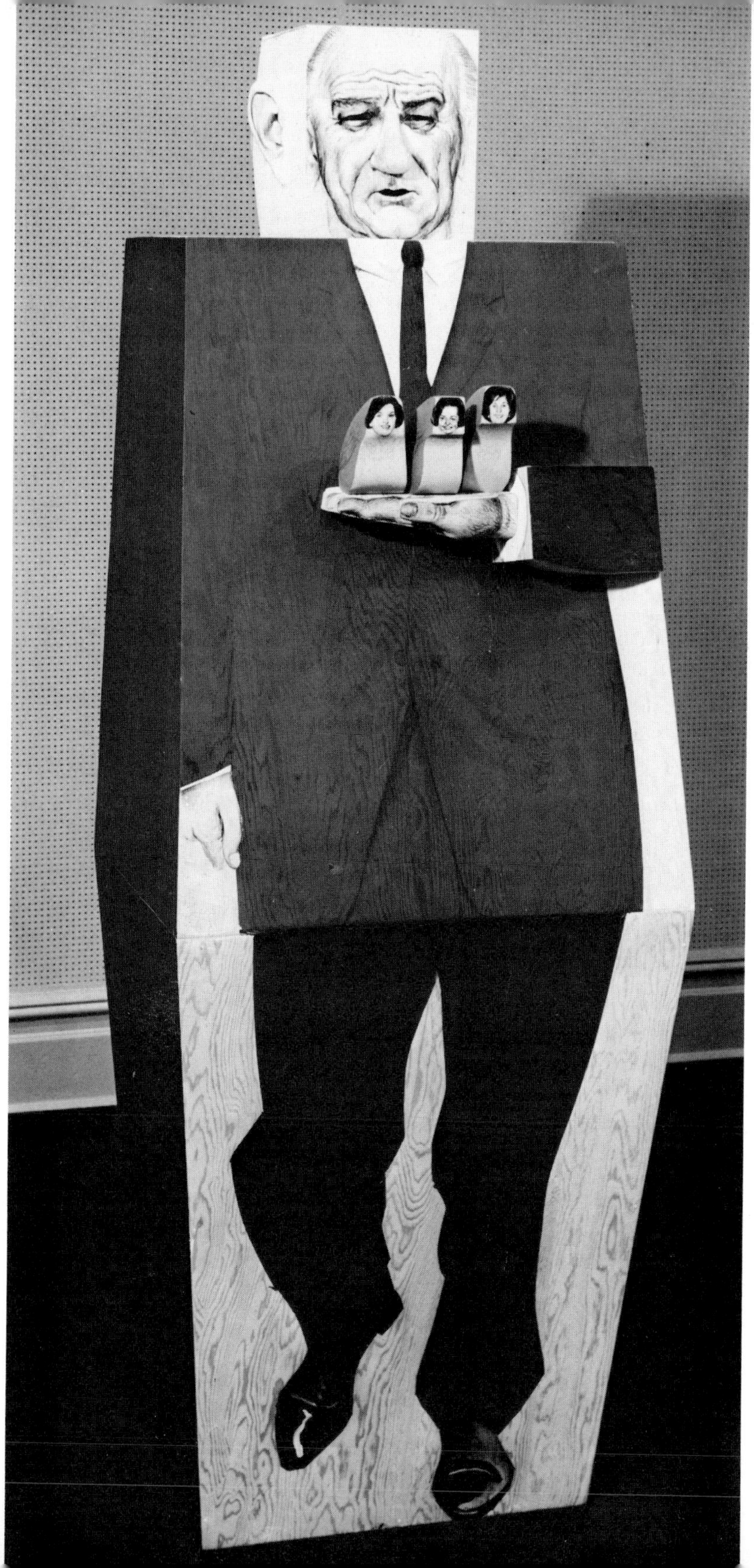

LBJ, 1967.

Barracuda, 1971.

Zebrasoma, 1971.

Eva Hesse.

EVA HESSE is a sculptor who died of a brain tumor at the age of thirty-three, in 1970. Her short life was both tragic and marvelous, alternating between external fears and interior visions.

Hesse was born in Hamburg, Germany, in 1936. She had a beautiful, gifted, but neurotic mother and an intellectual father, both of whom she adored. There was also one older sister, Helen, to whom she clung desperately throughout the strained events of her life.

The Hesse family was forced to flee Germany in the late thirties and made their way to the United States in 1939. Life was hard and uncertain for the refugees and childhood was a time of nightmare terrors for the sensitive Eva. A rebel at home, Hesse took a job at *Seventeen* magazine at the age of eighteen and then went on to Cooper Union and Yale where she was acknowledged as an outstandingly gifted student.

In 1961 she married Tom Doyle, an artist quite a few years older than herself. They were separated in 1966. While living with Doyle, her work went through a series of transitional explorations, but she never abandoned her own developing form of personal expression.

In 1965, while living in Germany with her husband under the patronage of a wealthy German collector, Hesse created pieces out of wood, rope, steel, and papier-mâché that opened up for her, and a generation of artists to follow, an entirely new series of possibilities. She constructed a piece called *Hang-Up* which was composed of a wooden frame wrapped in a painted rope out of which jutted a steel rod of about ten or eleven feet. In this work Hesse articulated all the crucial elements of her work to come: the desire to move the figure off the canvas into actual space in order to dissolve the boundaries between drawing, painting, and sculpture; the need to explore all sorts of non-art-associated materials; the wish to temper the geometric with the organic, the ordered with the chaotic, the logical with the absurd, the detached with the engaged.

Hesse's explorations and discoveries in these areas in the next five years, up until the time of her death, were extraordinary. She combined latex, rubberized cheesecloth, rope, clay, metal, wire mesh in the most daring, innovative manner. By a repetition of circular, cylindrical, or rectangular forms, she created sculptural works; each shape in the series, however, was different in size and detail, giving the total piece a sense of individual organic growth and change, rather than the mechanical repetition of an arithmetic progression. *Repetition 19* with its fiberglass, cylindrical columns in various stages of elevation and deflation has undeniable sexual connotations. One might consider *Expanded Expansion* with its flexible elasticity a visual metaphor for a gigantic respiratory system. Hesse's last untitled works of 1970 made out of plaster, fiberglass, and iron mesh have the vitalism of some forms of amoebic life enlarged to human scale and beyond. With trailing cords and petal-like formations, these works create situations that compellingly draw the viewer into their intensely personal ambience.

From her student days onward, Hesse responded to the tragic, explosive paintings of the Abstract Expressionists. Completely self-absorbed, she resisted the cool, detached, ultracerebral attitudes of the so-called Minimalists of the middle and late sixties, although she responded to their obsessive repetitions of geometric form. Her contribution was to transform the geometric into the organic, the rigid into the flexible, the detached into the personal, while constantly eschewing any tendency toward the sentimental by maintaining an intellectual awareness of the task at hand.

Hesse was one of the pioneers of her generation to acknowledge the need for restoring spontaneity, sexuality, and emotional reaction to an art form grown sterile and rigid in its theoretical and intellectual entanglements. In asserting her need to be subjective, idiosyncratic, emotional, absurd, Hesse opened a huge vein that others have been mining more or less successfully ever since. In her work she broke through the pseudomasculine cult of detached intellectualism, giving license to female and male artists alike to explore and openly reveal their interior sense of themselves.

CINDY NEMSER   Tell me about your family background.

EVA HESSE   You won't believe it. I was told by the doctor that I have the most incredible life he ever heard. Have you got tissues? It's not a little thing to have a brain tumor at thirty-three. Well my whole life has been like that. I was born in Hamburg, Germany. My father was a criminal lawyer. He had just finished his two doctorates and I had the most beautiful mother in the world. She looked like Ingrid Bergman and she was manic depressive. She studied art in Hamburg. My sister was born in 1933 and I was born in 1936. Then in 1938 there was a children's pogrom. I was put on a train with my sister. We went to Holland where we were supposed to be picked up by my father's brother and his wife in Amsterdam but he couldn't do it, so we were put in a Catholic children's home and I was always sick. So I was put in a hospital and I wasn't with my sister. My parents were hidden somewhere in Germany and then they came to Amsterdam and had trouble getting us out. Somehow they got us to England. My father's brother and his wife ended up in concentration camps. No one else in my family made it. But we did. We got from England to America via one of my father's cousins who had an import-export firm, one in England and one in America. He got us in very, very late. We came in the summer of 1939. It was the last chance. And when we first came here we lived across from the Nazi party on Eighty-sixth Street until our cousin could get us a place to live. My father got trained as an insurance broker and my mother was sick all the time. Then we lived in different homes because my mother was in and out of hospitals and my father was studying to be an insurance broker. So I used to be alone at night and I used to be terrified. My mother was there but not there —there, but not there. I was shifted from home to home. I was raised in different places and so was my sister. My mother was in and out of sanitoriums. She had a psychiatrist who told her to divorce my father and fell in love with her. The last time I saw my mother she was living with a doctor and his wife. My father remarried a *bitch* whose name was Eva (she became Eva Hesse) who had a brain tumor two years to the day before I did. Sounds incredible? Let me finish the story. She got out of the hospital two years to the day I went in—same hospital, same doctor; in three years, two people not related but with the same name. Well, the story goes on. It doesn't end there. My father was sick for fifteen years. He died three days after his sixty-fifth birthday but he was sick the fifteen years. I think my family is half like the Kennedys. I don't mean we have that extreme of wealth or fortune but it's all been extremes. I have no one. No one in my family has lived. I have *one* healthy sister. There's not been *one* normal thing in my life—not one —not even my art. I never tried to get into a show. Art is the easiest thing in my life and that's ironic. It doesn't mean I've worked little on it, but it's the only thing I never had to. That's why I think I might be so good. I have no fear. I could take risks. I have the most openness about my art. My attitude is most open. It's totally unconservative. It's total freedom and willingness to work. I'm willing really to walk on the edge, and if I haven't achieved it, that's where I want to go. But in my life—maybe because my life has been so traumatic, so absurd—there hasn't been one normal, happy thing. I'm the easiest person to make happy and the easiest person to make sad because I've gone through so much. And it's never stopped.

Then I lived with a stepmother whom I just couldn't stand and I love people, I have no trouble with people, but I hated her and she was terrible to me. My father was terribly sick. He had his first attack when I was thirteen—like Eisenhower—a terrible coronary attack. And my stepmother used to say, "You can't tell him anything or you'll make him die." And he loved me with a thing that was almost incestuous. So I had a lot of trouble with men too because my father and I were very close, but it was very quiet. It wasn't talked about because he was constantly ill and he was getting crippled and they had to operate on his spine and there was the danger of the heart. My stepmother who was a thorough, unadulterated bitch did one good thing in her life. She loved my father; she really cared. They went to Europe and he died like that [snapping her fingers], which was good. She brought his body back and put herself in the hospital. She had said for the last three years that he was alive that she didn't want to go in but she knew something was wrong. First they couldn't find anything. Then finally it came out that she had a brain tumor. My sister and I really took care of her and unfortunately, when I got mine [laughter], she'd come to the hospital to stay with me and I couldn't stand her. I had to cope with that. And she still calls me. When I'm sick she's very good to me, but if she thinks I'm better she's not.

In between it was pretty much hell. I used to feel a fraud all my life. The world thought I was a cute, smart kid and I kidded them. But at home I was called a terror. I was miserable. I had trouble—tremendous fear—incredible fear. I had my father tuck my blankets in tight into my German bed which had bars at the bottom which I would hold at night and he would have to tell me that we wouldn't be poor, and we wouldn't be robbed, and he'd be there to take care of me in the morning. As a child it was a ritual every night. There wasn't one day of security and it never really got any better.

So that gave me whatever strength I have. I've been a giant in my strength and my work's been strong and my whole character has it inside. But somewhere I'm a terribly frightened person. There was a whole abandonment syndrome because my father had to leave us all the time and I was left without my sister and I went from home to home. And my marriage split up which created another terrible abandonment problem. Then my father died. I think I had two relatively happy years. But as bad as things that have happened are, and maybe because of that, I can have tremendous happiness. Even this year I had good things. Though it's a miracle I lived through this first operation. (I had a few hours left to live—there was so much pressure—the whole brain tipped over and all the intelligence in the front.)

C.N. Where did you study art?

E.H. When I was sixteen I went to Pratt Institute and I didn't like it very much at all. The only painting I knew, and that was very little, was Abstract Expressionism and at Pratt they didn't stress painting at all. When you started painting class you had to do a lemon still life and you graduated to a lemon and bread still life and you graduated to a lemon, egg, bread still life and this was not my idea of painting. The rest of the classes were two-dimensional and three-dimensional design. I was also much younger, at least emotionally, and chronologically too, than everybody else. I was sixteen, an immature sixteen, and I didn't like it. I waited until I was getting "A's" instead of "C's" and declared I was quitting. I had to know that it wasn't because I wasn't doing well.

C.N.   What happened after that?

E.H.   I quit in the middle of the year and I had lived away from home so I had to go home. As soon as I got there my stepmother said, "Get a job." So where do you go at sixteen-and-a-half knowing very little, but having an interest in art? I took myself to *Seventeen* magazine and for some strange reason they hired me. I think it was just because of the gall of coming up there. So I got the job at *Seventeen* magazine part-time and afterwards I went a few times a week to the Art Students League just to draw in a class without a teacher—just from the model. And the days I didn't do that I went to the Museum of Modern Art and went to the movies. They changed them almost every day and I saw a *lot* of movies. Then I took the middle of the year test for Cooper Union. I was very frightened of the examination and that was the only plan I made. I never made more than one plan. I always counted on whatever I tried. I had to make it. I got in and the following September I went to Cooper Union which I loved from the very start. I moved out on my own again, went to Judson. Then I finished at Cooper Union doing very well and I went to Yale. I didn't like it, but because of the combination of being afraid to get out of school—because that was frightening—and not being defeated, I stayed. In retrospect I don't think I should have stayed. I did well there but schools depend on both faculty and students and the faculty was poor. It was a bad time and the students responded to the tension and friction and uninterest in this thing that was going on. There was Albers who was being forced into retirement, but they let him stay because they had no one to replace him, and Bernard Chaitin and Rico Lebrun. It was ridiculous clashes of personality and they fought each other through us and the result was that the work wasn't very good there.

C.N.   Were any of your fellow students the people you now know in New York?

E.H.   No. The irony is that as I was leaving there a lot of people who are now in New York—Bob Mangold, Sylvia Mangold, Brice Marden, Richard Serra, and Frank Lincoln Viner—were all there immediately after I left.

C.N.   Do you feel any of your teachers influenced you?

E.H.   I don't think so. I loved Albers' color course but I had had it at Cooper. I did very well in it. I was Albers' little color studyist—everybody always called me that—and every time he walked into the classroom he would ask, "What did Eva do?" I loved those problems but I didn't do them out of need or necessity. But Albers couldn't stand my painting and, of course, I was much more serious about the painting. I had the Abstract Expressionist student approach and that was not Albers', not really Rico Lebrun's nor Bernard Chaitin's approach either. And if you didn't follow their idea it wasn't an idea. And in color you had to. You were given coloring papers so your choices were less and you had to work within certain confines.

C.N.   Since you didn't feel any strong influence at Yale, were there people in New York who influenced you when you came back and started working on your own?

E.H.   I think at the time I met the man I married. I shouldn't say I went backwards, but I did, because he was a more mature and developed artist. He would push me in his direction and I would be unconsciously somewhat influenced by him. Yet when I met him I had already had a drawing show which was much more me. I had a drawing show in 1961 at the John Heller Gallery which became the Amel Gallery. It was called "Three Young Americans." The drawings then were incredibly related to what I'm doing now. Then I went back one summer again to an Abstract Expressionist kind of tone—that was really an outside influence. I think that struggle between student and finding one's self is, even at the beginning level of maturity, something that cannot be avoided. I don't know anyone who has avoided it. And my struggle was very difficult and very frustrating. I was conscious of it all the time, and if I ever had any worry in my development, then it was in finding myself. I used to worry: Am I just staying with a "father figure"? Where is my development? Is there a consistency? Am I going through a stage and will I reach there? I was very aware of that and it was a very frustrating, difficult time. But I worked. I never had the touble of not being able to work although there would be, say, three months where I would work all the time and then maybe there would be a break and that would be very frustrating. But after a while I could always get back. It is true, there were stages, but in retrospect—the steps—Oh, it's so *clear*.

C.N.   When did you start working in soft materials?

E.H.   I started working in sculpture when my husband and I lived for a year and a half under an unusual kind of "Renaissance patronage" in Europe. A German industrialist invited us to live with him and I had a great deal of difficulty with painting but never with drawings. The drawings were never very simplistic. They ranged from linear to complicated washes and collages. The translation or transference to a large scale and in painting was always *tedious.* It was not natural and I thought to translate it in some other way. So I started working in relief and with line—using the cords and ropes that are now so commonly used. I literally translated the line. I would vary the cord lengths and widths and I would start with three-dimensional boards and I would build them out with paper mâché or kinds of soft materials. I varied the materials a lot but the structure would always be built up with cords. I kept the scale, in Europe, fairly small, and when I came back to America I varied the materials further and I didn't keep to rectangles. Even in Europe I did some that were not rectangles, and then they grew and grew. They came from the floor, the ceiling, the walls. Then it just became whatever it became.

C.N.   How do the soft materials relate to the subject or content of your work? Do they embody unconscious ideas? Looking at your works they seem, to me, to be filled with sexual impulses or organic feeling. I feel there are anthropomorphic inferences.

E.H.   It's not a simple question for me. First when I work it's only the abstract qualities that I'm really working with, which is to say the material, the form it's going to take, the size, the scale, the positioning or where it comes from in my room—if it hangs from the ceiling or lies on the floor. However, I don't value the totality of the image on these abstract or esthetic points. For me it's a total image that has to do with me and life. It can't be divorced as an idea or composition or form. I don't believe art can be based on that. This is where art and life come together. Also I have confidence in my understanding of the formal to the point that I don't play with it. I don't want to make that my problem. I know it so well. I have complete confidence in my ability. I don't want to be aware of it or conscious of it. It's *not* the problem for me. Those problems are solvable, I solve them, can solve them *beautifully.* In fact, my idea now is to discount everything I've ever learned or been taught about those things and to find something else. So it is inevitable that it *is* my life, my feelings, my thoughts. And there I'm very complex. I'm not a simple person and the complexity—if I can name what it consists of (and it's probably increased now because I've been so sick this year)—is the total absurdity of life. I guess that's where I relate, if I do, to certain artists who I feel very close to, and not so much through having studied their writings or works, but because, for me, there's this total *absurdity* in their work.

C.N. Which artists are they?

E.H. Duchamp, Yvonne Rainer, Ionesco, Carl André.

C.N. Let's talk about some of your early sculptures.

E.H. There was a piece I did for that show in the Graham Gallery, "Abstract Inflationism, Stuffed Expressionism," in 1965 or '66. It was called *Hang-Up*—a dumb name. I did the piece when I came back from Europe and I wasn't totally aware of how "hang-up" was being used here. It's unfortunate, but I can't change it. I think it was about the fifth piece I did and I think the most important statement I made. It's close to what I feel I achieve now in my best pieces. It was the first time where my idea of absurdity or extreme feeling came through. It's huge —six feet by seven feet. It is a frame, ostensibly, and it sits on the wall and it's a simple structure which if I were to make again I'd construct differently. This is really an idea piece. It is almost primitive in its construction, very naive. It's a very thin, strong metal, easily bent and rebent. The frame is all tied like a hospital bandage as if someone had broken an arm, an absolutely rigid cord around the entire thing. That dates back to those drawings I told you about. I would never repeat that piece of construction but there's a nice quality about it. It has a kind of depth I don't always achieve—a depth and soul and absurdity and life and meaning or feeling or intellect that I want to get. And I think that I believe in this piece enough that I have it in the back of my mind (and I never wanted to do this before) to redo it. Not to reconstruct it physically. I think it would be a different piece but I would like to do it again because I think it's valid. Don't let anyone hear this. This is the piece that Richard Serra called about. He said that he saw it and he really thought it was good. It is also so extreme and that is why I like it and don't like it. It is so absurd. This little piece of steel comes out of this structure and it comes out a lot. It's about ten or eleven feet out and it is ridiculous. It's the most ridiculous structure I have ever made and that is why it is really good. It is coming out of something and yet nothing, and it is holding. It is framing nothing. And the whole frame is gradated—oh more absurdity—very, very finely. It really was an effort. And it's painted with liquitex. It is very surreal, very strange. It is weird. It is like those things I did in Europe that come out of nothing in a very surreal and yet very formal way and have really nothing to do with anybody.

C.N. In a way this piece makes me think of Picasso's sculpture—his wire pieces which were really drawings. They were related to his Cubist work and he tried to three-dimensionalize them. Perhaps this was a similar impulse with you in the drawings?

E.H.   Yes. But this was a long time after the drawings. This was done the first year of being back in America. The drawings and the first series of sculpture were done a year or two before in Europe. But I was still using cord and rope, though about this time I started dropping it and not using it so rigidly. At first I used it rigidly like lines in my drawing.

C.N.   Here's another rope piece from the Sidney Janis show, called *Ennead.*

E.H.   Now let's see. It's an early piece. It says 1966. I think I did it in 1965 when I first came back from Europe.

C.N.   You talked about the idea that this piece started out with perfect symmetry, the whole thing was perfectly planned, yet as the cords worked down from the board from which they were attached they became entangled and ended up in chaos.

E.H.   One of the reasons is the strings are very very soft. I dyed them and they were gradated in color and each string came from the center of a circle, and by the nature of the structure of this piece, as they started falling down, even though they were in perfect order, the strings were so soft they went different ways, and the further they got to the ground the more chaotic it got. Although I wove the string equally in the back (you could see they could be moved to be perfect), none of them are. They are all different lengths. And the further you get away from the structure the more chaotic it is. But then I have always opposed content and form or just form to form. There's always this divergency. It has always been so consistent. Even if the interest in material and scale are different, that element has always been in my work even as an Abstract Expressionist.

C.N.   How about motifs? I notice that you use the circle quite frequently. What does it mean to you?

E.H.   I think that there is a time element. I think that that was in the sequence of change and maturation. I think I'm less involved in it now. I guess if you are going to pick a motif, you would say that before I got sick I was working with squares and rectangles. At that time when I really worked, the last works I did were just about a year ago, I was less interested in a specific form as the circle or the square or rectangle and was really working to get to non-anthropomorphic, non-geometric, non-non, where you can't make any reference as a circle. I'll try to get back to your question. I think the circle is very abstract. I could make up stories of what the circle means to men, but I don't know if it is that conscious. I think it was a form, a vehicle. I don't think I had a sexual, anthropomorphic, or geometric meaning. It wasn't a breast and it wasn't a circle representing life and eternity. I think that would be fake—maybe on an unconscious level, but that's so opposed—to say it was an abstract life symbol or a geometric theory. There you have the two in opposition and I don't think I had that conception. One memory I have: I remember always working with contradictions and contradictory forms which is my idea also in life. The whole absurdity of life, everything for me has always been opposite. Nothing has ever been in the middle. When I gave you my autobiography, my life never had anything normal or in the center. It was always extremes. And I think, I know that, in forms that I use in my work that contradiction is certainly there. When I was younger or a less mature artist, I was always aware that I could combine order and chaos, string and mass, huge and small. I would try to find the most absurd opposites or extreme opposites and I was always aware of their contradiction formally. It was always more interesting than making something right size, right proportion. Back to the question—within the circle I remember taking this straight perfect form and then putting a hole in the center and dropping out a very, very flexible surgical hose, the most flexible rubber I could get. I would make it very, very long and then it would squiggle and wiggle. That was the extreme you could get from that perfect, perfect circle.

C.N.   I was reading Lucy Lippard's article on "The Dematerialization of Art," in which she talks about how the most rational ideas as they begin to work themselves out appear visually chaotic. So one must begin to question the whole concept of what is rational and what is irrational. She mentions your work in those terms and also Bernard Vernet, people who begin with rational ideas.

E.H.   Or it can go the other way round. The original idea can just be intuitive, right? So that it is just an emotional thing. Then you calculate from there and follow through without any divergency.

C.N.   There is a certain element of chance or openness of possibilities in your work—say in a piece like *Sequel* in which everything can be manipulated.

E.H.   Everything is loose, totally at random. Yet it's sort of rigid. They're half-spheres and they're cast from half-balls and then they were put together again but not put together completely. They were put together with an opening so that the whole thing was sqooshy. It was a solid ball but it wasn't a solid ball. It's collapsible because it's rubber and then it's cylindrical but yet not. Then they could be moved. The only limitations are the mat and they could roll off the mat because they are basically cylindrical. The whole thing is ordered yet they're not ordered. But this is an old piece and it interests me less, which doesn't mean that I think it's negative or less interesting as a problem. Yet I've said I was not interested in formal problems—again that duplicity—since *Sequel* obviously represented a formal problem to me.

C.N.   Morse Peckham in *Man's Rage for Chaos* defines art as a desire for chaos, a kind of opening up of the unknown. The artist is seeking the unknown, seeking it to give it order but he or she has to find the chaotic before it can be given order. Art basically makes people aware of the chaos that surrounds them so that they become alive to it.

E.H.   It's definitely both ways. When Van Gogh first did his paintings, that was fantastic chaos. Now it's so conventional. Jackson Pollock showed us that. What is more chaotic than those drips, but he made his order out of that, so it was the most ordered painting. That piece I did at the Jewish Museum and now the rope that I started is completely chaotic, but yet you can give it an order.

C.N.   The artist makes the viewer aware of a chaotic situation perhaps as a sort of reference to something of which he has never before been aware. It's as if the art is a searching tool. It makes me aware of something I never thought was esthetic before. But it is not only esthetic. It makes me aware of an area of my surroundings or life that never dawned on me before.

E.H.   That's the point. It's what's important to me—finding a quantity for myself and whatever problem I might get with it. I might find something else, answer some question, or find some new form or thought.

C.N.   It's the idea of extending out into something that doesn't exist yet—almost like falling off.

E.H.   That's a nice way of putting it. Yes. I would like to do that.

C.N.   Repetition is very prevalent in your work. Why do you repeat a form over and over?

E.H.   Because it exaggerates. If something is meaningful, maybe it's more meaningful said ten times. It's not just an esthetic choice. If something is absurd, it's much more greatly exaggerated, absurd, if it's repeated.

C.N.   Max Kozloff in talking about a Cubist painting described it as a series of planes placed one on top of the other or slipping out from behind each other, as layers of memory of the mind. The painting becomes a kind of layering on, and building up, of experience. Somehow that interpretation seems analogous to what you are doing. Do you think there's anything obsessive in your work?

E.H. I guess repetition feels obsessive, and that box—not that I think it's an important work—where I had 4,500 holes . . .

C.N. Which box was that?

E.H. That huge box. It was called *Accession.* I first did it in metal, then in fiberglass. That's obsessive repetition but the form it takes is a square and it's a perfect square. Then the outside is very, very, very clear and by necessity it just works that way. The inside looks amazingly chaotic although it's the same piece of hose going through, so it's the same thing but as different as it can possibly be.

C.N. It's a kind of inner-outer dichotomy.

E.H. In that sense the piece is one of the best examples, but it becomes a little too precious, at least from where I stand now, and too right and too beautiful. It's like a gem, like a diamond. I think I'd rather do cat's eyes now or even less than cat's eyes, dirt or rock. I'm giving an analogy or metaphor. It's too right. I'd like to do a little more wrong at this point.

C.N. It's a very tactile work. My experience of it was that I wanted to get inside it.

E.H. I lost one of the pieces because people got inside of it in a museum and the piece came back wrecked. It was promised to someone and I had to repeat it. And *there's* great irony and absurdity—the day that I finished that piece was the day I collapsed.

C.N. All your work is extremely tactile. One wants to touch it, handle it.

E.H. I see everybody does. I'm not aware of it. I'm not asking everybody to, but every time I've been in a place where I've seen my work there were hands on it. I guess it was a greater involvement but I'm not aware of it. I don't intentionally do it. I really feel that the most truth is that it just happens.

C.N. I feel there is so much of the unconscious in your work, things that are coming out of you that you don't even realize. I guess that's true of every artist, but your work seems to have a release in it that some art doesn't have.

E.H. I let it. I want that release. I can't go on a sheer program. At times I thought "the more thought the greater the art," but I wonder about that and I do have to admit there's a lot that I'll just let happen and maybe it will come out the better for it. I used to plan a lot and do everything myself and then I started to take a chance. I needed help. It was a little difficult at first. I worked with two people but then we got to know each other well enough and I got confident enough and just prior to when I was sick I would not state the problem or plan the day. I would let more happen and let myself be used in a freer way. They also—their participation was more their own, more flexible. I wanted to see within a day's work or within three day's work what we would do together with a general focus but not anything specified. I really would like, when I start working again, to go further into this whole process. That doesn't mean total chance or freedom or openness.

C.N.   It seems to me that kind of working together has something to do with expanding art to include other people as participants—not mere spectators. It's as if the artist incorporates others and makes other people part of the art. Did working with others, this new open-ness, change your art?

E.H.   I can think of one thing it changed. The process of my work prior to that had taken a long time. First, because I did most of it myself and then when I planned the larger pieces and worked with someone they were more formalistic. When we started working less formalistically or with greater chance, the whole process was speeded up and we did one of the pieces at the Whitney that I love the most, the ladder piece [*Vinculum II*], in a very short time. It was a complex piece, but the whole attitude was different and that is the attitude that I want to work with now—in fact, even increased, even more exaggerated.

C.N.   That's a later piece, isn't it?

E.H.   It was one of the last pieces before I got so ill and it was one of the pieces we started working on with less plan. I just described the vague idea to the two people I worked with and we went and started doing it. There were a few things that I said to one of the people that I worked with—I said I wanted a pole. He made a perfect pole. It wasn't what I meant at all. So we started again and then he understood.

C.N.   How is this piece made?

E.H.   It's reinforced fiberglass, and then the structure underneath (I shouldn't say that because it's part and parcel) is wire screening in fiberglass and then rubber hose.

C.N.   You directed making the piece?

E.H.   No. We did it together. Now I have to learn to do that even more because of the illness. I can't work at all now, and when I *can* it's going to be limited. My physical capacities are going to be limited for some time and it's unreal to think I can handle it all. So I'll have really to give more and more for other people to do, and there's such a personal idiom for me, such a personal involvement, that it's not going to be easy for me to conceive of other people handling—I guess if I'm well enough to participate or at least verbally be there—

C.N.   It's like accidentally you opened something up.

E.H.   Yes. Fortunately, because it would have been harder to conceive of doing it if I hadn't already started.

C.N.   When I looked at *Ishtar*, the piece that had the half-cups with the cords going through it, it seemed to me that it had sexual connotations and there was a joining of the two sexes. And it's the same in a work like *Repetition 19* where you have container-like forms that are tall and could also be tower-like or phallic.

E.H.   You mean they're both male and female symbols?

C.N.   Because they're containers and they're also cylindrical forms.

E.H.   And the next version gets taller—greater erections. No! I don't see that at all. I'm not conscious of that at all or not even unconscious. I'm aware they can be thought of as that even in the process of making them, but I am not making that.

C.N.   What comes next?

E.H.   It's *Area* and I have a personal thing about this piece because it's made out of the mold of *Repetition 19.* It is the insides that we took out and then made into another piece totally. There is no connection whatsoever—except if you really saw it, it is very clear. You see it's the bottom of the can and this is around this wire mesh; it looks like the curve. That is its parts and then I rubberized and attached them. I sewed them with wire and that is the piece. The only thing is that there are only ten. I think I got lazy and it was a hot summer and I just couldn't get nineteen done. I also had to give it to Lucy Lippard for a traveling show. Actually it is very long. The heights of these are twenty inches and it is twenty feet long. It would really have been good if I added all of them. It's totally irregular and yet it is all connected. I have a personal attachment because I took one piece and made it totally another one. This one was empty containers where you have that sexual connotation. It's anthropomorphic, and these aren't, or in a totally different way. They couldn't be more different. *Area* is so ugly. It's rubber. *Repetition 19* is clear fiberglass. They are totally disconnected. Yet to me it is like an inside joke.

C.N.   It's an extension of your whole outlook: out of the same thing comes something different. Here's a piece which you showed in the Castelli warehouse exhibition in 1968.

E.H.   One of the two pieces which was often, by certain people, connected as one piece. But if anyone looked, they had two titles and I don't think it even looked like one piece. The title is *Aught.* I had another piece on the floor. It was called *Augment.*

C.N.   I remember the piece on the floor. It was lapping over and over. Those pieces got short shrift from some of the people who wrote about the show—like Max Kozloff.

E.H.   I read that. That's the only time I've been bombed. I really wasn't bombed before, just neglected. It was very sarcastic but at least I was in good company. He dumped Nauman worse than me.

C.N.   Yes, I noticed. But then he took the whole article to write about himself and he just mentioned the artists in passing. Anyway, *Aught* is a kind of serial piece.

E.H.   It's canvas rubberized and there are two sheets and they are stuffed and they just hang there and they're four in a row—all slightly different. It has that quality and I guess it's intentional. It's ludicrous. Oh, you could say, "Okay, it's process, it's hanging stuff," but you know it's something else. It's like banal—then saying it four times.

C.N.   Do you have an impulse to satirize?

E.H.   I think so. I think that piece does and I think that other piece that was on the floor does too. It was the same mats just repeated over and over and over again.

C.N.   Do you think you were satirizing Minimal art?

E.H.   No, I don't think so. I don't think I'd get mean. I don't think I was punning anything except my own vision. I think that piece is strikingly ridiculous and that is it's best quality. They are very large and they sit there.

C.N.   What about the idea of environmental art? Do you think of your work as environmental?

E.H.   No. I don't make them for the outside or the inside. Yet I guess they're for the inside because they are much closer to soul or introspection—to inner feelings. They are not for architecture or the sun or the water or the trees and they have nothing to do with color in nature or making a nice sculpture garden.

C.N.   I was thinking of it in another way. Large pieces take up a great deal of the actual space in a room. They control the spectator and in a sense they demand more of one and one has to bring more to them. It's the idea of perception and perceiving.

E.H.   I think that is mainly scale and you have to walk in and around something and it covers or connects to the four walls and the ceiling and the floor. And some can be very, very inconspicuous. No, I am not interested in that. I could control the environment if I meant to do that through another means. I think I could control the environment if I wanted to with something the size of a book.

C.N.   How about the relation of light and color in your work?

E.H.   I think they are less important. Color is whatever comes out of the material and keeps it what it is. The light—I'm not too concerned with it, because if you use reinforced fiberglass clear and thin the light is there by its nature and the light does beautiful things to it. It is there as part of its anatomy. I am not interested in dramatics and so I de-emphasize the beauty of the fiberglass or the light and just make it natural. I don't highlight it with extra light. It's a by-product, built in there. Maybe dark does beautiful things to it.

C.N.   You mentioned that when you came out of your last operation you thought that you might make films.

E.H.   I had gotten to love Jean Godard and I had just seen *Weekend* and I was moved as I could be by anything. When I woke up from the operation one of my second or third thoughts was film. I had never tried to make a film and I don't know why or what made me think that was physically easier.

C.N.   Do you think there is a relationship between making films and the rest of your work?

E.H.   I never really did think so except it is connected to my idea of the absurdity of life. I have so little content in my work in terms of reality. For me it is very much that—but it is not visible. It is abstractly that way. And in film, although I'm sure my film would be very abstract, there is some closer connection. I mean you have to use some kind of imagery to do it—through connectiveness of people or whatever I would choose. And it would be another vehicle of content that I have never used in my art.

C.N.   Getting back to the chronology of your work, next comes the piece you did for the show at the Jewish Museum.

E.H.   I could tell you background about that. I have to go to my past years a little bit because it is relative to it. I had started the initial idea a year ago, before I was sick, and it was sitting, it was strung up, in my studio for a whole year. Once I got sick I canceled every commitment except this one show which was being done by a friend who I had really promised and if I were sick he said that he would take an old piece and I didn't want that. So I was committed to this show called "Plastic Presence." In July I was in Woodstock and I was feeling absolutely better so I came back to New York to work on this piece. The idea totaled before I was sick. I wasn't in touch with it that much because it was almost a year, but I visually remembered what I wanted to do with the piece. At that point I should have left it as it was because it was really daring. It was very, very simple and very extreme because it really looked like nothing. I wanted so much to be able to throw myself into a vision that *I* have to learn to adjust to, learn to understand. And that is really what I had, but coming back to it from Woodstock and not having seen it, I felt it needed more statement, more work, more completion, and that was a mistake because it left the ugly zone and went to the beauty zone. I didn't mean it to be that. And it became for me—I don't even want to use the word in any interview of mine—decorative. That word or the way I use it or feel about it is the only art sin. The material is beautiful and the original statement of irregular wires was so simple and there wasn't that much there. But it was very large in scale and it was really absurd and looking strange. I lost it, I lost it. So now I am attempting, but I haven't been well enough yet, to do it in another material and I think I'm going to get much better results with this one. It ain't that attractive.

C.N.   Here's this piece I like so much from the Whitney's "Anti Illusion, Procedures, Materials" exhibition. What's it called?

E.H.   *Expanded Expansion.* It has also been called *Untitled* because I hadn't really completed it when I went to the hospital. They didn't know it had a title. I never call things "Untitled" since things need to be titled as identification. I *do* title them and I give it a lot of thought most of the time because things being called "Untitled" is a sign of uninterest and I am interested. I try to title them so that it has meaning for me in terms of what I think of the piece and yet it's just like a word. I use a dictionary and a thesaurus. I usually use a word that sounds right too but that doesn't have a specific meaning in terms of content. It's straight but not another word for it. Anyway, this [photograph of *Expanded Expansion*] was taken in my studio when we just had this section. You could see we had the rods for the next section on the floor. We were working on it.

C.N.   How big was the piece?

E.H.   About ten feet high. How wide depends—it is flexible, you could push it. You could put this very narrow or you could put it wide apart. This is about juxtaposition. It is rubberized cheesecloth and reinforced fiberglass.

C.N.   You were insisting your pieces aren't environmental before, yet this piece is so large-scale.

E.H.   Its scale would make it environmental but that is not enough to make something environmental. Then it is leaning against the wall and it looks like a curtain. Those things make it superficially environmental but I don't think that was the purpose. I thought I could make more sections so they could be extended to a length in which they really would be environmental but illness prevented that.

C.N.   I look at this piece and I think of the Ku Klux Klan because of its threatening quality.

E.H.   This piece does have an option. It has connective associations. Maybe that's not so good. The Ku Klux Klan, for me, is a terrible thing to look like. But again it has that feeling—I can't use that word any more—absurdity. Because it potentially has quite a few associations and yet it is not anything. So maybe that increases its silliness. And then it is made fairly well so it contradicts its ridiculous quality because it has a definite concern about its presentation. You think, "Well really—it can't just be a whim, you know, it's too considered." There's a great.deal of concern and it's visible.

C.N.   Are you interested in craftsmanship in the sense of something done in a right or wrong way?

E.H.   But my right or wrong isn't to have a pure or fine edge. I do think there is a state, quality, that is necessary but it is not based on correctness. It has got to be based on the quality of the piece itself. That hasn't to do with neatness. Not artisan quality for the sake of craft.

C.N.   But you are concerned with the idea of lasting?

E.H.   Well, I am confused about that as I am about life. I have a two-fold problem. I'm not working now, but I know I'm going to get to the problem once I start working with fiberglass because from what I understand it's toxic and I've been too sick to really take a chance. I don't take precautions. I don't know how to handle precautions. I can't wear a mask over my head. And then the rubber only lasts a short while. I am not sure where I stand on that. At this point I feel a little guilty when people want to buy it. I think they know but I want to write them a letter and say it's not going to last. I am not sure what my stand on lasting really is. Part of me feels that it's superfluous and if I need to use rubber that is more important. Life doesn't last; art doesn't last. It doesn't matter. Then I have that other thing that I should use—I can't even say it because I believe it less—but maybe that is a cop-out.

C.N.   Good craftsmanship is very hard to deny. One's whole upbringing is that things should be good and last.

E.H.   I think it is both an artistic and life conflict. I don't know about the validity of keeping. I feel that if I make something, I'd like a photograph of it and then I could keep it or give it away or sell it, but I would like some record. I have this partial thought about it and it's also interesting how life and art merge because I've been so sick, to the point where I could have died during all that time, that the whole idea of art and making something last is put into another perspective. I'm not sure how I feel about it, if it matters (it probably shouldn't), but I'd like to try the rubber that will last.

C.N.   Here is that other piece you had in the Bern show in Germany.

E.H.   It's called *Vinculum*. It means links and connections. This piece went to Europe to the Bern exhibition "When Attitudes Become Form." I had three pieces in that show. But *Vinculum* is prior to the piece that I made at the Whitney—the ladder piece. That piece is connected to this piece. That is solid and staid and inflexible except for the hose. This one is similar but it is totally flexible. There isn't anything staid or put. All these can be moved, every connection is moveable, so it has a fragile, tenuous quality except that it is very, very taut. It's attached from two angles so there's a lot of tension, yet the whole thing is flexible and moves. I like this piece very much.

C.N.   What's it made of?

E.H.   This is wire and this is wire mesh with fiberglass and they're turned over and stapled so they can either go up or down. They are positioned but they can be moved and through the wire and fiberglass is a hole and these irregular rubber hoses go through it. It moves because they are very thin hoses. It's rubber but not really a hose. They are all different lengths. Everything is tenuous because they're not really knotted very tight and they can change and I don't mind that within reason—the potential change—but I'm not asking anyone to touch them and handle them and change them.

C.N.   You said that about the other piece, *Sequel*—the one with the half-balls—the potential for change is there too. Emily Wasserman did a review of that piece when you showed at Fischbach. She said she saw you, when somebody straightened out the balls, make them irregular again.

E.H.   But *Vinculum* has greater tension, greater possibilities. That's intentional.

C.N.   The soft material that you use, does that have something to do with your idea of contradiction too?

E.H.   I think so. But now the material that I am really still eager to work with is rubber. I want to try to work with other rubber than latex. First because you build that up in a certain way, layer over layer over layer, and I used it almost as paint. I want to try other possibilities and work more direct.

C.N. Does your work concern itself with the process, in the sense of Richard Serra's saying he is concerned with pushing or pulling or lifting, etc.?

E.H. Well, process—that is the mold I felt I was going to be *put* in. I don't really understand it. Everything is process and the making of my work is very interesting but I never thought of it as "now I am rolling, now I am scraping, now I am putting on the rubber." I never thought of it for any other reason than the process was necessary to get to where I was going to get to. I do have certain feelings now to keep things as they are. I have very strong feelings about being honest, also heightened since I have been so ill. And in the process, I'd like to be —it sounds corny—true to whatever I use and use it in the least pretentious and most direct way. Yet you could say that it's not always true, for instance I rubberized cheesecloth . . .

C.N. Then it's not the old truth-to-materials doctrine.

E.H. Yes. It partially is because rubber needs more strength than rubber alone for permanency. And if you like to keep it very thin and airy you have to figure that out. There is a very, very fine plastic glued to a very cheap plastic to get some of those very, very close lines, because cheap plastic is so thin and it clings together well, so when the rubber dries you have all this clinging, linear kind of thing. And I make things too. If the material is liquid, I just don't leave it or pour it. I can control it but I don't really want to change it. I don't want to add color or make it thicker or thiner. There isn't a rule. I don't want to keep any rules. I want to change the rules. In that sense processing the materials becomes important because I do so little with them. I do so little else with the form which I guess is the absurdity. I keep it very, very simple, so then it's like a hanging material. But I don't do that with any thought. Sometimes I feel there is something wrong with me. I don't have that kind of precise mind or I just don't feel that way. I don't know if I stand alone but I don't have that kind of system. Maybe mine is another kind of system.

C.N. About the piece called *Contingent* in the Finch College exhibition "Art in Series," 1969, could you describe how you made it?

E.H. I started the piece before I got sick, which was last year. It was latex rubber over a cloth called ripple cloth which resembles another version of cheesecloth. It has a more interesting weave (I guess I have some kind of interest in the material) and reinforced fiberglass—clear. Actually it is a casting. There were two or three made last year and then the ones that were worked on presently were done by some students and were quite direct. And I believe they all have some kind of differences which was all right. I used them. They were supposed to fit. There are eight of them and they hang fairly regularly but there is great divergency from one to the next.

C.N.   They are serial but they are not serial?

E.H.   Right. They are geometric but they are not. They are the way they are and the way the material and the fiberglass worked out. Maybe a little self-conscious—maybe that was not so good. They are all different sizes and heights, but I said "Well, if it happens, it happens." One was too long and I could have cut it off but I said, "No." So it will stand different.

C.N.   What about the relationship of the drawing to the piece itself?

E.H.   Well the drawing was very honest. It was one of the first ideas for the piece. This was the orginal idea and I changed it. It's the same piece but it's got all sorts of subtle variances. The pieces were much thiner and on either end they had wire mesh underneath the fiberglass and they were going to be on hardware that turns. There were going to be many in a row.

C.N.   I think you said it was the first time you did a sketch for a sculpture.

E.H.   I did a whole group at one time—in one or two weeks. I did ten sketches and I think I worked them all out or they are being worked out—every one of them.

C.N.   That was unusual for you because previously the drawings were separate.

E.H.   Yes. I always did drawings but they were separate from the sculpture or the paintings. I don't mean in a different style but they weren't connected as an object, a transference. They were related because they were mine but they weren't related in one completing the other. And these weren't either. They were just sketches. It is also not wanting to have such a definite plan. It is a sketch—just a quickie to develop it in the process rather than working out a whole small model and following it. That doesn't interest me. I am not even interested in casting. The materials I use are really casting materials. I don't want to use them as casting materials. I want to use them directly, eliminating making molds but making them directly at the moment out of some material. In that sense I'm interested in process.

C.N.   Recently I read an article on Keith Sonnier where the author talked about the way Sonnier used material so that layering was almost a form of painting—one color on top of the other.

E.H.   That is my drawings. My last series of drawings—I call it series because one was done after the first operation, one was done after the second, but there were five—were painted. They were inks, layer over layer, very, very fine washes on paper. They're absolutely paintings. Even those very careful ink drawings were layer over layer. These were very careful too, but they are looser. Those five circle drawings were washes, one over the other.

C.N.   And that extends to the three-dimensional work too?

E.H.   Fiberglass and rubber are layers. Fiberglass less, but it builds up and if I need any thickness it is one fine layer over the other. And rubber is certainly that way. The rubber that I've been using you can't pour on very thick.

C.N.   So your work has more relation to painting than to sculpture which one thinks of as carved-out or molded.

E.H.   But I never did any traditional sculpture. I don't think I ever did any traditional paintings except what you call Abstract Expressionist. I didn't even do much sculpture in school and once I started out there wasn't anything traditional about any of my pieces. I don't know if I am completely out of the tradition. I know art history and I know what I believe in. I know where I come from and who I am related to or the work that I have looked at and that I am really personally moved by and feel close to or am connected or attached to. But I feel so strongly that the only art is the art of the artist personally and found out as much as possible for himself and by himself. So I am aware of connectiveness—it is impossible to be isolated completely—but my interest is in solely finding my own way. I don't mind being miles from everybody else. I am not, now, possibly. Critics, art historians, museums and galleries do like to make a movement for their own aims and for art history and to make people understand, but I wonder about that. In that way I have been connected to other people but I don't mind staying alone. I think it is important. The best artists are those who *have* stood alone and who *can* be separated from whatever movements have been made about them. When a movement goes, there are always two or three artists. That is all there is.

C.N.   Do you feel then that you've broken with the tradition of sculpture?

E.H.   No. I don't feel like I am doing traditional sculpture.

C.N.   Then your art is more like painting?

E.H.   I don't even know that. Where does drawing end and painting begin? I don't know if my own drawings aren't really paintings except smaller and on paper. The drawings could be called painting legitimately and a lot of my sculpture could be called painting. That piece

Contingent I did at Finch College could be called a painting or a sculpture. It is really hung painting in another material than painting. And a lot of my work could be called nothing or an object or any new word you want to call it.

C.N. In a sense, though, isn't there Abstract Expressionism in what you are doing now? You have the idea of exploration, of letting the material take its own form in the way that the Abstract Expressionists allowed the paint to spread out.

E.H. Well, only maybe the good ones really allowed that to happen. I think the other ones took on a lot of mannerism.

C.N. Kline supposedly never knew what size his canvas would be until it was actually finished.

E.H. Yet even with the Abstract Expressionists a lot of that was the idea. I think the ones that we consider important had an idea and they followed through on it. I know Kline is historically important but I don't really like his work. There are people like that.

C.N. Whose work did you really like?

E.H. Well, not necessarily the best ones. I loved most de Kooning and Gorky but I *know* that was for me personally. You know, for what I could take from them. I know the importance of Pollock and Kline and *now,* if you ask me *now,* I would probably say Pollock before anyone. But I didn't in growing up.

C.N. What about Minimal art, so called?

E.H. Well, I feel very close to one Minimal artist who's really more of a romantic, and would probably not want to be called a Minimal artist and that is Carl André. I like some of the others very much too but let's say I feel emotionally very connected to his work. It does something to my insides.

C.N. What do Carl André's floors represent to you?

E.H. It was the concentration camp. It was those showers where they put on the gas.

C.N. I wonder what would be André's reaction if you told him your response to his work?

E.H. I don't know, because we like each other maybe he'd understand, but it would be repellent to him that I would say such things about his art. You can't combine art and life.

C.N. Sure you scare people with that kind of talk . . .

E.H. But it's a contradiction in me too because I can't stand romanticism. I can't stand mushy novels, pretty pictures, pretty sculpture, decorations on the wall, nice parallel lines—make me *sick.* Then I talk about soul and presence and guts in art. It's a contradiction.

C.N.   Are there other artists you admire?

E.H.   Oldenburg is an artist, if I have to pick a few artists, that I really believe in. I don't think I was ever stuck on Oldenburg's use of materials. I don't think I have ever done that with anybody's work and I hope I never do. I can't stand that. But I absolutely do like Oldenburg very, very much. I respect his writings, his person, his energy, his art, his humor, the whole thing. He is one of the few people who work in realism that I really like—to me he is totally abstract—and the same with Andy Warhol. He is high up on my favorite list. He is the most artist that you could be. His art and his statement and his person are so equivalent. He and his work are the same. It is what I want to be, the most Eva can be as an artist and as a person.

Ishtar, 1965.

Hang Up, 1965–66.

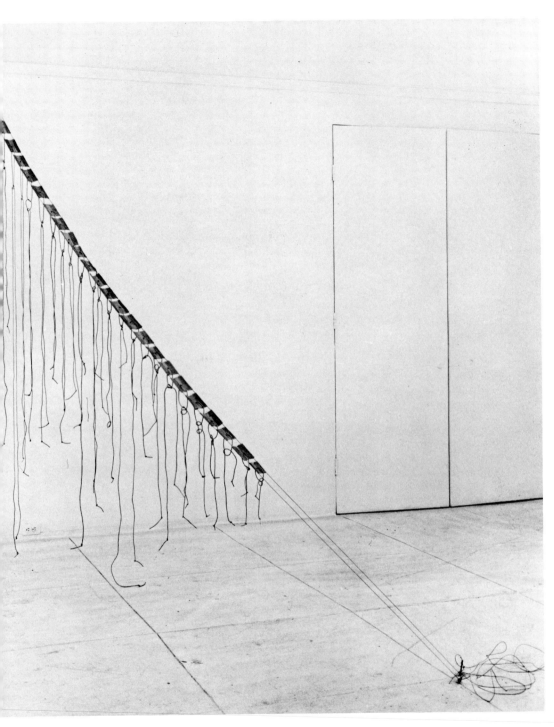

Vinculum II, 1969.

Expanded Expansion, 1969.

Contingent, 1969.

L ILA KATZEN is a sculptor who has always worked in a monumental way. She has constructed total environments out of plexiglass, vinyl, fluorescent and black light, iridescently colored liquids, and other unusual materials.

In her early forties, the artist has been married to Philip Katzen for over twenty years and has two grown children, Denize and Hal. Five feet-nine in height, an imposing physical presence, Katzen is a woman of amazing energy and intellectual prowess. She has been teaching three-dimensional design and mixed media at the Maryland College Institute of Art in Baltimore for the past twelve years and at the same time has maintained intimate contact with the New York art world. Affiliated with the Max Hutchinson Gallery in New York for the past four years, the artist moved in 1973 into a loft space in the Soho area of New York while continuing to commute to Baltimore in order to fulfill her teaching commitments there.

Katzen has always maintained a completely individualistic approach toward her art, frequently setting herself against the popular trends of the day. As a result of being in the forefront she has often found herself struggling in an unsympathetic milieu not yet ready to accept or recognize her daring innovations. A creator of contained forms at the height of Abstract Expressionism with its emphasis on the explosive brushstroke, an explorer of shallow space when spatial depth was all the vogue, it was only in the late sixties that the art world and Katzen actually reached an area of mutal understanding.

Seeking to free herself from the confines of the canvas, Katzen, originally a painter, began in the early sixties to make freestanding, painted acrylic sculptures. Then, obsessed with the need to discover a more intense way of transmitting color, the artist began to explore the potential of black, or fluorescent, light as a medium. In a piece called *The Pressure Light* Katzen discovered that light was infinitely more complex as soon as it began to interact with the environment. Following this lead she was soon immersed in environmental concerns. Black light, which is held in its sculptural containers yet simultaneously has the capacity to extend beyond its immediate boundaries and interact with elements around it, was utilized in several sculptures. Presented in a darkened room, the black-lit pieces caused the white apparel worn by the spectators to appear to glow, thus making the viewers part of the total sculptural effect.

Lila Katzen

Next, seeking to create a complete light ambience which would simultaneously hold its sculptural form and float freely, Katzen built her celebrated *Light Floors.* These constructions were first exhibited at the Architectual League in New York in 1968 and then traveled to museums throughout the country. The floors were contained in three rooms, geometrically shaped out of mathematical proportion, and as the visitors moved through these areas they had the sensation of being enveloped in a beautifully transparent chrysalis of light.

From this exciting project Katzen moved on to her equally fascinating *Universe as Environment* in 1969 at the Loeb Student Center, New York University, in which she transported the viewer to a world beyond time and space. Then in 1970 she created her sensuous *Liquid Tunnel* which was exhibited at the Smithsonian. This piece consisted of an octagonal Plexiglas structure intersticed with vinyl pouches filled with fluorescent water. One enthusiastic viewer who had transversed the tunnel reported that he felt as if he had entered the heart of an amethyst.

After building the tunnel, Katzen became fascinated with the contrasts and similarities of liquid and solid materials. These concerns eventually lead to the creation of large-scale Corten sculptures composed out of several sections. Monumental works such as *Slip Edge Bis* (1973) and *Trajho* (1973), which require as much as sixteen square feet to house them properly, are designed to relate with flexibility to whatever site is selected for them. The open-ended possibilities inherent in their formation plus the humanly scaled proportions reveal Katzen's continual preoccupation with the interrelation of art and the essential human environment.

Coinciding with Katzen's esthetic commitment to human concerns is her commitment to the feminist movement in the arts. She is as outspoken in her indictment of sexual discrimination in all professional areas as she is generous and supportive to the younger women who are her students and admirers.

CINDY NEMSER   When did you decide you were going to become an artist?

LILA KATZEN   I never had any doubts about what I was going to do. I was going to be an artist even when I was in kindergarten. I used to bring drawings home to show to my mother and she was always interested and encouraging. My grandfather was an artist. I found him a fascinating man who showed me all kinds of things when I was very young. He was always an ideal to me.

C.N. Did you get encouragement from your parents as a young woman when you told them art was going to be your profession?

L.K. My father died when I was very young. My mother just accepted my interest in art in the early years until I became a teenager. She knew I was preoccupied with it and used to call me the dribbler and smearer. She was always very proud and excited about what I did but she never thought that I would get so involved with it. She thought this interest would ultimately fit into the background of what she believed would be my major life—that of wife and mother.

C.N. Did you study art at school?

L.K. I was always considered the class artist. I had various female art teachers and they were always very encouraging to me. The art club would meet after school and we would do various painting and drawing projects. At that time there was an interest in art appreciation in the New York public schools. Small reproductions of well-known paintings and sculptures were bought and booklets were made out of them. We did our own scrawling art history and it was a stream of interest running through my early years. When I graduated from public school I looked around for a high school that would be of interest to me. My mother had heard of two schools, Music and Art and Washington Irving. However she was not keen on my going from Brooklyn to Manhattan to study. But I was adamant about going to a school that concentrated on art and finally decided on Washington Irving.

C.N. That's where Lee Krasner went to school. How was your experience there?

L.K. Washington Irving was an enormous all-girls school with a tremendous number of students. I found it exhilarating. I worked for a commercial artist after school and did all her line drawings and layout work for the great sum of five dollars a week. I also got very involved in doing theater design at that time.

C.N. How did you end up going to Cooper Union?

L.K. I had gotten a scholarship from Washington Irving to Parsons but I couldn't take it because of financial reasons. I decided to get a job and started working for an advertising agency. The art director thought I was talented. It was actually he who suggested that I should get more training so I started to go to Cooper Union at night. I became more and more interested in art and decided that somehow I must manage to go to school full-time. As it happened my mother convinced my step-father to give me a small allowance and I worked part-time as well.

C.N. You told me that there was a problem about your doing your art work at home then.

L.K. Very definitely. My stepfather was adamant about my not working at home. He was a very settled individual who had specific habits. He would go to sleep exactly at 9:30 in the evening and get up exactly at the same time each morning. I talked it over with my mother and she said, "If you can arrange some way of working so that he isn't aware of it, it's all right with me." So I would put out the papers and coverings all over the floor, set up my work, paint sometimes until two or three in the morning, and then clean everything up and try to get the smell of paint out of the room. I would put things back in a cupboard that I used as a secret place to keep my supplies. This went on for quite a while.

C.N. How was the instruction at Cooper Union when you were there?

L.K. That was around 1950 and the instruction was good. It was difficult to get into Cooper and I was very proud to be there. The teachers were professionals and I took many subjects. I found it stimulating but then as I began to be interested in certain areas I ran into obstacles. I never worked well in a group situation but I worked very well privately. There was a group of eight or ten students sharing a studio across the street. We all took turns using the space because it was so small. I was the only woman allowed into the group because I was to do the cooking. I used to cook spaghetti because it took a long time to make the sauce and it would give me a longer time to work. But while I stretched my time in the studio I was constantly in the dean's office at school for not being in class even though I maintained a very high average. As far as the work itself was concerned, I ran into obstacles there too. I had a sculpture teacher by the name of Hovannes who gave us an assignment of carving a lion out of a block of wood. Originally I was quite interested in sculpture and I had done the drawings, set it up, and started carving. It took me a couple of weeks to carve out the snout and an ear. I spoke to a fellow student who was doing something else. We agreed that I would help him work out some of his pieces, plan them and arrange them, if he would do the carving for me. I was bored stiff with all that carving. Then I went to Hovannes and explained to him what we had decided to do. (I didn't want to do anything behind his back.) This was the way I felt about the work. I had conceived it and I would direct it to look exactly the way I wanted it but I didn't feel that my hand was important in the work. Hovannes was enraged and told me that I definitely was not a sculptor and that I must be a painter because I wanted things to happen too quickly. He convinced me. I decided to go into the area of painting.

C.N.   That's very interesting because your attitude toward sculpture plays a part later in the kind of work you do and the way you do it.

L.K.   That's right. It's funny how certain things stand out in your mind. I remember once I was trying out for a Rosenwald Foundation Grant and I was painting all kinds of pictures. One fellow in my class came over to me while I was washing out some of my brushes and said, "Are these the brushes that are going to win the grant?" I didn't realize that he was putting me on. I just said to him, "Yes, what's the matter with these brushes?"

C.N.   What kind of painting were you drawn to at that time?

L.K.   Everybody then was being pushed toward Cubist painting. Then Abstract Expressionism was moving in so we all gravitated toward more gestural painting. I always worked abstractly. I did semi-figurative work. I would cull from the figure and relate it to some spatial concept, worked out in a formal way in relation to shapes and colors.

C.N.   Did you ever have any contact with the Abstract Expressionists who attended *The Club* and were so influential at the time?

L.K.   I was not part of that generation and I didn't know too much about them but I did bump into a few of those people accidentally. Everybody had heard about the Cedar Bar and I went in there once and met Franz Kline and got to talking with him. I also met Grace Hartigan briefly.

C.N.   What was your impression of her?

L.K.   She was very beautiful, blonde, quite gorgeous, and very vivacious. After that I was introduced to de Kooning by Sam Francis.

C.N.   When did you get married?

L.K.   I must have been nineteen. My husband was from Baltimore.

C.N.   Did you find that it was difficult for you to continue your career as a professional and be married.

L.K.   I met Philip, my husband, when I was still at Cooper. He actually commuted back and forth to New York from Baltimore to see me. He was very involved and interested in what I was doing. My mother warned him that this was a total preoccupation of mine and that he couldn't expect very much from me as a wife—that I wouldn't do anything around the house. But she did say that he would never have a dull moment!

C.N. And I know he hasn't.

L.K. Fortunately he loved me enough so that she didn't scare him off. Philip is a very helpful, interested, and stimulating person who has encouraged me at all times. During our first year in Baltimore he was remarkable. I went on an orgy of working. It was like a dream come true in which I worked all day long, every single day, and he would come home and nothing was done. I never made a bed or did a dish. He would come in and find me absolutely an utter mess and everything a wreck; but he never complained. He always thought it was very exciting. We had a chance to get one of those lovely little garden apartments with everything set up rather neatly and I almost fainted with dismay. I said I couldn't live there. I could never work in that kind of a setting. I had to have a place that I could just mess around in and not worry about. We took an old dilapidated apartment—a kind of railroad flat—just the type of place I feel comfortable working in. Philip's parents were just stunned.

C.N. Even when you had children you didn't feel you had to make your art secondary to being a wife and mother? Many women artists say they have a terrible conflict in this area.

L.K. I guess I was very fortunate, although I do feel that we choose and pick what we want. I never felt, in any way, secondary. I suppose what happened was that my work became the focal point of the entire household. The children too were always made to understand that this was important and their father took that stand from the beginning. There was never any kind of bitterness or irritability about it, so as a consequence they saw this as natural. They often kid me about it now. I used to have my studio on the second floor of the house. When people ask my daughter Denize and my son Hal, "How did your mother keep you busy while she was working?" They say, "She used to yell down, 'Here are some crayons and paper,' and throw them down the stairway."

C.N. So many women say that their household duties take up so much time and their fears of neglecting their children create such a sense of guilt that they can't find the time to work.

L.K. Let's face it. It does take a lot of organization and you do have to decide just what you want to do. I have a strong sense of duty. I felt that I wanted the children and I wanted them to have a happy home life. I didn't want my husband harassed either. On the other hand, I had to make certain decisions about how I was going to do it. I worked from eight in the evening to two in the morning. I also set up a schedule of work knowing that I wanted to put in a forty-hour week. I felt that I had to do that. In the beginning it was very hard and I used to chalk out the hours that I got out of the week. This week I only got four hours. Well that is very bad. This week I got eight hours. That is better, but it is nothing. And I made up my mind that even if I didn't do anything, even if I just sat there or if the things were messes or if I destroyed things (and I went through real rituals of making nothing and destroying lots of stuff that I had made), regardless of anything, that time was going to be spent in the studio. That is the way I did it. I spent the days with my children. I enjoyed going outdoors with the kids. We played and my daughter used to throw me out of her sandbox because I liked to play there more than anywhere else. When they napped, I would nap too or I would go upstairs and work.

C.N.   What you have just recounted counteracts this whole notion that women are so overwhelmed by their domestic duties and children that they cannot function as artists.

L.K.   I think it is a myth. After all when you think about it, there are men who after they have worked all day come home, fix household appliances, work in their own shops, go out and bowl, and so forth. If they can find the time to hold a job down and come home and do all these things, I can't see why not the reverse. Nobody's work is ever done.

C.N.   What do you think of the idea that some people have that women must chose between marriage and a career.

L.K.   Why should it be assumed that you can't be a serious artist if you cook a meal, have children, and take care of the usual things? If you organize the household and do your work, whatever it may be, they assume you are a dilettante and that the household duties are the major work and the artistic endeavors are just the left-overs. That is something that has been put upon women and they shouldn't accept it.

C.N.   During those years you also began to go to Provincetown in the summer, didn't you?

L.K.   Yes. It's really weird because Hans Hofmann had a school on Eighth Street, not far from Cooper Union, but I had never heard of him in New York. When I moved to Baltimore I met a woman there whose work interested me a great deal. She said that she had studied with Hans Hofmann and that I must go and meet him. On a lark, Philip and I drove up to Provincetown and took an apartment there for the summer. I got into the Hofmann School. This must have been about '49 or '50. I was fascinated with the setup of the school. There was no instructor around all the time. You worked on your own and Hans came in two days a week, Tuesdays and Fridays, to do a critique. Otherwise a monitor set everything up. Then in the winter time I stayed with my mother and went to the Hofmann School in New York. My husband was back in Baltimore working.

C.N.   All throughout your career as a painter and sculptor you lived in Baltimore and yet maintained a residence in New York.

L.K.   Yes. I made it a point to get to New York at least once a month so I wouldn't die of esthetic starvation. Then I could come back.

C.N.   You were willing to make great financial and physical sacrifices to be in the center where the stimulation was.

L.K.   There was a brief period in Baltimore when Kenneth Sawyer who was a poet and art critic for the *Sun* paper came on the scene. He stimulated the city as it had never been stimulated before. It was strictly him because it never has happened before or since. He brought people like Sam Francis and Paul Jenkins among others down to Baltimore.

C.N.   What was Hofmann's attitude toward you as a woman artist?

L.K.   In the studio he seemed quite interested in my work and would hover over me and discuss it. At that time I was doing hard-edged drawing in which geometrical, carefully balanced color forms were being placed in different arrangements. Most of the other students were working more expressionistically. I seemed to have Hofmann's respect and interest during the school time. I don't think that he slighted me or anyone in the class. What made him a great teacher was being able to take any student on any level and deal with him or her. After all his class was a mixed-up situation: dilettantes and curious young idealists, old timers and teachers who were there to open themselves up, and so on. But as I got to know him more, I think the more serious he felt I was getting, the more irritated he became. I had that feeling.

C.N.   You once told me about a time that you invited him to dinner in Provincetown.

L.K.   Oh yes. I invited him to dinner one night with some of his German friends. I thought it would be a nice, friendly evening. We were all feeling pretty good and I think we had a bit to drink. Then Hans got up and made some kind of a toast and said, "To art" or something to that effect, and "Only the men have the wings." Of course I was outraged. I told him that if those were his sentiments he could take them and himself elsewhere.

C.N. Beautiful.

L.K. An argument did *ensue.* Those other people were very annoyed with me because they thought it was terrible even to say what I did. But I was bitterly hurt. I had been encouraged by him all this time. Then underneath, I discovered that he felt women were just not there. His ideas were obvious to me. What else could a remark like that mean?

C.N. Lee Krasner remembers that at one point he said to her, "This is so good you would not know it was done by a woman." How did your painting develop from that fifties' period?

L.K. I moved from that geometric form into a more open but very flat unfolding surface in which there were no compositional elements but rather an unfurling and unfolding of the forms in and out of the surface. The space was very shallow. Often the work was attacked by the other students for being decorative because it played across the surface and at that time they were all very involved with deep space. I realize now that I was dealing with areas that were the groundwork for much contemporary painting. In any case, I didn't want to remain in the Hofmann School because that influence was too strong. So I told Hans that I would show him work from time to time but I would not continue as a formal member of the school. But he had an amazing eye. No matter what I put in for critique without his knowing it, he would look around (I would be hiding somewhere) and he would always say, "Ah, Katzen, I see you are here."

C.N. How did your work develop from painting back to sculpture?

L.K. When I was about twenty-three years old, I had my first one-woman show at the Baltimore Museum. I had done an enormous amount of paintings. Some of them were one-tone and others were paintings that had calligraphic or linear elements interwoven and stained into the surface. I was staining and opening surfaces then.

C.N. That was very revolutionary painting. Was anyone else besides you doing that kind of work?

L.K. Yes. Morris Louis was living in Baltimore and we shared our mutual ideas. Kenneth Sawyer was also very excited by what we were doing. He went to New York and told Clement Greenberg about it. In the end Louis got the attention from Greenberg and he then brought Louis and Frankenthaler together.

C.N. So you and Louis were involved in doing stain painting around that same time. But you didn't continue in that direction?

L.K.   No. For me painting was like something I could walk past, and look at out of the corner of my eye—the sweep of the arm, putting it on the floor—I could straddle a canvas and pour paint so easily. I just had to get into something that was more of a challenge. I felt the major thing that was constricting me was the surface or two-dimensionality of the canvas. So I looked around for some way to get the canvas out of the way. I did a lot of collage and assemblage and got more satisfaction out of working this way. I came across nylon canvas which was semi-opaque and semi-transparent and I started to stain and work with that. I didn't like that either. Finally I dropped the canvas. I started painting on acrylic sheets on which I felt that the paint could stand in the world without having to be tacked on to something.

C.N.   Many artists in the last ten years have been trying to take that paint and make it an independent entity. I think that happened with Eva Hesse's work. She wanted to make the surface stand without a support.

L.K.   Yes. Give it a reality, a factuality. That was it. Acrylic presented all kinds of problems to me. Yet even though I cried and sweated over it, it appealed to me more.

C.N.   What are acrylic sheets?

L.K.   Plexiglas, plastics.

C.N.   Specifically when did you start to work with it?

L.K.   In the late fifties going into the sixties.

C.N.   How did those Plexiglas sheets evolve into sculptures?

L.K.   It was a very strange development. About 1960 I had a dream that repeated itself over and over again. I was walking around this darkened room and this incredible luminous color was springing from the wall and springing from the floor as I moved to certain positions in the room. It seemed that I had a relationship or confrontation with these colored areas. In the dream I was overwhelmed with the beauty and factuality of this color. I guess it was something that must have been in my head. When, in the dream, I came out of the room, I saw a man in uniform standing by the door and I said, "This is incredible. Whose work is it?" He said, "Don't you know?" I answered, "No." He said, "It's Lila Katzen's work." I had that dream over and over again for a week and it was driving me batty. Then I set out to try to find how I could make this color which was so luminous and glowing a reality. I played around with fluorescent dyes and tried different suspension methods with acrylics to make my own fluorescent paints—and I did.

I painted with them on acrylic sheets. I used to put on an underlay and then just paint over it. I drilled holes into some of those sheets and hung them on wires or chains. Still I didn't like that. That still related to the wall and to the architecture of the room. So I devised some bases, wood shapes, that had grooves in them and I dropped the sheets into them. At that time I was sharing an apartment in New York with a painter. (It was over a fish market and the smell used to come up. Philip used to visit me and say, "My God! How do you stand it?") I kept some of those works there and I showed them to the critic Irving Sandler. I gave a small piece to the Kulicks as a present. It was then that Sylvia Stone asked me how I did these works. She had seen the piece at the Kulicks' apartment. In the summer I still continued to go up to Provincetown because of Hofmann, and Walter Chrysler became very interested in those free-standing works.

C.N.   Who is Walter Chrysler?

L.K.   He is a collector who took over a church in Provincetown and turned it into a museum. He collected works from various artists who happened to be in that area then and he bought all those early works.

C.N.   So these were free-standing, acrylic paintings.

L.K.   Yes, some of them were made up of two, three, or four sheets, four-by-eight feet in size, one in front of the other in a wood base. One shape could be seen through another so that the shape seemed to float. Some were in two sections one staggered in front of the other.

C.N.   What happened after you developed this?

L.K.   I was working in Provincetown in 1964 and I met George Segal. I asked him to look at what I was doing and he talked to me at some length. He felt that I was in transition and that I really wanted to get my work off the surface into a three-dimensional, more sculptural experience. He felt that for me painting was something that was left over from other things. He said I had to make a decision. I thought about it at some length, did some experiments, and dropped the painting completely. I went into constructing Plexiglas sculptures. That experience of talking to George is an example of why it is so important for artists to see each other's works. They stimulate each other.

C.N.   But many women haven't felt confident talking to men artists about their work. They haven't been welcomed by them which means that women haven't had the opportunity to interact with the art community which is male-dominated.

L.K.   That is true. Fortunately for me, I had two older brothers. We had to take care of each other as my mother was always working. I suppose I related very well to them, particularly growing up, and there was a camaraderie and exchange of ideas between us. They were always very proud of me though eventually they became puzzled by what I was doing.

C.N.   This gave you a feeling of confidence. You could talk to men and not feel inhibited?

L.K.   No, I never felt inhibited that way. I just accepted it as a matter of fact.

C.N.   So you changed your direction from painting to sculpture. What happened next?

L.K.   At that time Grace Hartigan came to Baltimore and we got to know each other. She came up to my studio in the house. I hadn't realized it but the whole second floor was covered with work from end to end—a ten by ten flat area was all that was left to walk in. We had even opened up the attic and I had stuff stored in there. There wasn't any space where there wasn't something. Grace said to me, "Don't you think you have worked your way out of here?" I looked around and I felt that the time had come for me to move into my own studio completely away from the house. I was ready for it. Another factor was that the children were getting older and they were bringing friends home. It was no longer possible to say, "You can't come upstairs." The kinds of rules that had been set down had to be lifted. They had to have more freedom for their own lives. So I took a studio on Baltimore Street which was then known as "The Block" where they had all the striptease joints and show bars. I had a second-floor studio, a very large place which was a delight to me, and across the street was a place called Murray's Show Bar. I was working on different things dealing with color and the sensation of physicality of light. But it seemed to me that no matter how or what I did every time that damned light from Murray's Show Bar went on (they would flip the light across into my studio) everything I did looked pale by comparison. Then one night something happened to change that. I remember Philip called me up at the studio at about eleven o'clock and said, "When are you coming home?" I said, "You won't believe what I have gotten into," and described the structure that I had started to do. Philip was fascinated by what I told him and he came down to the studio. I remember that he helped me with some of the wiring and we stayed there until two o'clock in the morning working. You see that is the kind of a guy he is. That was my first kinetic light structure.

C.N.   What did it look like?

L.K.   I made a box out of canvas which I painted black and used a relay of Christmas lights inside. I opened up holes in it, placed acrylic sheet over it, and put layers of colored papers with different shapes inside. The light underneath one area made the shapes appear to come from inside, to seem to flow up to the surface, and then to drop back again. This was getting close to the image I had once visualized. I was very excited about it. Finally I had the whole form with another lighting system come completely up to the surface. This was the beginning of my being able to make lights stand within a physical housing. From there on it was just a question of moving in one direction or another.

C.N.   When did this discovery take place?

L.K.   That was in 1964.

C.N.   Then you began to work with black light?

L.K.   Yes. I made several structures in which black light became an integral part of the piece.

C.N.   What is black light exactly?

L.K.   It is a long-wave, black fluorescent light which has built-in filters which are not damaging to the eyes. This light has a chemically reactive effect upon materials that have fluorescent matter in them. Often they use it to show up laundry marks or lint on various things. The light fascinated me because the actual emanation from it wasn't far from the source. In other words, with an ordinary fluorescent light you have a housing which is the tube and the light goes past the source of the housing and floods. Black light will not flood but will hover close to the housing which contains it.

C.N.   It is almost as if the light becomes the form.

L.K.   Exactly, and there is at the same time the possibility of making an environmental contact to any substance in the room that has fluorescence in it without the light having to leak or transgress past its physical housing in an obvious visual way. I was so completely fascinated with the light that I worked with it more and more. In that early period I remember showing some slides of these things to Dick Bellamy who sent me over to the John Daniels Gallery. Dan Graham was the director then and David Herbert was working there with him. They got interested in what I was doing and showed my work along with that of Robert Smithson, Donald Judd, and Sol Lewitt, among others.

C.N.   What kind of form was this black light contained in?

L.K.   In the beginning I used containers in which I placed fluorescent forms and paper that seemed to be activated or kinetic. Then I lost interest in the idea of movement of forms and became much more interested in the light itself. Light by nature has to be housed in a fixture. But rather than have a fixture show, I would put it in a black plexiglas container. The constructions were vertical black plexiglas slabs in which the black light was situated maybe a half inch or an inch above. The tube itself would have this strange hovering light, and the whole dimension of the space had broken down so that you couldn't tell whether the tube was inside or outside the form. The *factuality* of the lighting existed but *where* it existed spatially was always a mystery.

C.N.   Did that lead you into environmental concerns?

L.K.   Oh, very definitely. I did a work called *The Pressure Light* at that time. It consisted of a black acrylic box with black drawers. There were yellow fluorescent tubes on the bottom of these drawers and they could be pulled out at various heights from the surface. Tremendous physical intensity existed between the surface where the light hit and the enclosure of this drawer. This intensity which could be compared to pressure forcing the light through an opening, was controlled by pulling the drawer out and extending the light or by pushing the drawer back and contracting the light. I was interested in that light going beyond the container and yet holding within the container, a kind of dualism. From there I wanted to do a situation in which the light was not separated from the experience of viewing it. I think that is what moved me into the concept of walking on light or being surrounded by it.

C.N.   This interest eventually led to your *Light Floors.*

L.K.   Yes, but before the *Light Floors,* I did some other things. There was the *Fan Piece* which was a series of black lights contained in a construction of wood. This was done as a separate module situation slipped into a base. The light was contained in interstices that were fan-like. Here again the black light hovered and held physically in there. This piece was shown at the Delaware Art Center and I asked everyone to come in black tie. The women were asked to wear white and it worked out beautifully because the piece emanated beyond its source. The white shirts of the men and the white dresses of the women looked as if they were completely floating around in relation to the room.

C.N.   You created apparitions.

L.K.   After that I was fortunate enough to be commissioned by Patrick

Lannan to do a piece that I had wanted to do for some time but couldn't finance. It was a staggered, large, free-standing, black Plexiglas piece, a very narrow corridor-type construction in which there were free-floating shapes of red fluorescent acrylic. It was called *Infinity Piece*. You stood at one end and looked down this alley and felt both the pressure of the light and the floating of the shape. You were aware of the physicality of the piece, but, at the same time, the sensation of light became the most important thing. I think that is a remarkable piece even today.

C.N. And that leads you into the *Light Floors?*

L.K. Right. Most of these things that we are talking about are works in which light is at one point and the person is at another. The contact is made either through viewing the work from one point or from the work making a contact through space clapping to the individual nearby.

C.N. Did you say "space clapping?"

L.K. Yes. You know how you clap your hands? Well this is a clapping of the space between the individual and the work. The clapping is the compressing of that space and time as well. I was interested in the idea that the physical presence of the work would become something that would exist and be activated by the person actually moving through the work. The individual would make the work take on different stances through his or her perception and contact with it, and thereby change, disorient, and rearrange the kind of physical situation that existed. I had set quite a big thing for myself because I wanted the work to exist as a work itself and not just as an effect. I wanted to house it much the same way as light is housed in an actual or factual way and still, at the same time, have it move.

C.N. The viewer becomes part of it or inside it and yet the work is still contained in its own form?

L.K. Yes. I wasn't interested in working a strip of neon which is a diffused form unless it was put into a particular configuration, nor was I interested in just having the effect of light without any formal concerns.

C.N. Such as a light show . . .

L.K. The idea of a light show would be exactly what I would be against. I wanted the physical form that had some kind of resonance and meaning and I was interested in the idea of stepping or walking through it. I did the floors in a combination of numerical components. Some floors were done from one to nine. Some, one to eleven. I don't know if everybody was aware of that but I always got a tremendous charge out of seeing this combination numerically, physically, and visually working together.

C.N.   There were three rooms weren't there?

L.K.   Yes and I treated them as an open space. I went from the very spare *Silver Diamond* in the front room to the *Horizontal Slide* which was a very compact numerical room, to the third room which was called *Oblique,* in which I used a mirror in the back. It was very open and illusionistic and seemed to repeat itself and to go back like a trapezoid in the other direction. The floors were very effective. People seemed to relate to them and enjoyed them.

C.N.   Those *Light Floors* were a phenomenon. I remember walking through them at the Architectural League. It was a very strange and exhilarating sensation to be moving through light. I was experiencing it in an entirely new way. I was enveloped by it and almost lost my equilibrium because the light was below me instead of above. Yet at the same time it created an aura all around me.

L.K.   Exactly.

C.N.   The *Light Floors* were originally built for the Architectural League?

L.K.   Yes. I was very fortunate. I had the idea of what I wanted to do and I thought it was a hopeless project and that I would never realize it. Then I was in a show in Philadelphia and I exhibited *The Pressure Light* there. During the show I met the painter Richard Anuskiewitz and he was very interested in the work and in my ideas. He said to me, "You ought to go over and see the people at the Architectural League. I think they would be interested in what you are doing." So I met John Margolis who was then directing a whole environmental series there. Margolis liked my *Light Floor* idea and presented it to the committee. I made a model showing them exactly what it would look like and eventually I got the grant and the work was built.

C.N.   Again this episode shows how important the contacts between artists are. About how much was the total cost of a project like that?

L.K.   They gave me a grant of $8,500 but I must have put in about $18,000.

C.N.   It's very costly to be a sculptor!

L.K.   Oh very. And that is just materials. I am not talking about labor. My husband helped me to build the floors. He did a lot of the work on them. We had some of the sections fabricated elsewhere but, for the most part, we did all the building. We were fortunate to get an old garage, rent-free. It was unheated, with no electricity, and we had to run lines in.

C.N.   You who didn't want to carve out the lion sculpture ended up having to do all that.

L.K.   That's true. But I did have a lot of help. We hired some students and it got to be a fun project. Still, plastic is very difficult to work with and takes a lot of sanding and grinding. There was a lot of stuff I did that I didn't care to do. But when you have an image in your head, you just have to do it.

C.N.   Before you did the floors in '68 you did some pieces called *Moon Markers* in 1967 which are also related to your environmental concerns.

L.K.   I was doing some polyurethane work. I was playing around with crater-like forms which seemed to me like strange other-world shapes. Inside the polyurethane shape I had a black light and the base of the crater would have a blown glass test tube with a fluorescent liquid in it. The light would come up and this ghostly liquid would move back and forth across these pieces. I thought of them as miniature landscapes. It seemed to me that maybe someday they would become huge markers on the moon for certain deposits, landing sights, housing sites, and so on. They would be seen as one came in for a landing. They were quite beautiful, but unfortunately some of them were destroyed.

C.N.   This was a time and space project.

L.K.   Yes. We were into space launching and that fascinated me too. The idea that we could conceive of contact with an extraterrestial situation—not be there but know all about it.

C.N.   If we skip ahead this leads to your *Universe as Environment* exhibition of 1969 where you create an entirely new world. We imagine ourselves on the moon or on some other planet and discover there all kinds of substances that are found here on earth.

L.K.   Yes. That was the motivating factor. I had done some things called *Light Emanating Cities* in which I used fluorescent materials to make buildings and their surroundings. The idea was that instead of tearing buildings down and putting up new ones, we would keep the bases and move the buildings in sections from one base to another. Instead of lighting streets, buildings would emanate their own light and by the color of the emanations you would know what section of the city you were in.

C.N. What fantastic architecture. How did you come to do the *Universe as Environment?*

L.K. New York University had gotten interested in some of my ideas. Ruth Bowman and some of the students came to visit me and said that I could have the Loeb Center space which was sixty-five feet to exhibit in. I decided to do *The Universe as Environment* which was an exchange between natural materials and technological man-made materials. I used shale, sand, various mica, and minerals and exchanged it with acrylics, vinyl, dyes, polyurethane and black light. Part of the environment contained my coal pieces in which black lights were suspended above beds of coal on which I had induced coal crystals to glow. I also had my *Material Wall* which was made up of sections of acrylic sheets, plexiglas, sand, and minerals. The minerals had various colors as well as fluorescent sawdust. The fascinating aspect of this piece was that as these sections were moved from the studio to another place certain strata in the material would change. Then if they were moved again there would be more changes. The forms and shapes, the pyramids of sand, changed with the fluorescent quality of the sawdust. To me that was what the *Material Wall* was all about. It was the transition which took place through the history of its own movement that related it to the strata of the earth and the moon.

C.N. There is a relationship between your work and that of Robert Smithson who took rocks and other material from land sites. He put them into containers and displayed them in galleries, along with photographs of the places from which they came. One had the sense of being simultaneously in the gallery and on the original site. In *Universe as Environment* you also transported the viewer to another place, the moon, through the use of photographs.

L.K. Yes. I had a super, very large slide of the back side of the moon that no one had seen. I wanted to present this image plus the possibilities of materials that could exist there.

C.N. You went further than Smithson since you took a site that was not imaginary but which you had never actually seen.

L.K. Well we hadn't seen it in actuality but we were seeing it through photography. That was the thing that was so fascinating. It was a site or an area that was unknown but known. I experienced it through data and materials that existed in relation to the site I was located on at the time.

C.N. You are a person who is very much aware of your surroundings. I remember once you talked about your relationship with television.

L.K.   Yes. The sense of being in two places at one time. You could be in your own living room yet have the awareness of being in Paris or London or on the moon. You could project yourself past your own physical housing. I think being able to move past limitations of physicality, of time and space, is what intrigues me.

C.N.   In *Universe as Environment* light still continued to fascinate you too.

L.K.   Yes. I was still exploring the different ways light could be perceived. The fluorescent liquids were housed in vinyl pillows. People who saw the show would sit and lie on them. They were essentially strange fluorescent markers and I situated some of them on very large blow-ups of certain craters and sections of the moon.

C.N.   In introducing man-made materials you were also asserting human identity on the universal landscape. After all, these are man-made objects.

L.K.   Woman-made.

C.N.   Right [laughter]. Then after you did those liquid vinyl markers you created that marvelous *Liquid Tunnel*.

L.K.   I did the tunnel for the São Paulo Biennial, the one that didn't go to Brazil. It stayed at the Smithsonian in Washington and was renamed *Exploration '70.* Instead of being outside the liquid, I wanted to move inside of it.

C.N.   Could you describe the *Liquid Tunnel?*

L.K.   It was a sixty-five-foot tunnel which I built in octagon shape. It was a combination of the geometric which is rigid and the soft fluidity of vinyl shapes. The octagon housed black lights that were staggered at intervals going around it. In between them were hung hundreds and hundreds of pillows of fluorescent liquid. They were graduated in scale from tiny to quite large so that the whole visual perspective was changed when you looked in—even before you walked through. The floor was made up of black acrylic sheets and looked almost like a river in that you could not tell its depth or where the edges would end. Someone said that it was like being in the middle of an amethyst. People just loved it. As they walked through they had a great sense of relaxation and a feeling of being inside a glorious never-ending space. I enjoyed watching them go through it. We had only one problem. At one point, they were denuding it.

C.N.   Everyone wanted souvenirs. The tunnel definitely relates to the *Light Floors.* One has the sensation of being immersed in it. Yet one is conscious of its forms at the same time. Then there is the ambivalence in discerning which is the solid and which is the liquid. The liquid is contained in the plastic which is very solid and formed while the acrylic floor is liquid in feeling because of its blackness and shininess. It gives the illusion of a deep flowing substance. The solid becomes liquid and the liquid solid.

L.K.   Very definitely.

C.N.   Then comes your 1970 exhibition in which you begin to combine metal with the liquid in the plastic.

L.K.   Yes, the area of liquidity and solidity interested me and I began to explore metal both in its flowing liquid state and as a solid sculpture. I think this was a transitional exhibition.

C.N.   That was at the Max Hutchinson Gallery.

L.K.   Yes. My work was moving again and I was fascinated with the things that happen when you work with metal. I found that this material needed a lot more coaxing than many of the other materials that I had worked with. I deal with steel in terms of its essence. I approach it as a living, growing entity in its own right. I don't want to structure it, cut it, weld it, torture it into some artificial situation. It has its own identity which lends itself to rolling and folding. This is the internal physicality of the work. These sculptures are not frozen moments in time but rather they are made up of a set of stacked parts. They have a variable as well as a site-oriented stance.

C.N.   What do you mean by site orientation?

L.K.   The work exists only when it comes to some kind of completion in terms of where it is placed. However one placement is not the only completed state. In other words, the work isn't static—it is not a completely finished entity, cut off from life. These works have built-in variables in them. But they are not endless. Some of the pieces may have only one or two variables.

C.N.   How do these variables work?

L.K.   The works are made of several components—sometimes two, sometimes more. These components set up a dialogue between themselves and their site as well as with the human encounter. As in all my work, the relationship between the human being and the art is very important. These works are monumental but they are within the context of human contact. They are not unapproachable or minimal works but, on the contrary, they are alive with a sense of becoming even while they maintain a certain form in time.

C.N.   What is the actual size of these sculptures?

L.K.   *Slip Edge Bis* is made up of a number of sections and is about fifteen feet in length and four feet wide. It weighs a little more than a ton and will encompass an area of sixteen feet by sixteen feet depending on the configuration. The work can be placed in a number of ways, either on a hill or on a flat area. This is not a one-piece work that must be situated on one specific part of the floor or the ground or remain static on a pedestal.

C.N.   Your large steel sculptures are fabricated aren't they?

L.K.   Yes. I conceive the work in wax and change it into the kind of images I have in my head. I make a discovery and work from it and make another discovery. I try to get as close to this inner image as I can. Then I work in steel with my own equipment. I can do some small bending and rolling myself. For the most part, however, even quarter-inch or eighth-of-an-inch steel casts have to be done by someone with the proper equipment.

C.N.   You need big presses and dies?

L.K.   Yes. The big pieces are done with huge presses and huge rolling equipment in which we will take a sheet of steel, which may weigh about half a ton, put it into the roller, and push or bump it along for maybe an inch at a time. This can tie the machine up for about a week. The fabricator does it, though I will be standing there watching and holding my breath. Sometimes he will say to me, "Come on, you do it." I will say, "No. You handle it. You have twenty years of experience as a craftsman with that machine." I'm not interested in my own hand doing the work. It is my total self I want in the work and I feel that this comes about by realizing something, by making something come into being as a complete entity. I can see things as totals and it isn't necessary for me to do the handwork to make them exist for me. Finally I have overcome my student days in which I was put down for not wanting to carve the wood. I have recently read that Henry Moore did marble work over in Italy and that he had a battery of carvers who were roughing out everything. I have never thought of touching marble because I always thought of it as slow-process handwork—having to tickle every surface. Now I think it might be very interesting to try to do something in terms of marble if I didn't have to spend a year carving it myself. I would like to do it solely in terms of the immediacy of the material. I am also thinking about using concrete with steel. The big problem is how do you get these works executed? How many large works can you realize? No matter what you see in your head it isn't enough. When the work is realized you see it as a totality. You see certain things that have opened up the progress and possibilities for other works. This moves your development as an artist ahead by a decade. Maquettes are fascinating in the sense that you are creating a Lilliputian world and trying to enlarge it in your imagination. But it is not the same as walking around the actual piece and having the physical experience of the work itself.

C.N.   How do you finance these large projects?

L.K.   I am in constant debt. I borrow from loan companies. If I get a grant, that helps tremendously, but it is a constant hassle of survival. Sometimes a collector will back a piece but he or she will expect a quick sale and will get upset if the money isn't paid right back. You really have to develop nerves of steel to keep your work going. I have spoken to other sculptors and they have the same problems. I can't do the work in inferior materials or mock-ups. I just don't want to do it that way. I can't put all of my tension, the poised moment, into the mock-up. I would rather retain the tension of the work inside of me for a period of time. Sometimes it is years before I realize the work.

C.N.   What is a mock-up?

L.K.   It is a full-scale model of the work but not done in the originally intended material. You would use cardboard or wood to simulate metal, or cardboard to simulate wood, or something to simulate something else. To me, however, the very essence of the work is the sense of the material becoming a configuration and maintaining its sensibility as material. I can never make a mock-up out of cardboard because it would be a cardboard sculpture I would be making.

C.N.   Do you think it is harder for you as a woman sculptor to finance these kinds of projects than for a man?

L.K.   There is a problem there. I think to get the funding you want from a dealer or collector you have to make them aware that the work has importance. Now the fact that you are a woman makes them suspicious immediately. While it might never be openly stated, there is always that underlying question, "Are you serious? Are you really that serious?" I think in my case I have overcome this suspicion to a large extent because through grants and loans I have managed to do a lot of work. I would rather live in a state of anxiety and discomfort if I can have the work realized. If you can get the work done, people develop more faith in you and are more prone to back you.

C.N.   In the past artists such as George Segal and Richard Anuskiewitz encouraged you in your work. Do your find the male sculptors who are doing large-scale works today sympathetic to you?

L.K.   I have tried to discuss ideas and make contact with other people who are doing this kind of work but many of the men don't want to hear about my ideas or discuss my work. Sometimes they will discuss *their* work, even then not too freely. But there have been a number of male sculptors who have been interested and encouraging to me—Ken Snelson and Marc DeSuvero among others.

C.N.   Do you think there is resentment on the part of many because you have invaded sculpture which is considered a male territory?

L.K.   I remember once a woman artist who I respect very much said to me, "It's bad enough that I am a painter working in a man's world but you as a sculptor are really entering an area the men consider out of bounds for a woman." I was astonished at the time by her remark, but now I am beginning to get an idea of what she meant.

C.N.   Do you think there are differences between a man's and a woman's approach to sculpture?

L.K.   I am not able to say that I see any difference in terms of genuine interests and attitudes. As a teacher of art I have seen just as many men work with ephemeral materials as I have seen women. I have seen both women and men work with heavy materials. However there is a type of male who believes his physical prowess, sweat, and ability to pick up weights and throw the hammer is the sign of the great sculptor. This attitude automatically excludes women. Yet this idea that physical prowess makes the sculptor is really a myth. Throughout history the great sculptors had helpers, assistants, students. This is a myth that has been put on women to keep them out.

C.N.   You mentioned that you finance your sculpture through grants and benefactors but you also support yourself and your art by teaching.

L.K.   Yes. I have been teaching at the Maryland Institute College of Art for the last twelve years. Before that, when my children were young, I taught in my own studio. I taught psychiatrists and doctors who wanted to relax and do a little work.

C.N.   Do you enjoy teaching?

L.K.   Yes. I guess I am one of the few artists who does. I enjoy dealing with young people because they are enthusiastic and demanding. You can't kid a kid. I find it stimulating because it's thinking out loud about all the things that you are interested in. You empty yourself out so that you leave yourself open for new things. It is exhausting, however, as

I now live in New York and have to commute weekly back to Baltimore to teach.

C.N. How are the attitudes toward women sculptors in the universities?

L.K. I don't think that sculpture departments are open to women in colleges and universities. I may be wrong but I don't think there is one sculpture department in the country with a woman at its head. You find very few women even teaching in the sculpture departments and there are a lot of good women sculptors around. I was told by the head of my own sculpture department that if I wanted to discuss my own ideas with the students they would love to have me do it but they wouldn't pay me. I declined. I have managed to bridge this problem by teaching a mixed-media class in which I work with both two- and three-dimensional forms, but I don't know if other women have been able to come up with this solution. I know of one or two women who are teaching in sculpture departments but they have been made so miserable that they can't function well. Art schools are feudal in their attitudes both toward the woman who is in sculpture as a student and the woman who is a sculptor and who could bring innovative and interesting ideas to that area—ideas that go beyond the "sweat and groan" school of working.

C.N. How about your relationship with the architects?

L.K. I believe most architects are the enemies of the sculptor, both male and female. The architect doesn't want sculpture to mar or deface the inside or outside of his building. He considers sculptures pimples on the surroundings and tries to do everything to eliminate them and all other art as well. Our buildings are conceived without any sense of the culture of the time or the sense that a human being would like to deal with an experience beyond the beauty of materials or the function of a building. Of course there are architects who fancy that they are sculptors too.

C.N. Like Frank Lloyd Wright? He sabotaged all the artists he could with the Guggenheim Museum.

L.K. The only one I ever saw overcome him was Calder with his mobiles that hang down through the Guggenheim. Calder won because he overcame the space through the top areas and wouldn't deal with the balcony or the architectural structure of the building at all.

C.N.   You have always been concerned with the relationship of your work to its environment and to people. Yours is an art that reaches out to interact with the world. Most of today's large sculptures have little interest or relation to their surroundings. They are egotistic at worse but they come out of an egotism of desperation.

L.K.   I think you are right. They are embellishments for big buildings, symbols of strength and largeness for corporations. Large overall structures is what these corporations want. Then people will say, "Oh, look at that huge thing in that huge building."

C.N.   Would you say they are typical of men's kind of work?

L.K.   No. I don't think that at all. I think they are indicative of the time we live in, of human beings, male and female, who find it difficult to have any sense of their own ability to move in the world. These works reflect our sense of powerlessness. I don't deride them but they are, as you say, works of desperation attempting to show the individual power of an artist to be able to produce and move in the world in some meaningful way.

C.N.   Yet these sculptures seem very remote from human concerns.

L.K.   They have nothing to do with the scale of human beings. They are scaled to buildings, buildings that are emptied at five o'clock, and located on streets where people can no longer see them unless they drive by quickly in a car.

C.N.   They are monuments to commerce.

L.K.   Yes. And I object to that. There is a tremendous need for sculpture to be opened up to people. It should enliven and enrich.

Penumbra, 1963.

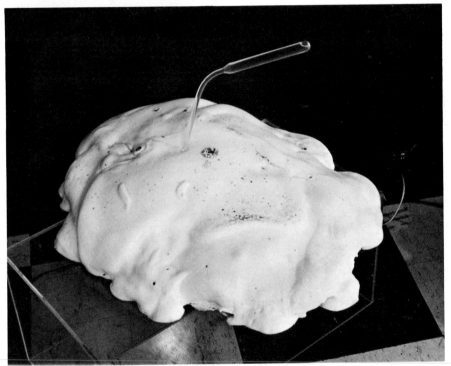

Moon Marker with Blown Glass Marker (Universe as Environment), 1969.

Liquid Tunnel, 1970.

Liquid Pouches, 1969.

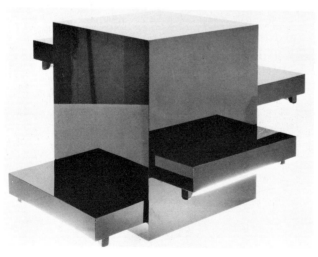

Pressure Light, 1967.

Little Curl (Liquid and Solid), 1970.

Insula, 1973.

Antecedent. 1973.

Slipedge-Bis, 1972.

Traho, 1973.

Representational Painting (Eleanor Antin), 1972.

LEANOR ANTIN is what has been recently labeled a conceptual artist. She combines assemblage, "happening," and performance techniques to present long narrative adventures and concise psychological portraits of both a fictional and factual variety. Drawing on materials from the lives of others as well as herself, Antin documents her presentations or pieces by means of photographic and video-taped recordings.

Born in New York City in 1935, Antin went through many painful years trying to find a satisfactory medium in which to express her esthetic vision. In the fifties she attended and graduated from City College, majoring in creative writing and minoring in art. The artist also studied phenomenology at the New School for Social Research. During this period she attended the Tamara Daykarhonova School For Stage Acting, joined Actor's Equity, and obtained dramatic parts on stage and television.

Finally, in the late sixties, Antin found a way of putting all these seemingly diverse interests and activities together into a series of unique art works. Following in the Dadaist, phenomenologically oriented footsteps of Duchamp (Antin is an accomplished chess player), the artist produced between 1965 and 1968 (exhibited in 1970) two *Consumer Goods* pieces known respectively as *California Lives* and *Portraits of Eight New York Women*. These assemblages, each named for an individual, consisted of between four to nine consumer items which offered clues to the person's identity.

Always drawn to large-scale projects, in 1971 Antin conceived her *100 Boots* piece. In this work, one hundred rubber boots become the hero of a picaresque novel staged in visual terms. Fifty picture postcards, representing a hundred boots in various *Easy Rider* adventures were mailed to approximately a thousand people over a period of two and a half years. The Museum of Modern Art became the hero's last "crash pad" and the boots themselves, along with an extensive documentation of their entry into New York City, were exhibited there in June 1973.

Antin was the first artist to bring sociologically oriented, fictional-narrative content to a form of conceptual art which had previously been conceived of by such artists as Vito Acconci, Scott Burton, and John Perreault as a series of psychologically introspective, short-term events. *100 Boots* served as a vehicle to present a wealth of familiar material in a strikingly original way. Avoiding popu-

Eleanor Antin

larization, Antin made a previously inaccessible art form immediately available to a more general public.

After this long involvement with what Antin calls the biographical, the artist next became fascinated with the autobiographical. Deeply affected by the feminist movement, even at the time she produced *Portraits of Eight New York Women,* Antin, in 1973, began with great intensity to concentrate on herself as a subject. Her first explorations of self were in a naturalistic vein. In *Carving: A Traditional Sculpture,* she displayed one hundred and forty-eight photographs of herself documenting the minute bodily changes produced by dieting over a period of thirty-six days, while in *Representational Art* she made a video tape of herself applying attractive street make-up of the type she herself admired but never wore. From these exterior transitionary works, Antin then moved into interior or psychological transformations. Convinced that everyone has a right to the richest, most expanded "autobiography" he or she can concoct, Antin has created several lives for herself: including one as a king, Charles I, and one as a ballerina in the company of the great Russian impressario Diaghilev. Dancing, dressing, being photographed and video-taped, as well as writing as ballerina and king, the artist enacts, in a totally concrete way, two universal fantasies of the female and male variety. With her imaginative artistry she shows the rest of us how it is literally possible to transcend the workaday world and "escape" to another realm of beauty and glamor. The artist is the grown-up child still playing "let's pretend," but doing it so exquisitely, with such attention to form and detail, that for a short time we believe that she really *can* escape and that we can go with her.

Eleanor Antin is thirty-nine years old and lives in Solana Beach, a small town near San Diego, California. She is married to the poet David Antin and has one son, Blaise Cendrars.

CINDY NEMSER   How did you come to invent the boots?

ELEANOR ANTIN   I was tired of coming into New York to put on shows that were always going into a vacuum once they were over. I wanted to do something that lasted longer, something that I wouldn't have to travel to do, that I could send out without moving from my nice, old, falling-apart house over the Pacific in California. So I thought of the mails which are an obvious method of distribution that reach everyone with an address. Besides, people like getting mail. So I decided to do a mailwork.

C.N.   You make it sound as if mailworks are a category unto themselves.

E.A.   I don't think of it as an art category so much as a distribution system. There are many kinds of art works that you can engineer in relation to the peculiar social and structural properties of mail. I wanted to make a complex structure taking plenty of time to unfold not because that's necessarily the best thing to do but it's the most practical. Artists are the most practical people in the world, that is, in the sense in which it counts. Dylan Thomas was a practical poet, wasn't he? To sustain the high his poetry needed he became a lush. That it killed him was unfortunate but his job was to make poetry not collect social security. Why should I waste my time inventing a work that would be over in a few weeks? I was also intrigued with the difficulties of what you might call the long form of the big single work. I thought I might try something in the nature of a picaresque novel. The great novels of the past by Dickens and Dostoevsky, say, were always in serial form, written month by month to make a deadline. Now in order to do a picaresque novel I would need a hero. Who would be my hero? Who would be sufficiently engaging so that he could carry this work through several years? I don't really know how it happened but I thought at this point that I could make a hundred boots my hero. Then I went out and bought "him" and started planning "his" adventures.

C.N.   What kind of boots are they?

E.A.   That was a problem. Everyone wears boots and they're marvelously elegant. I didn't want anything like that. They had to be neutral. They had to be black rubber, bland enough and yet boot enough that all you could say about them was that they were boots. Finally, I found them, Hong Kong made, because America no longer makes that kind of boot, and I just bought all hundred of them.

C.N.   How about the mailings?

E.A.   Preparing the mailing list was a very complex thing. I amassed a large mailing list, almost one thousand names from various people. Then at intervals, ranging from one month to several days, depending upon what I took to be the internal necessities of the narrative, these people received another installment—or postcard—of this picaresque novel. People were occasionally taken off when I decided I didn't like them or that they really weren't with it. I had to do that every now and then for my soul. The work took a little over two and a half years to be presented.

C.N.   What do you mean by "the internal necessities of the narrative"?

E.A.   Well, I played with "real-life" time as if it were an accordion. I would compress or expand the time as needed. For example, at one point, *100 Boots* trespassed, and since this was their first crime I couldn't wait for another month to pass for them to make their getaway. They would have been caught. So a week later, I sent out the next card: *100 Boots on the Road,* which was *100 Boots* on the lam—fast. Do you remember the five installments of *100 Boots Taking the Hill?* Ending with *100 Boots Take it?* There they are in a burned-out house. Well, they were seen slowly moving up to the top of the hill where there were some houses. The terrain didn't look like Korea so I figured that they should get up pretty fast. I mailed out those cards every three days.

C.N.   I remember those war cards were numbered one to five.

E.A.   Yes, that was near the end of the work and I wanted to call attention to the narrative, to force people to see the difference in their spatial position as they advanced up the hill. I also figured such rapid mailings might get fucked up in the mails and the numbers were a form of insurance. I still got a letter from somebody telling me my mailing list was screwed up and they were getting repeats. There were times I played games with the other players—the recipients. In one adventure *100 Boots* were in and out of some industrial jobs. Then they got a job in a carnival. At one point I sent a card reading *100 Boots Up* which was a Ferris wheel shot from below and you couldn't see them. I did that sometimes, by the way. They didn't have to be around all the time. The postcards had already been established as their space, their story, whether they were in the picture or not. After *100 Boots Up* I sent out *100 Boots Down* and they were standing around a new grave in a little Mexican cemetery. I waited about six weeks before the next installment. I knew people were thinking it was all over. I got letters from people telling me how sorry they were that the work had ended. The next card arrived a week before Christmas—*100 Boots Move On* —a cheerful image of them walking one way and a group of regal ducks walking in the opposite direction.

C.N.   How many cards were there altogether?

E.A.   Fifty-one.

C.N.   And the structure was completely worked out from the beginning?

E.A.   The day I did the first card I did the last card. Of course, that wasn't sent out for two and a half years. In between there was room for improvisation, digressions, games. I wanted this work to be very leisurely and I could take all the time I wanted and end it when I wanted to end it. It was like an arrow on the way to the bull's-eye choosing to make a series of gay loops instead of moving in a direct line. Essentially this kind of leisurely feeling dictated everything in the work and also helped to take a lot of weight off individual images. Images I may have thought were weaker than others could be carried along by the others. In the overall context they sometimes even turned out to be very strong. There were always surprises in it for me. That's what kept it from becoming boring for me.

C.N.   The way one image in *100 Boots* was carried along by its spatial and temporal relation to the others makes the intervals between the images as important as the images themselves.

E.A.   That's true. I thought of them as conceptual gaps in which the images set up a gravitational field into which they drew meanings. If an image really has possibilities for meaning, it just charges the ground all around it right up to the next image and then you have a whole charged space. After *100 Boots* had been all over the suburbs, doing what good suburbanites should do, I had them go to the empty parking lot of a drive-in theater. Then they circled, turned a corner, trespassed, and one week later were on the road. That was a single adventure. People didn't know that an adventure was taking place in this work until it was over. Then the sub-set of smaller adventures— perhaps I should call these events—that had occurred prior to the final one indicating it was over suddenly made sense. Frequently the scenic and tonal shift of the card immediately following the final one was necessary to frame the events preceeding it as a single adventure.

C.N.   Like many other artists today, you seem to be involved in work-ing out the relationship of the part to the whole, in time as well as in space.

E.A.   That's absolutely true. I thought of each image as a conceptual clue. What I called the conceptual gaps—the space between the images —is the time gap which is filled when you have one clue and then you get another which immediately changes the first. This whole mystery just played itself out without my dictating a specific tight narrative which I think would have been tedious. Of course, the whole process depended upon the ability of the recipient of the work to hold it to-gether in his head over a period of time.

C.N.   It's almost the way I think of certain painting relationships in which one color changes the other color, and when another color is put on they all play back and forth. Cézanne worked that way, laying on time as well as actualizing space.

E.A.   True, but whenever you put in something next to something else it changes. It's like the earlier movie pieces I was doing. They were not actual movie stills, but pieces of photographs, high gloss, blown up into standard movie-still size. I put them into two foot by three foot manufactured cases which are actually identical to the ones that were outside of old-fashioned movie theaters before they got fancy and built them in. My idea of a movie is that it is only two or three images with all the other stuff as featherbedding which connects it together. Now that featherbedding is fun and I'm not against sitting in a movie theater and watching a whole picture, but when you remember the movie what essentially charges it for you are those two or three images. That's why I always laugh when people say they like a particular boot image better than another. To me, one image is meaningless. It's too heavy, too direct. It doesn't have enough ambiguities and possibilities for meaning. Two images are even more direct; they belong together too neatly like a hand and a glove. Now three is more interesting because it widens the field and has more potential. Four becomes quite complicated. Ambiguities are built in. It gets harder to hold together. There's an old Zen story about this but it stops at three as the magic number. *100 Boots* was never meant to be a haiku.

C.N.   I noticed that you used words as well as images in the *Movie Stills.*

E.A.   What I did there was to use a word like *Soon* or *Coming* or *Tuesday,* the kinds of words you would find in coming attractions outside a movie theater with a particular image. The image I had for *Soon* turned out to be a science fiction movie and it actually looked menacing.

C.N.   Are you investigating the relationship of the verbal and the visual in your works?

E.A.   I've been very interested in playing with this relationship. I consider my work—the visual as well as the verbal material—to be texts. There's not a direct correlation between a sentence and an image but if you place them together a relationship happens. There is a definitely charged space in which they move together. I think works of art are cue systems and the fantasy about masterpieces and immortality is that there was an inexhaustible supply of cues to turn the mind on. All art sets up a system of cues to set the mind thinking and the mind has to be invited or begged or kicked or cajoled or seduced or whatever. You might call an artist's style the manner in which he seduces or forces the viewer to play his game. All art works are conceptual machines.

C.N. Do you consider yourself a conceptual artist?

E.A. In a way, no art is bigger than my postcards. All art exists in the mind. Even Michael Heizer's cut into the earth exists in his mind in the same size as it existed in my cards. The most obvious corroboration of this is the fact that the works of Carl André and Robert Morris are talked about by people who were never in New York when either of them were showing. They've seen little pictures of their work in magazines and believe they can discuss them with perfect impunity.

C.N. Art magazines have almost made the museums superfluous.

E.A. You might consider art magazines a perpetual exhibition. Not only because they're showing pictures but because of all the talk that's engendered in the magazines. That talk, in its way, is an artwork and it's charging the whole space. That is, of course, if people attend the show—that is, read the magazines. Unfortunately, though those magazines are conceptual art, they are often bad art, that is, boring art. Oh well, how many interesting paintings do you find in any given Whitney Annual?

C.N. How did people react to seeing your boots placed in the actual environment when you were photographing them?

E.A. I didn't photograph them. Philip Steinmetz did. Reactions varied I suppose, from pleasure, through cool interest, down to outright hostility. Hostility was rare though. Sometimes pecuniary interest was evoked. Like the surfer who responded to my joke that the boots fell off the train—they were walking along the railroad ties in Del Mar—by measuring his bare feet against them and starting to walk off with a pair.

C.N. Did you feel that your boot cards were a challenge to today's commercial marketing of art? After all, you've managed to by-pass the gallery system of art distribution.

E.A. They were artworks that nobody paid for as I sent them out to one thousand people free of charge. Occasionally people asked if they could either buy a particular card in bulk or the whole set and I told them they weren't for sale. They were bio-degradable in their environment, the environment being the mailing list. I actually have very few complete sets left. Of course I have the negatives. We will probably do a book one of these days. At the moment I'm too into my other work to bother about old work. But the presentation of the complete set of images without the real-time interruptions built into the original system, along with the digressions such as the sequence of twenty-seven images done for the Museum of Modern Art, makes for an interesting narrative work in itself. The picaresque narration becomes clearer as well as the work's cinematographic properties. It certainly looked that way in the MOMA show.

C.N.   Don't you think that ending the work as you did in a major establishment institution destroyed the original iconoclastic intention of the work?

E.A.   Oh, no. I always knew it had to end up in a museum. It had such a polemically small and unhurried presentation that it needed an official framing device to stamp it as "authentic" art. The work was, after all, didactic. The museum was necessary to close the system. In fact, they printed up the five cards immediately preceeding the final one and mailed them out to my mailing list which was their necessary inclusion into the distribution system. There was some talk of them doing a bulk printing of their five cards and selling them in their bookstore but this would have been an alien intrusion into the system. It would have made each image its own artwork—like *Picasso's Girl in the Mirror* or the other cards they sell—which was not how the work operated at all. I nixed it.

C.N.   What about the actual fact of seeing the boots there in the museum? Didn't that interfere with their previous presentation through photographs?

E.A.   I was aware of that problem. Photography is a glamorous medium. *100 Boots* had acquired over the two and one-half years of its presentation what Doug Heubler called their "mythology." A head-on confrontation in the museum would reveal them for what they were —one hell of a lot of rubber. I think I solved that problem by having the museum build them a crash pad complete with Puerto Rican green walls and molding, a bare light bulb hanging from the ceiling, a sink built into the wall, sleeping bags, mattresses and bedding, and a radio playing. You could only see them through the chain-locked black apartment door we built for the room, or the door's peep-hole. By keeping them within a fictional context and making it impossible for people to do anything but spy on them through the crack in the door they retained their glamour.

C.N.   Did you think of the boots as saying something about the way we exist in today's culture? I was very struck with how neutral they are, so nondescript—the most anonymous thing you could find. They seem related to Ernest Trova's robots, the alienated, nameless, faceless people who wander around the faceless, suburban landscape. The only way they can stand out is to do something outlandish, like trespassing, or they'll just fade into the background.

E.A.   I like to think of them as my "beat" heroes. Out of Kerouac. The romance of my childhood, I guess. I had begun to anthropomorphize the boots, you know. I remember being insulted *for them* when the museum refused to insure them. Then they changed their mind and did insure them. It's probably ridiculous how happy that made me. Not for myself but *for them.*

C.N.   I saw the piece as a series of incidents, situations where boots normally shouldn't be, yet somehow belonged.

E.A.   Of course they belonged. I'm not a random invader. I always asked myself the question, "What does this place have to add to *100 Boots* and what does *100 Boots* have to add to this place?" It's a content based upon juxtapositions of already meaningful but incomplete elements. I combined the features of landscape with the features of boots and together they made an image of meaning. This was partly determined, of course, by the position any given image had in the narrative, but at the same time the narrative grew out of the running sequence of images. Remember I am an image artist and I'm primarily interested in content and *content* is such a polemical word. We're always surrounded by so much potential content—like the pictures of My-Lai. When you've seen thousands of pictures like that you ignore them. "Oh another war." "So the Indians are massacreing everybody in East Pakistan." If you want to deal with that material you have to deal with it through the insane, cumbersome system which takes so long that while people are discussing cease-fires everyone is being slaughtered. Through this bizarre series of hypocritical situations, the horrific content comes through the gaps of this maniacal system. The dead speak through the gaps. All the material is there, but you have to work into it obliquely. You have to concentrate on the machinery, then the other will come through and that has strong possibilities for an artist to work with.

C.N.   That happened when you did the *Library Science* piece, didn't it? That work was a metaphor for the whole series of categorizing or segmenting systems under which we live.

E.A.   I have a special affection for my *Library Science* piece. I did it for a women artists' show at San Diego State which was held in the

Love Library. Doesn't that name freak you out for a women artists' show? I asked all the women in the show to give me some information about themselves, their work, their history, their life, their art, whatever they felt most represented themselves at that time. Twenty-six women responded and I got everything from a resumé to a pair of shoes. I presented the pieces of information on a table and catalogued them according to the Library of Congress classification system. I just used a system normally used to classify the world of books, to classify the world of people. I catalogued each piece of information as if it were a book, by subject and call number. It was a lot of fun and the system allowed me to make some interesting and meaningful connections. For instance a plant was classified as "Guerrila Warfare." I don't have a green thumb. Plants just wither up and die when I look at them. Presenting me with a living plant was an assault on me. I had to be responsible for it, or it would die.

C.N.   Even though you consider yourself an image artist, you have been very concerned with creating a style through which your image would present itself as fresh and new.

E.A.   That's right. I used to think what I wanted to do was to get a kind of neutral style, what Roland Barthe calls the style at degree zero. I wanted people to read out my images and I thought that what I was doing was trying to subtract all obviously stylistic elements that would interfere with the reading. But now, as I see it, subtraction is only reverse addition. It's a negative addition. You take away one style and you wind up with a piece of another. You want to remove obstacles and you put in a banister. There's no such thing as neutrality. You do what you have to do to get the job done. One thing I found I did have to do, though, was not to make appearance attractive for itself; style is meaning. It has to pay its way. That's why I couldn't have all the cards be so seductively beautiful. I put in a beautiful one every six or seven cards just to suck the tired people back in again but it would have been both misleading and boring to have all the cards beautiful. I deliberately tried to keep them neutral enough to force a reading.

C.N.   Are there any contemporary artists who influenced you?

E.A.   How about Michael Heizer. If Heizer made a cut into the ground it was a big one. If I'm going to do a work that plays itself out in time it's going to be a long time. But you know influence is a loaded word. I don't really know what it is. Something is in the air, for me, for Gilbert & George, for David Bowie. Maybe it's the stars.

C.N.   Your boots utilized the serial ideas that come out of recent avant-garde developments. Remember an article entitled "The Razed Sites of Carl André" by David Bourdon? I think your work has a real affinity with Carl's path-making pieces. However, your pieces are not just about the process of moving along. Rather they are using this stylistic device to move a whole narrative content along with them.

E.A.   You're right. My idea of structure or sequence is that, though I can take any direction, there is some place I want to go. And it's not an abstract concern. I don't want to get to a cube.

C.N.   Tell me about your background. When did you discover you were an artist?

E.A.   I always knew I was an artist but I didn't know what kind. I didn't have the problems most people have—having to live down an academic painting or sculptural background. I did study in those areas but my interests in college were as a writing major. I did some years of graduate work at the New School in phenomenology and I worked for several years after that as a professional actress. As a matter of fact, my current work has been pulling all those things together. I don't think I could have survived the conventional art education most people have.

C.N.   But you went to Music and Art High School in New York. From there did you go on to any formal art schools?

E.A.   I minored in art at college but I found it totally tedious. To me there is nothing more tedious than worrying about problems of color. I don't see how I could have survived it, although I did have some of it. But even when I was doing paintings they were always more bizarre and Dada-like.

C.N.   Could you describe those early paintings?

E.A.   There was one series in which I was doing valentines for people. They were large canvases. I would ask the people what color they wanted for their valentine. If they said, "blue and green," I could use any value of blue and green or I could make the ground green and the valentine blue or vice versa. I remember a black valentine on a six-foot canvas in which the shoulders went off the painting like a zoot suit. Next to the six-foot black valentine on a white ground was an unpainted three-foot by two-foot rectangle with a strip of white paint in a "Z" down the center. It was the back flap of the envelope, but, of course, that large valentine would never fit into that envelope. That was the kind of painting.

C.N.   You always get a unique slant on even the most prosaic activities.

E.A. My drama teacher said that if on stage I had to pick my nose, instead of sticking my finger up my nose in a normal way, I would put my arm around my head and come in at the other nostril. She thought she was putting me down because she found my attitude disconcerting. But I would say that is what saved my life.

C.N. How did your studies of phenomenology effect your work?

E.A. I had been very turned on by the prose style of existential writers like Sartre and Camus. I really like that kind of romantic prose style but at the New School they were into the Germans who are totally tedious. I stuck it out as long as I could, but it wasn't productive for me at all, so I finally quit.

C.N. You respond to the dramatic and the concrete.

E.A. I guess I am a romantic.

C.N. You did a piece called *The Blood of the Poet.* Could you describe it?

E.A. I collected blood specimens of one hundred poets and put them into a box. You could read the names of the poets with these smears of blood on a slide. If you thought there was a relation between the blood and the name there was one; if you didn't, there wasn't. That piece actually took several years. It was about '65 to '68. I had been writing poetry during the time I did *The Blood of the Poet* boxes and I started to do the "consumer sculpture" then. It was about this time that I really knew "where I was at."

C.N. Was that when you were still living in New York?

E.A. Yes. Then I went to California and was very turned on by the sociological scene there.

C.N. Where did you live?

E.A. Outside of San Diego in Solana Beach which is a little beach town. Southern California is such another thing from New York where I was brought up. It was like being turned on to the country music here which is a kind of soap opera. People here buy things from catalogues. Now I hate to shop but I was very turned on by things like the Sears Roebuck catalogue. I would order things from Sears and they would send them to me. It really freaked me out. I worked out sculpture from items, consumer goods, in the catalogue. *The Consumer Goods* sculpture were configurations of anywhere from four to nine brand-new, American-manufactured consumer goods which were placed in relation to each other. Each configuration had a name of a person.

C.N. Your first set of configurations was *The California Lives?*

278

E.A.   Yes. Then it was suggested to me that I use people that everyone in the art world knew.

C.N.   Weren't the California people real?

E.A.   Many of them were and many weren't. But, of course, nobody in New York knew them so it didn't matter if they were real or not.

C.N.   These sculptures were a grouping of items that revealed the person's identity?

E.A.   Yes. They gave some aspect of the person. They were linguistic structures and you could read out that person's particular life-novel from them.

C.N.   But if you didn't know who the person was ahead of time wouldn't that be difficult?

E.A.   Well, Southern California culture is a little different from New York culture, but we all live in the same world more or less.

C.N.   Then they are types rather than individuals?

E.A.   But they were very specific—sometimes they worked on an anecdote, sometimes on an irony. But let me give you an example. There was a pair of large black men's shoes, the type no hip guy would wear, and a pair of rolled socks in the shoes. The shoes were placed in the middle of the floor and there was a watch placed inside of them too. They freaked me out. An aunt of mine, who didn't know what the show was all about, had gone to see it and she said, "That's terrific, there are some men like that. They lie down in bed with you and before they do that they place their shoes and rolled-up socks very neatly under the bed." The title of that piece was *Howard*.

C.N.   Then you did a second series of portraits of New York people.

E.A.   Right. It was *Portraits of Eight New York Women* and they were in the art world—artists, writers, etc.

C.N.   It is interesting that you chose to do only women.

E.A.   Yes. In *The California Lives* it was about half men and half women. I was getting turned on to feminism then.

C.N.   What year was that?

E.A.   About late 1969 or early '70.

C.N.   Many women artists, at that time, didn't want any part of the women's movement.

E.A.   I was aware. I was first turned on to feminism and then to how it related to me as an artist.

C.N.   Some of the women you picked were quite well known like the dancer Yvonne Rainer and the artist Carolee Schneeman. Who else did you chose?

E.A.   There was Lynn Traiger who does public relations in the art world and Hannah Weiner who is a poet and the art critic Amy Golden.

C.N.   These configurations also were filled with clues to the individual's identity?

E.A.   Right, and some of my favorite pieces of this series were very heavy. The *Lynn Traiger* piece was an apartment door painted black (like New York City apartment doors are), leaning against the wall with one of those little footmats in front of it. It also had fat-free milk and fat-free cottage cheese at the foot of the door and an envelope tucked between them. Her name was in the slot and the *pièce de résistance* was a bunch of keys which was stuck in the lock. It didn't need much intelligence to know that the milk was already delivered so it must be morning. And in New York City you don't leave your keys in the lock unless you have a strange compunction to be raped or murdered.

C.N.   These pieces are still kind of cryptic. It seems that as your work develops it becomes more narrative, easier to read, like *100 Boots* or the video pieces you conceived after the boots piece was set into motion.

E.A.   Well, when you look back on your *oeuvre,* or, as it were, autobiography, you see things precisely falling into place. My interests always were narrative because narrative gives you a way of moving. You don't have a past. And then they were always psychological, which I guess was most clear in the *Consumer* pieces. When I was doing the *100 Boots,* I knew that an interesting hero would be the only thing to carry me through that long a period of time, so that was a biographical novel. Then I started working with autobiography. At first it was, what I like to think of as, naturalist autobiography. *The Carving Piece* depicted a weight loss of ten pounds over thirty-six days. It consisted of one hundred and forty-eight photographs of my naked body, refining itself down, as it were, to an esthetic Greek sculpture. I had myself photographed each day: front, back, right, and left profile. When these photographs are placed along the wall there are about twenty running feet of nudity and you can read the weight loss. There is a very minimal change from day to day and you can read it for each single pose horizontally and for each single day vertically.

C.N.   That was a photography piece?

E.A.   Yes. I did a number of pieces of what I like to call my naturalist transformations and then I went into my more psychological pieces.

C.N.   It seems to me in this piece with its aim of weight loss there is a commentary on how women are always concerned with the need to improve their bodies. Did you think of this work in those terms?

E.A.   The piece has been shown a lot, but the first time I put it up on a wall in a gallery in 1971, combined with the other works I had there, there was so much female flesh around that I started freaking out. Then I said, "Fuck it. That is my body." This piece was actually done when the Whitney Museum asked me to tell them what I intended to have for one of the Annuals. I thought it was a sculpture Annual and since I figured the Whitney was academically oriented, I decided to make an academic sculpture. I got out a book on Greek sculpture, which is the most academic of all. (How could they refuse a Greek sculpture?) This piece was done in the method of the Greek sculptors . . .

C.N.   Who carved the marble.

E.A.   Yes. And it is called *Carving: A Traditional Sculpture.* They would keep carving around and around the figure and whole layers would come off at a time until finally the esthetic ideal had been reached. I stopped after ten pounds. It looked to me as if they were as ideally esthetic as I wanted them to be.

C.N.   After you did the *Carving* piece you said you did other more psychological works.

E.A.   There was the *Domestic Peace* in which I played not with changing my physical self but with changing the image of my psychological self. A couple of years ago I had to stay at my mother's house in New York for three weeks. I told a series of stories to my mother every day and made notations on the psychological relations or the things that transpired between us as a result of these stories. (Sometimes things happened and sometimes they didn't.) I also noted the length, in terms of time, of the conversations they engendered between us. I told one story each day. They were stories geared toward representing myself in an alien image, "the good daughter, the good wife and mother."

C.N.   To take a slight detour, that piece brings us to the question of your parents' attitude toward you as a woman and as an artist. As you were growing up did they encourage you to be an artist and take you seriously?

E.A.   My mother encouraged me when I was a young girl to be an artist. But to her an artist was someone who put up paintings. The stuff I was doing was so alien to what my mother considered art she just couldn't take it seriously. Now I think she has changed somewhat. This work was called *Domestic Peace* because it was supposed to have engendered real spontaneous natural conversations which would create domestic peace in the household so I could go about my real work. I like to call it my *Domestic Peace* playing on the pun.

C.N.   Could you describe some of the stories that you told?

E.A.   Some of them were little narratives, some were gossip, some were about my husband and child—what a genius he is.

C.N.   And you graphed your mother's reaction.

E.A.   Yes, I made a graph notation which is like an oscilloscope. It was a representation of the kind of psychological reaction the piece engendered.

C.N.   So when the lines on the graph really oscillated, it showed that the tale you were telling wasn't bringing peace at all.

E.A.   By the way, everyone has to play this game with their parents all the time. When I first put the piece up I got a corny reaction to it. People said it was such a bourgeois image of myself and totally alien to me. I thought, "Oh God, this is not good for my image!" It turned out that men as well as women just freaked out because everybody has a mother.

C.N.   You are demolishing the whole romantic myth of the artist as someone who doesn't have the same normal family connections as everyone else.

E.A.   Yes, we all have this romantic image of the artist. For example, a lot of people have this romantic image of Robert Morris. He told me once that his mother used to call him up every week and ask him when he was going to have a child. You see everyone has the same problem.

C.N.   Artists are now beginning to use the materials of their own lives very candidly to make art. Roger Welsh was one of the first people to do this. He did a piece consisting of films of three generations of his family. I would be loathe to say that the exploration of identity is only for women although it could be called feminist if one equates the term with being fully human and having a strong sense of self.

E.A.   Welsh helped bring this kind of exploration back into the art world.

C.N.   Just as your work brought real narrative back into art content.

E.A.   This takes me into the work that I have been doing for the last two years. I think that we women helped bring real psychological and sociological information back into the art world which was in a total cul-de-sac—talking about what is an artwork all the time.

C.N.   You mean discussing only the formalistic aspects of a work— how the plane relates to the edge and so on.

E.A.   That's baby stuff. Now everybody knows anything is art if you call it art to frame it. That's no problem, but we have been going over it ad nauseam. I think we women brought in these other elements and the results are very curious. What has happened is that people are having a very deprived idea of what autobiography is. The autobiographical material that I have been doing really treats one's life as a novel. It is everyone's novel. I was telling Germano Celant, who wrote *Arte Povera,* that everyone is his own artist in that he is responsible for his own life and it was the poor man's art. (I was punning on his term.) Even the slave has it though he is more confined in his possibilities. But I think that things like "Three Generations of My Family" as a particular image of autobiography is a shabby kind of naturalism. It is a picture of deprivation. I figure that since autobiography is about past events, it is only fiction because the events are over.

C.N.   You mean the selection of events becomes a matter of choice.

E.A.   Right. You could say anything and who is to know whether it is true or false and what does it matter? I decided that there was no reason, when I do my autobiography, to have an underprivileged fantasy. It is all fiction anyway, since it is obvious that autobiography is not written by a dead person writing about his past. It is written by a passionate person living in the present. He has got something to sell, an image of himself, which he considers adequate or which, for some reason, he wants to convince people is true. I don't care if it's Billy Rose or Saint Augustine. They both do this number on the world because the mind is literary and the soul is pragmatic. This is known as your life after the fact.

C.N.   Could you talk about specific works that you did? How about the *Make-up* piece?

E.A.   That was called "Representational Painting" and was part of the more naturalist works. It was a video tape in which I changed myself from my everyday self into a sort of *Vogue* hippie, a glamorous woman, putting on make-up on camera. It was very simple make-up and the kind I respect on other people but just never bother using myself because I don't use any make-up.

C.N.   Then it was a transformation piece.

E.A.   Right. And a perfectly reasonable one because you could see me walking around the street that way if I chose to do it. Then I went into more exotic transformations.

C.N.   Could we say this was a transitionary work because you go from the *Carving* piece in which you are stark naked in the most naturalistic way to the *Make-up* piece in which you transform yourself. It could be read almost as a feminist parody—the stages of woman.

E.A.   Well, it wasn't a parody because I do everything perfectly straight. I don't want to rip myself off. I made myself as glamorous as possible. I rather grooved on looking so good.

C.N.   What came after the *Make-up* piece?

E.A.   When I started moving out of those more plausible or expectable transformations like dieting, putting on street make-up, or changing my regular artist's self into a more bourgeois image, all these things we do all the time, I moved into perfectly plausible but less expected and perhaps more exotic transformations. I got interested in the transformational nature of the self and the possibilities of defining my limits, such as age, sex, space, time, talent, what have you, all the things that restrict our possibilities. I mentioned the slave before and how restricted his novel of himself would be. Well I wanted perfect freedom.

C.N.   To transcend space and time.

E.A.   Why not? If autobiography is fiction—and it is because it is history, the past—you don't have to be restricted to your own past. You might come up with someone else's fiction. One of my selves is a king.

C.N.   Does that refer to your piece *The King and the Ballerina?*

E.A.   I have been putting those two together.

C.N.   Which did you do first?

E.A.   Well they all started with *Carving* and the naturalist transformations and then they went into exploring the limits of my possibilities.

C.N.   What was the first exploration?

E.A.   First I decided to see what I was like as a man. I did this first as a video piece. I thought a beard should make all the difference, so I didn't do anything but apply, in an old-fashioned, manual, stage-actor's method, a hair-by-hair application of strands of hair to my face. Now I didn't want to rip myself off. I wanted to be as handsome a man as I could be. I have small bones and a rather delicate face so I wasn't going to take the beard of an arctic explorer. It turned out it was just natural to have a cavalier's beard. Then I discovered that the man I was going to be was a king. That was great. Why should I be a beggar? Or why should I work in a factory? So I became this cavalier king and the resemblance of my face as king to the face of Charles I was very strong. I have done a number of pieces called *January 1649*. That was the date his head was removed. In those pieces I change the facial expression and make it sadder and sadder—as I suppose the poor man looked on that day. This piece refers back to the fact that you can claim to be anything or anyone as your autobiography. Well my claim to be Charles I comes up against that previous claim of a short egotistical guy who had his head chopped off, or a portrait by Van Dyke. But that's all history. I come as Charles I with video, photography (everybody knows photography can't lie), this whole personal presence as Charles. Why shouldn't that be more meaningful or more real than some historical gossip? This led me to the very powerful realization that documentation wasn't some tedious listing of facts but was actually a reincarnation or a re-creation of what you know you are dealing with. Everyone knows us by the public report of ourselves. That is what the documentation does and it is always there, no matter what. You know me only by how I talk to you and how I look. Therefore when I document myself as Charles I it is just as reasonable as what the history books will say.

C.N.   I think everybody at some time fantasizes about being in some great character's place or living someone else's life.

E.A.   Well we always try to show ourselves off in the best light we can. Why should I be underprivileged?

C.N.   People read novels to escape their own world and go into some other world. In your next piece *The Ballerina* you were actually getting into another life. Haven't you actually been studying ballet?

E.A.   What happened there is that since I had taken what I thought of as an extremely masculine image, I thought that I wanted to play with an extremely feminine one, which is what I think of *The Ballerina*. Ballet had always been my passion but they say that after ten or twelve you can't be a ballerina anymore. I said to hell with that.

C.N.   That was Zelda Fitzgerald's tragedy.

E.A.   I think Zelda's tragedy was being a woman.

C.N.   I remember the accounts of her in Nancy Mitford's book trying so hard to be a ballerina. I couldn't help thinking of that when I read that you were studying ballet at your age.

E.A.   You see you used the wrong documentation. She really went out into the world and danced. I sent out reports, photographs, drawings, and that is different.

C.N.   I'm not saying you are doing the same thing as Zelda.

E.A.   But actually it's related. She just chose the documentation that recorded things that weren't relevant to the glamorous image that she wanted to present as a dancer. I wanted to be a glamorous Russian ballerina in the old style, not the new Balanchine gymnastic ballerina. What I did was study the old Cechetti method. I got myself on toe three hours a day and then, interestingly, I realized that documenting that process was totally tedious and I was not going to do it. The interesting thing was to make myself into a ballerina and show the final product.

C.N.   That's what you always wanted anyway.

E.A.   Right. So I had these marvelous stills of myself taken in a long *Les Sylphides* costume and in a short tutu looking very glamorous. Then I made a video tape that shows how the photographic session was done (and, poor thing, I have to hold onto a broomstick in order to get into the proper position and things like that). It is the lie or perjury that glamour photos really are that is made clear in this video tape. I am not out to make it clear but there was no other way to take those photos. Then I did a whole series of drawings of recollections of my life with Diaghilev and I am actually in the process of writing the full-length autobiography of my student days in Paris (where I have never been). That's why when I saw the Poirer show at the Sonnabend Gallery, which is a beautiful show with photographs of Roman ruins, I did a funny take. When Elon Wingate, the gallery director, told me that the Poirers spent a whole year doing archeological studies with maps and records and so on, I looked at him very ingenuously and said, "You mean they didn't make it up?" Not that making something up is better, it's easier.

C.N.   It's strange to think of you living in San Diego in a house with your husband and child . . .

E.A.   And being all these grand people.

C.N.   Your work could be interpreted as taking all the women's fantasies which have always been scoffed at and elevating them to artworks. Something previously devalued becomes something to be revered through your artistry.

E.A.   And an artist's life is very hard. You don't measure out your life in coffee spoons, you measure your life in art-making. There is no time for all these grand and noble possibilities because you are a workman.

C.N.   You also make choices. If you were the ballerina you would actually have a hard, miserable, grueling life practicing all the time. You didn't really want that at all.

E.A.   Absolutely not.

C.N.   The thing that is most intriguing to all of us are those wonderful ballet costumes.

E.A.   Yes. I noticed that every time *The Ballerina* goes up in a gallery people just go around with faces filled with orgiastic pleasure. I think many women are still closet ballerinas and men find the exhibit glamorous. When I had the shows in Europe, I was a ballerina at the openings and everyone thought it was the most beautiful thing. If you are a ballerina you're beautiful.

C.N.   Your work goes under the category of conceptual art as we mentioned earlier. But that's a term that's hard to define. How does it relate to the work of such artists as Joseph Kosuth and the other linguistic artists who do nothing but present esoteric writings most people find incomprehensible?

E.A.   I think that's a kind of mad poetry they have in their heads. It's like when I went to the New School to study phenomenology because I liked the prose of the Romantic Existentialists. These people you refer to like the particular sound of thinking in the particular language they use.

C.N.   You mean it's not meant to be understood.

E.A.   It sounds to me as if it is a perfectly sexy love affair with language.

C.N.   And with each other exclusive of the rest of us. However, your work seems at the other end of the spectrum of what is called conceptual art. It has concrete visualization in the form of photographs and video tapes.

E.A.   James Collins is making the word conceptual art a bad word. *Artforum* is into post-conceptualism. I was recently called that in a review.

C.N.   What's that supposed to mean?

E.A.   It's supposed to mean the good guys as opposed to the bad guys.

C.N.   Who are the conceptualists?

E.A.   They were the old Minimalists, and the post-conceptualists are the people with a light, more graceful touch.

C.N.   Certainly "post-conceptual" art is just as hard to classify as "conceptual" art. Most people wouldn't know whether to put it into the category of painting or sculpture. And doesn't it enter into the realm of performance?

E.A. Yes. The king went for a walk in Solana Beach about a month ago. I was wearing a cape and a bush hat, which looked like a cavalier's hat, and my beard, and there were my breasts hanging out through a frilly blouse. I wondered if I would have a heavy reaction from people who could see I was a woman walking around with a beard. I had a beautiful reaction. Everyone loved me and asked, "What's going on here?" I said, "I am a king visiting Solana Beach. Solana Beach deserves a king." I guess Americans love kings because I gave flowers to the ladies and discussed politics with the old gentlemen.

C.N. Didn't they think you were a little eccentric?

E.A. I think they thought it was strange. You know, there is something lovable about *The King.* I think I'm a bit of a Chaplin. I don't try to be but I think it comes out. I just said, "I'm a king visiting Solana Beach," and the surfers said, "Far out," and that was it.

C.N. This whole episode makes me wonder how your boots exhibition was received by the public at the Museum of Modern Art.

E.A. I got a letter from Kynaston McShine the curator saying this was the only project show that didn't have a single complaint letter. I am still getting fan mail.

C.N. I can see why. Your work is really exceptional because it transcends the very tight little art circle. It has a universal content and a clear presentation. It communicates on many levels.

E.A. I think comedy is at the heart of everything I do. I don't do it on purpose but I think that it's straight in line with romanticism. I think at the heart of all romanticism is a kind of absurd comedy that lies side by side with the really beautiful aspects of it. This makes it a funny, shabby, fragile thing which has never been played out. I think that is all there in my work, it is something innate, and people respond to it.

C.N. There is a whole escapist, fantasy element in your work, a Walter Mitty kind of thing. You wanted to be a ballerina without having to work for it.

E.A. But I did work for it—three hours a day.

C.N. You worked at it so you could present it as an artwork. The real artistry was not in your newly acquired skill as a dancer but in the presentation of yourself as a dancer. That was where the real creativity and artist's work came in. You are not an amateur ballerina; you are a professional artist presenting us with a wish-fulfillment image that is as life-like as possible.

E.A.   Right. And when you present the fantasy image with precisely all its possible ramifications of meaning, it's real. It doesn't matter whether it actually happened or not. Someone in England asked me if I really worked with Diaghilev. I said, "How old do you think I am?"

C.N.   So when you are talking about autobiography, for you it's one's fantasies, one's imagination, how you would *like* to live your life as well as how you *do* live it.

E.A.   Whether they know it or not everyone lives their life that way. But why do it in a deprived way? Why remain in an underprivileged country?

C.N.   To get back to more prosaic kinds of questions, you are not represented in a New York gallery are you? I have always seen you as a little at odds with the art establishment.

E.A.   I guess I'm a sort of buccaneer which bugs a number of people who work so hard to be "in." But I'm actually represented in Europe by Galleria Forma in Italy.

C.N.   I remember that when you had *The Consumer Goods* show in New York it was not in an established gallery.

E.A.   The first one, *The California Lives,* was shown at the Gain Ground in New York, which was an avant-garde gallery (if the term ever had any meaning, it had there). Gain Ground was run for a year by artist Robert Newman, and Vito Acconci had his first show there as well as Robert Newman and myself. My second show, *Portraits of Eight New York Women,* was shown in New York months later. I was supposed to have it in a gallery in Soho and I had the stuff all ready. Then it turned out that the gallery didn't have the money to open. I said "To hell with it, I've got all this stuff in the studio and I'm going to put this show up and then be able to forget about it." Otherwise it haunts you. I took a place in the Chelsea Hotel and did the whole thing myself. The Gain Ground had closed but Robert Newman said he would back me with the Gain Ground name for whatever it was worth. I said, "Thanks Robert, but if I am paying for this whole thing and doing it myself, I'm going to do it myself." I guess in those days, which were still academic in New York, it was an independent thing to do.

C.N.   It certainly was. There is a stigma in backing oneself, especially if you are a woman. But women with spunk have often backed themselves, Virginia Woolf and Gertrude Stein for example.

E.A. Poets do it all the time. Now I don't mind having European representation because they get the work around. But I rather like representing myself in America which is my country. I've had more shows than I can count lately.

C.N. You've just come back from a European tour.

E.A. And I have a video show up at the Everson Museum in Syracuse. I have a show going up in Buenos Aires in a couple of weeks. I can't keep track of them all.

C.N. But you're still an underground person compared to the other women in this book: Lee Krasner is at the Marlborough Gallery and Nevelson is at Pace and so on.

E.A. It's very nice if I still make people uncomfortable. I think that is a good thing.

C.N. I think the younger artists in this book—women in their late thirties and early forties—have a different attitude toward themselves as women artists than do some of the older people. You, for example, openly use yourself, your body, the fabric of your life and fantasies, as your material. You also had the confidence to take your career into your own hands and have made a success independent of the gallery system—although I guess you wouldn't turn down a top New York gallery if it came your way, would you?

E.A. I'm not a purist. I'm not impure enough to be a purist.

C.N. We just mentioned that you use your own body and life to make your art. Many male artists have done this in the recent past such as Bruce Nauman, Denis Oppenheim, Vito Acconci, and Chris Burden who recently shot himself to create a body artwork. Do you think, in general, that a woman's approach to this kind of "body art" is different from a man's?

E.A. At the time the whole "body works" thing started I remember writing to John Gibson that I didn't think an artist could be a body artist because it was like asking a Black Panther to go into insurance or become a minstrel. Those were always acceptable professions for Blacks. I was wrong, very wrong. But I like Vito Acconci and I think he is a very interesting artist. He is infinitely more expressionistic than I am but he is also much more manipulative.

C.N. Yes. Many of those men are abusing themselves or abusing the audience. But when you use the term expressionistic how do you mean it in this context?

E.A. When I used it in reference to those male artists I meant it as a word that describes a totally manipulative way of violating people's privacy by forcing heavy emotional feelings on them. I think Vito is very good at it but I find it totally bizarre that people take him for real (of course he's real), that they believe every number that he pulls. Everything he does is a violation of the audience. He dredges up all these fictions about himself and uses them constantly over and over to manipulate the audience. I don't do that.

C.N.   Vito and those other men are after control. It seems to me in the *Carving* piece and in all your other works you were not seeking to manipulate the audience but rather they were invited to empathize with you and to participate.

E.A.   It's seduction on a different level. If you hit upon images and ideas that are basic to enough people they will want to play your game because there is something in it for them. They groove with it. When I was in Florence, I made a tape in which I was the *Bearded Ballerina* which totally freaked out the technicians and people I was taping with. Instead of seeing me as a comical figure, believe it or not, they saw me as a totally romantic sexual image.

C.N.   There you have a classic androgynous situation.

E.A.   Not unlike one of my favorite artists, David Bowie.

C.N.   Getting back to the question about women artists dealing with their bodies and minds as material for art, do you feel there is any specific women's approach?

E.A.   I teach out here and the kids are very into working with autobiographical materials. I stand for an autobiography that is privileged.

C.N.   I was on a panel with a woman artist who absolutely declared her art feminist because she created it out of her own personal background. Do you think autobiographical and feminist are the same thing?

E.A.   They could be but they don't have to be. There is a difference between feminist art that is directly polemical and didactic and a feminist art which is, as in the case of my *Carving* piece, made up of female flesh. It gets to be very much part of a woman's work when it's a woman's body.

C.N.   You mean the idea of a woman specifically concentrating on her own body is feminist?

E.A.   Right, and without glamorizing it. The pictures I did are head-on. Someone called them "Gothic."

C.N.   But unidealized nudes have been done by men.

E.A.   Yes, both these have the coolness of passport photos. Although in my current work I am actually romanticizing and glamorizing the stuff.

C.N.   So you feel that there is a recognizable woman's art as opposed to a recognizable man's art?

E.A.   I tell you I don't know. My art turns out to be very much of a woman's autobiography. I don't do it on purpose, but that's the way it is. I really don't know. I know there are people working seriously on female iconography and I respect the attempt. Judy Chicago has been doing some interesting things in her own autobiographical materials and a number of people have reversed themselves and gone into this. It's hard to say. I think we will know better later when we look back on the scene. I certainly know a great number of women artists who are using autobiographical materials seriously, but then there are a lot doing it because it's a bandwagon.

C.N.   But though your art is, of course, a woman's art because you did it, can it really be called *woman's art*—in the sense that *only* a woman could have done it? After all, couldn't some man have had the idea to do a piece of a woman dieting, taking all the pictures and putting them up just as you did? If you didn't tell me, you, a woman did it, how would I know the sex of the artist?

E.A.   Oh, I see—a man artist could do a piece on her. Of course.

C.N.   I am only saying that if I can't identify a work of art as being done by male or female, before I am told the name of the artist, I remain skeptical about the value of putting art into sexual categories although I think it is extremely important to focus on what women artists, past and present, have produced.

E.A.   I really don't know. I know it is in the air for everyone to do his or her own thing. It's true we women have a different history and life experience than men, but then every woman has certain differences from every other woman. I really don't know how it will look later on —how history will rewrite it in that particular fiction that will become the art history of the period.

C.N.   It's interesting that in our conversation we haven't talked very specifically about your real biography—the actual facts of your life.

E.A.   My real biography? All I do is make art and have a little time left over for my personal life. It's not very interesting. An artist's work is hard.

C.N.   Before I asked you if your parents were supportive but you gave few details in regard to your actual experience with them. Yet I felt you answered my question in a different way when you told me about the *Domestic Peace.* Obviously you couldn't have made that piece if you hadn't had certain kinds of experiences with your mother which called for the kind of behavior which is expected from a "proper type" woman.

E.A. True, and part of it may be that though my mother encouraged me as a girl in my art, a girl is treated differently than a woman.

C.N. It's very true that to a girl from an educated middle-class household all possibilities seem open, but when you reach a certain stage you are expected to settle down and do what is expected from a woman—be a wife and mother.

E.A. Part of it was probably because what I was doing looked so weird to my mother.

C.N. It's interesting that you were supported in being an artist at all since that's hardly considered a sensible career for anyone.

E.A. Well, my ethnic background is Russian Marxism.

C.N. A very different orientation from someone who comes from a conservative middle-class background.

E.A. Yes, but that old-time Stalinist Left was actually very bourgeois which is why they fell apart in the fifties. They didn't like being disreputable.

C.N. You're always so light-hearted. I'm sure there were difficulties in your past.

E.A. That's quite true. I had a piece I wanted to do recently in which Eleanor of twenty years ago, of 1953, would meet on TV the Eleanor of 1973. We would confront each other and she would insist upon claims to me. It turned out to be a very heavy piece that I planned for about a month and found myself totally unable to do. Oh, I could do it but I didn't want to do it. I didn't want to assault myself just as I don't want to assault other people. You keep talking about the past. I always used to think of myself as a person without a past, with no history. The past was too painful. I led too heavy a life and I never really like to think of it. It was too unbearable. Instead of brooding about it, I have just forgotten about it. I just made everything new. I find very little difficulty in stamping out things that aren't useful to remember. This confrontation piece would have dredged up all those things that I wanted to forget. I'm not Vito Acconci. And I don't mean that putting myself down. It's a whole other relation to art and to the self. It's not mine.

C.N.   I know what you are talking about. In the women's movement some people keep talking all the time about how oppressed they are and after a while you feel that by doing this they are really perpetuating the oppression. The more you dwell on it the more stuck you are in it.

E.A.   I think so. The art I respond to has a more graceful touch to it. This other kind of heavy brooding assault is art that in general I don't like to look at, or to read, or to deal with—except that in Vito's case I find it interesting. It's sort of like the eldest Karamazov—comical, he is a total clown. It's not that I'm Pollyanna. It's just that it's not useful. Like all romantics, I'm a pragmatist.

C.N.   You have shown in your art that what is important is where we choose to look and what we choose to emphasize. We can go backwards or forwards or sideways or into another realm altogether. Getting back to Vito Acconci, if he weren't able to image his fears and neuroses so strikingly he wouldn't be an artist, he would be a nut. There is a relationship between you and Acconci in that you both have the artistry, the vision, the dedication, to pull it all together. He takes universal fears, while you take universal fantasies, but you both give them coherent form.

E.A.   Yes. And like all romantics, I'm an opportunist.

C.N.   That doesn't sound so nice.

E.A.   No, except, as I said before, I am not impure enough to be a purist. Those things that I forget or don't want to deal with are not useful to me or my work. You know we all manipulate our lives. Hopefully we can learn to manipulate them in a way to give ourselves the most satisfaction.

Portrait of Lynne Traiger, 1970.

The Ballerina, 1973.

" She was a dancer of the old school and after posed for our greatest painters."

" All of Paris rose to salute our modernism "

100 Boots on the Job, Signal Hill, Calif.,
Feb. 15, 1972, 12:15 P.M.

100 Boots out of a Job,
Terminal Island, Calif.,
Feb. 15, 1972, 3:00 P.M.

100 Boots in the Street,
Long Beach, Calif.,
Feb. 15, 1972, 4:45 P.M.

100 Boots Enter the Museum,
11 W. 53 St., New York City,
May 15, 1973, 10:50 A.M.

100 Boots Visit the Egyptian Gardens, 29th St. and 9th Ave.,
New York City, May 15, 1973, 4:35 P.M.

Carving: A Traditional Sculpture, 1972.

The King (Portrait), Jan. 20, 1649, 1972.

The King Visiting Solana Beach, Calif., 1974.

Black Is Beautiful, 1974.

UDREY FLACK has been a rebel ever since she was a child. The daughter of a middle-class New York family, she was torn between her desire to conform to their image of a proper woman, one who became a dutiful wife and mother, and her overpowering commitment to her art.

Determined to follow her artistic imperatives, Flack attended Music and Art High School and went on to study at Cooper Union in the early fifties. Again she found herself pulled apart by the external mores that conflicted with her own conception of what it meant to be an artist. In the macho world of The Club, an organization formed by the major Abstract Expressionists, a woman was expected to behave as "one of the boys" or to view herself as a sexual vessel for the servicing of the great male geniuses. Flack was unable to play the game on either level and therefore felt herself to be condemned as bourgeois even while her middle-class associates disapproved of her as a Bohemian.

Flack brought her rebellion into her art as well as into her social attitudes. Defying the strict dictum of those Abstract Expressionist days which absolutely forbade any traffic with recognizable subject matter, Flack, after graduating from Yale in 1952, was set on becoming a realist. She subsequently studied the figure with Robert Beverly Hale at the Art Students League and took to drawing with other like-minded artists, among them Philip and Dorothy Pearlstein, Sidney Tillim, and Harold Bruder.

Flack continued on her unfashionable, realistic course throughout the sixties, selecting her subjects from her immediate environment as well as from the social and political events of the day. Her grandmother; her aunt, Tante Feige; the Black boxer, Davey Moore; Mexican women potters; nuns on a Civil Rights march with southern Blacks; anti-war demonstrators; all take their places on her canvases although the art world at the time had little interest or enthusiasm for such subjects.

In 1965, Flack took a step which drove her into further isolation. By using a color photograph to paint the *Kennedy Motorcade* and failing to disguise her source she cut herself off from the small supportive circle of realists with whom she had, up until then, felt a camaraderie. But with this adaption of the photographic image she opened herself up to a completely new vision of reality which the art world today calls Photorealism. With the execution of *The Farb Family,* a commissioned portrait, the painter experimented with color slides and began to explore a whole new way of seeing. By projecting the colored slide onto the canvas scale was immediately achieved and drawing was eliminated. In such later works as *Jolie Madame, Royal Flush,* and *Spitfire* the artist, working with a spray gun, began to render in paint the rich-colored light which is projected through the color slide. Often using only the primary colors, pigment is sprayed on top of pigment in an effort to explore the actual nature of vision itself. Flack's daring challenge of conventional means continues to lead her into innovative visual territories.

In choice of subject matter as well as technique, Flack has also remained at odds with the reigning order. Ivan Karp, the owner of O.K. Harris Works of Art and the chief promoter of Photorealism has defined this painting style as a tough, cool, non-emotional (read "masculine") art consisting primarily of depictions of automobiles and motorcycles. Going against this trend, Flack defiantly paints emotionally charged subjects like the *Macarena,* a seventeenth-century Madonna, with tears streaming down her cheeks, and sumptuous still lifes, filled with crystal and jewels, personal items such as her own paints, card tables, and foodstuffs. Hers is an art which celebrates feelingly the essential loveliness and wonder of the prosaic substance of everyday life.

In her middle forties, Flack lives with her businessman husband, Bob Marcus, and her daughter, Hanna, in a New York apartment on the upper West Side. She tends to remain aloof from the intrigues and manipulations of art world politics, seeing only those artists—Harold Bruder and Richard Estes among them—with whom she feels connected personally and ideologically. Although Flack identifies with the women's movement, she asserts now, as she always has in the past, her right to carve out her own art and her own life style.

CINDY NEMSER   When did you decide you wanted to be an artist?

AUDREY FLACK   Art always seemed to be a part of my life. When I was about seven years old I saw a man in the park who was drawing and begged him to give me art lessons. His price was twenty-five cents. My parents wouldn't allow it. At such an early age it seemed absurd to them that I should have art lessons. During the period that I was growing up and even after that they could never really grasp the idea that a human life could be seriously involved with art. Ideally, I was to have gotten married, preferably to a doctor or a lawyer. I very deeply wanted to be accepted by my friends and my parents but my needs to persist as an artist created a barrier between me and the people I grew up with. I never fulfilled the role my parents projected for me.

C.N.   Very often artists are caught in this painful conflict. They feel themselves to be outsiders. I remember the beautiful story *Tonio Kröger* by Thomas Mann in which the narrator always feels cut off from the happy bourgeois family circle. How about your experiences as a student?

A.F.   I went to Music and Art High School and was the school rebel artist. I won the St. Gauden's Art Medal there and then I went to Cooper Union.

C.N.   Were you treated any differently because you were a woman student?

A.F.   No, not as a student. Nicholas Marsicano was my teacher. He was excellent and I don't feel that he discriminated against me because I was a woman. When I was a student I was a wild Abstract Expressionist—throwing paint and making huge canvases. The Artists Club, the club for Abstract Expressionists, was going strong then (I graduated in 1951) but it was a very tight, "in" place. They had a membership, to which you had to be elected, and each member could bring one or two guests. Marsicano took me there one night and I was to meet Jackson Pollock, my idol. I was so passionately in love with art that to me meeting Pollock was like a stage-struck person meeting Clark Gable. I wanted to ask him how he painted? What he did? How he thought? My intellect was geared for it. When I did meet Pollock I was thunderstruck by his deeply lined, worn face. To me it was the face of a debauched human being.

C.N.   How did he treat you?

A.F.   He could only relate to me as a female. There is no doubt in my mind that if I had been a male art student I would have been treated differently. I don't know how much better but certainly not in a sexist way. But in those Abstract Expressionist days the men had to prove their masculinity. Machismo was a great part of the Bohemian mystique.

C.N.   Women were treated like sex objects?

A.F.   Yes, they were. And unless they played the game they were not allowed into the inner circle. I was prepared to handle the art aspect of the scene but I wouldn't play the game.

C.N.   In general, a young woman who was a student and committed to becoming a professional artist was not taken seriously?

A.F.   Absolutely not. I don't know any young student who was. There were a few instructors who didn't allow sexism to interfere with their judgment, but for the most part women art students were not taken seriously.

C.N.   So a woman artist had to be very committed to withstand those kinds of pressures?

A.F.   Yes. The art world pressures you into acting out a wild Bohemian scene—as if that made you a "Real Artist"—while family pressures are just the opposite. Very often the art student is caught in the middle.

C.N.   The art world has its own conformist code. Many of its members feel impelled to act out the romantic role of the rebellious, impoverished, unconventional individual all the while concealing a basically middle-class life style. Artists who have achieved success without the Bohemian trappings expose this hypocrisy and are frequently resented for their honesty. It's ironic that artists, the very people who should be the most tolerant and accepting of all kinds of life styles, often turn around and become as narrow in scope as the most conservative segments of our society. But getting back to your development as a painter, at Cooper Union were you doing Abstract Expressionist work because that's what they taught you?

A.F.   I don't know if that is just what they taught me. That was the mythology of the time. When I graduated I got a scholarship to Yale University. Joseph Albers had taken over the Yale Art Department that year and the students from the previous administration were painting in a very poor academic manner. He recognized the need to infuse new life into the student body and came to Cooper Union asking for the ten top students. He offered some of us scholarships. He was using us and we were getting accreditation from him. I think Albers expected to control the students and make them into "square" painters. He got more than he expected. He couldn't control me and we really did battle it out. He was trying to force me into his kind of painting; I refused to let him criticize my work since he didn't understand it. Eventually we stopped talking. Albers respected me and kept away from me and I kept away from him. I wasn't required to take his class.

C.N.   Why did you decide to become a realist painter?

A.F.   I always wanted to draw realistically. For me art is a continuous discovery into reality, an exploration of visual data which has been going on for centuries, each artist contributing to the next generation's advancement. I wanted to go a step further and extend the boundaries. I also believe people have a deep need to understand their world and that art clarifies reality for them.

C.N.   When did you begin to work as a realist?

A.F.   In my high school years at Music and Art, Picasso and Braque totally dominated the art world and one learned to draw in their style rather than classically. At Cooper Union I still wanted to work realistically but Abstract Expressionism was popular; one learned brush movement—using the brush as an extension of one's arm and expressing one's inner emotions. Drawing courses were offered, which I took, but they were never sufficent in number or quality for me to draw with the kind of mastery I was looking for. After graduating from Yale, I went to study anatomy with Robert Beverly Hale at the Art Students League. I drew a great deal from the figure and my paintings became more and more representational. They evolved out of my early Abstract Expressionist work with heavy brush strokes, painterly surfaces, dripping and paint accidents applied to the realist subject matter. I was in a show at the Tanager Gallery in 1956 where I exhibited several figurative paintings; there weren't many artists working realistically at the time. Then the Stable Gallery had an annual and I submitted another figurative painting. It was the only one in the show and it was hung upstairs in the back. It was heretical then to do any figurative realistic art.

C.N.   It must have been a difficult time for you. Were there other artists involved with realism then?

A.F.   Yes. We had a group who drew together. Sidney Tillim, Harold Bruder, Arthur Elias, Sam Gelber, and occasionally Philip and Dorothy Pearlstein joined us. I began to use subject matter which was thematic. I made a painting called *The Four Horsemen of the Apocalypse.* Then I did a whole series of thematic paintings: *Dance of Death, The Three Graces,* and others. This kind of painting later on was labeled narrative.

C.N.   But the other members of the group avoided officially crediting you with contributing to the concept of narrative art?

A.F.   Yes. Even though I helped to formulate it.

C.N.   This is typical of what happens to women artists. As in the case of Hepworth and Krasner your innovative ideas were used but you were not given credit for them by the men in your circle.

A.F.   I have no doubt that it was because I was a woman. But I was not aware of it then. While I was aware of my worth in the group and equality as an artist, I was, nevertheless, happy to be accepted by these men. I was still playing the game. I was still signing my name A. L. Flack. Never using the name *Audrey.*

C.N.   How did your art develop into the kind of realism you are doing now?

A.F.   President Kennedy's assassination had a great effect on me. I wanted to make a statement about it. I made my *Kennedy Motorcade* painting in 1964. It got the most incredible reviews. People were horrified at the subject matter. Now it looks like such a mild painting. It was just a picture of Kennedy riding in the Dallas motorcade with Jackie at his side holding a bunch of roses and Connally riding in the front. Everybody is smiling, and, of course, you know that one moment later Kennedy is going to get shot. This event solidified and confirmed the direction in which my art was going to go in terms of subject matter and style.

C.N.   You were making work which conveyed your feelings about outer reality?

A.F.   Yes. And I had also begun to use the photograph. I had never seen Kennedy in person and now I couldn't get him to pose for me with his head blown off. I needed specific pictures of him. Before that, Harold Bruder and I had been experimenting with photographs. The *Kennedy Motorcade* was the first painting in which I used a color photograph for reference. I had used black and white previously. Many people in the art world were upset because I was using photographs. Of course now we realize that everybody has used the photograph—Vermeer with his *camera obscura,* Victorian painters, the Pre-Raphaelites, the Impressionists.

C.N.   But weren't other artists using photographs for reference at that time?

A.F.   Some artists considered it acceptable to use the photograph as a reference (Muybridge was used often) but it was not acceptable if the painting looked like a photograph. We hear that one must not copy. Yet the old masters worked from one another. They copied from plaster casts. I always encourage my students to copy, particularly something they admire. One learns through imitation. Originality will always come through.

C.N.   The creative part is to invent a structure in order to represent what is out there. In the past truly original artists took the structures created by earlier artists and modified or restructured them to meet their own needs. In the twentieth century that tradition has been lost and artists have had to invent schemata from scratch. The whole concept of originality has been distorted.

A.F. The public has been brainwashed to believe that any kind of eccentric behavior is "art" and the more far out and extreme it gets the more original it is. Conversely the public has been led to believe that it is wrong to use illusionist imagery to make art. Unfortunately this way of thinking came from Abstract Expressionism and developed into a mythology of "Modern Art."

C.N. So you were countering the concepts of what was considered original art in the sixties?

A.F. Yes. But despite the opposition there was no doubt in my mind where my work was going. I went to Mexico, took photographs, and did a whole series of Mexican paintings. I did a painting of a Mexican farmer, one of Doña Rosa the potter, and a double portrait of two women weavers from Oaxaca. I went into a kind of social protest realism. I made a painting of Davey Moore, the Black boxer. He was sitting in the back of Madison Square Garden after a match, talking to *Life* reporters, when he dropped dead. Ironically his boxing trunks said "Everlast," which is what is printed on all boxing trunks. I saw his pose as Christ-like. I painted three nuns, *The Sisters of the Immaculate Conception,* leading a Black people's freedom march. The sisters are frightened—you can see the fear on their faces, but they stand their ground.

C.N. You were one of the few people in the sixties who openly dealt with the political and social issues of the time.

A.F. Yet, interestingly enough, many artists and galleries who presented themselves as socially conscious and put on benefit exhibitions for liberal causes veered away from work with any powerful subject matter. Many of these exhibitions were promotional not for the minority group but for the artists and the galleries.

C.N. I notice, at this time, you also did many paintings of women.

A.F. For many years I painted women I considered beautiful—not in the sense of being sex objects but because they were strong and intelligent with great character and feeling. I painted my grandmother who had seven children and had a tragic life. I painted my father's aunt who lived to be ninety-six. She was only five-feet tall, but she was a strong woman who ran a farm, baked, cooked, shopped, plucked chickens, and outlived all her husbands. I also painted Marilyn Monroe and *Two Black Women Grieving over Kennedy.* One woman is pregnant and the other is comforting her.

C.N. These are monumental paintings. In their empathy with the women they relate to the paintings of Mary Cassatt, Paula Modersohn-Becker, and Käthe Kollwitz.

A.F. It was only after I read Sarah Witworth's article about my treatment of women that I became aware of what I had done. I was obviously concerned with being a woman and it came out in my art.

C.N. Did you use photographs for these paintings too?

A.F. I painted them from snapshots. It is interesting to look back and see my progression—black and white photographs; snapshots and journalistic photographs; black and white eight-inch by ten-inch photographs; color photographs; and finally, the Farb portrait where I used color slides. Oriole Farb, then the director of the Riverside Museum, commissioned me and was a very important, supportive force in my career. I was positioning the image of the Farbs on a rather large canvas and trying to scale it up (I don't graph—I have a good eye and I don't have the patience for that mechanical kind of work); then I got the idea that if I projected this slide onto the canvas it would save me a lot of time. I would see the scale that I wanted to paint.

C.N. How did the use of the slide change your art?

A.F. When I projected from a thirty-five millimeter slide, as I did in the Farb portrait, I got the scale rapidly (as a matter of fact it eventually eliminated the need for drawing altogether). It also got me interested in volume and mass and not the linear edge—that hard-cut edge which is not real. Then I began to study how light comes through the slide. I began to see little dots of color blending and combining. As I am standing in the dark room, color is passing through a tiny film and breaking into red, yellow, and blue. I am trying to translate that light into color. Color squeezed out of a tube isn't color to me anymore. Now color is the actual scientific definition—the length of the light waves hitting various surfaces before our eyes. I think we have the three primary colors before our eyes and we mix these colors in terms of light waves. If I mix the three primary pigmented colors in the same way as light waves, my colors are more brilliant. I can load the airbrush with phthalocyanine blue, and spray blue over yellow and it will turn green. If I spray blue over white, it becomes lighter blue. When it hits red it becomes purple or black. I'm mixing colors on the canvas and it's really exciting. Many of my canvases are painted with just the three primary colors, although sometimes it is necessary to use a two-base mixed color. For example, the face of the *Macarena* was painted pink because I would have had to spray red dots at too great a distance and I wanted a smoother surface.

C.N. Your work seems most related to that of Chuck Close who has been investigating what happens when you put one primary color on top of another.

A.F. I admire what he does. His technique is extraordinary. But I don't think Close is as involved in light and reflection as I am. He is interested in color process. One of the big differences between a slide and a color photograph is the brilliancy of the transparency. No color photograph gets that kind of luminosity. I am involved in the way a light hits a surface and creates form. In a painting like *Jolie Madame,* I am painting a piece of glass and, of course, you can see right through the glass. So where is the form? The light in the middle of that bottle is the form. Those crystal beads don't have color. In what color do you paint crystal? I am painting them from the way light reflects on them. In that painting there is a light over the whole surface and you can almost lift it up.

C.N. Is it difficult working with slides?

A.F. When I start positioning the slide on the canvas, setting it up and matching the colors, I am working in the dark. It's very hard and I hate working in the dark. I feel like a mole. But I am seeing as I have never seen before. I see halos and edges.

C.N. It's fascinating how you have eliminated the line and the brush stroke and yet your work is still painterly.

A.F. I have no line because there is no line in nature, but I do believe in the isolation of objects. I think my painterliness comes out of my Abstract Expressionist background. I have a smooth surface but it is a painter's surface. I also use the airbrush to get that transparency of color that I am after. You get that by glazing—red on top of orange, crimson on red, etc. I'm putting on films of color, working in layers, and the little sprayed-on dots blend together visually.

C.N. *Jolie Madame* is an extraordinary painting not only for the way it is painted but also for its subject matter.

A.F. This still life has an angel in it, which is a very favorite subject of mine; a wine glass; fruit; a broach that I wear—a very elegant jeweled thing; a vase that I love; a ring my husband gave me; my Cooper Union ring; a watch that I wear with bracelets; two little salt shakers; a rose; and lots of reflections and glitter which is what interests me. The reason I am inventorying all these things is that they are everything I love. They are part of my world. I wouldn't paint Harnett's rabbit hanging from a barn or a gun or a hunting cap. However in the contemporary art world it has been more acceptable to paint so-called "masculine" objects like motorcycles and cars. Any objects associated with "feminity" have been derided. We all partake of so-called "mas-culine" and "feminine" attributes. Besides *Jolie Madame,* I also painted *Royal Flush,* a poker table still life which could easily be construed as a "masculine" painting.

C.N.   I can't see the still life as masculine or feminine. Think of Char-din's kitchen scenes or Fantin-latour's roses. Great artists are not afraid to paint what they care about. You are asserting your particular preferences as an individual. I think Artemesia Gentileschi, Rosa Bon-heur, and Mary Cassatt painted what was around them with great authority. That is what makes for great art—the courage to speak and write and paint what you know and care about.

A.F.   The subjects of my 1971 exhibition at French and Company were very important to me too. Each painting had a universal symbol, a kind of Jungian archetype. To me, Michelangelo's *David* is the archetype of masculinity—the hero. He is strong but gentle, a comforting figure; he is not a violent figure.

C.N.   This is a unique and feminist approach to the male nude. You see the *David* as beautiful and sensuous as he is. He is a man truly sexually attractive to women and men. There are very few figures like that in art history.

A.F.   Yes. I also painted eight hundred bricks behind him. That's my Baroque detail. I think my art has always been very Baroque. I love multiplicity, curves, detail. But *David* is also a symbol. It's something that everyone can relate to and I want my work to be universal.

C.N.   You have also tapped a universal source when you did the *Macarena.*

A.F.   I think there are symbols that people have gravitated to for cen-turies. Macarena is the patron saint of Seville. (I also painted *The Leaning Tower of Pisa.*) But before I tell you about her I want to talk about kitsch because all these symbols have become kitsch. They have been put down and abused. You have seen *David* in little plastic stat-ues that are out of proportion and ugly. You can buy the head of *David* in a florist shop to put a flower in it. When I was in Pisa I saw *The Leaning Tower* as an ashtray. I saw a miniature toilet bowl with a young boy leaning over urinating in it and a picture of *The Leaning Tower* was printed inside of it. When we arrived in Seville I saw this polychromed, life-sized, wooden statue of the *Macarena.* It's a great work of art; the carving on the face, the patina, the pink cheeks are utterly beautiful. I went around asking who did this statue and when I found out it was done in the seventeenth century, by a woman, Luisa Roldan, you can imagine how I felt. Then, another aspect of this sculpture that flipped me out was that since the seventeenth century people have been worshiping it. On her full-length robe they have pinned emeralds; they have put rings on her fingers, strung pearls around her neck, attached lace to her. They have been kissing her, touching her, and all that love has become attached to this statue and is part of its greatness. There is the mass of humanity in this statue—the feelings of millions of people. All that kitsch, all that love poured into it. That is not just crap kitsch and I don't want people to laugh at it. It might be cheap lace, but it is love lace.

C.N.   How do you feel about the subject matter of many other Photo-realistic paintings—the preponderance of motorcycles and cars?

A.F.   The car and the motorcycle are supposedly male power symbols. There has been an attempt on the part of certain dealers to make cars and motorcycles, as well as other banal subject matter, synonymous with Photorealism. This is not true. There are many aspects to Photo-realism. It is not necessarily "cold," "brutal," "non-human." This kind of stereotyping is unfair and misleading. Photorealism embraces every kind of subject matter and attitude depending on the individual artists. Certain artists who paint cars and motorcycles do not approach these subjects with non-human detachment.

C.N.   What do you think of Photorealists who say they aren't interested in subject matter at all but only in making a replica or a fac-simile of the photograph?

A.F.   A lot of Photorealists are saying that they just render a surface. I don't think it's possible just to render anything. Set up a still life and tell everybody to copy it exactly. No two paintings will be alike because no two people's eyes are alike. We don't perceive color identically nor will we have the same composition any more than we will have the same feelings or attitudes. When I painted the *Macarena* or *Jolie Madame* or *Royal Flush,* it was my decision as to which photograph I would use in the painting. I can have as many as one hundred and fifty slides before I select *the* slide. (I work with a very sensitive photographer, Jeanne Hamilton, who understands my vision.) I think about it for months and months. I set up my still life as a master would set up a still life. I set up the light. I spot it. For example, the coins in my new painting *Royal Flush* were lit from the center. I wanted the cards to show through the bottom of the glass. The cigarette was lit and relit. I took many shots until I got the essence. It is interesting to watch the set-up develop. On a round poker table there are card hands and money around the outer edge. There are no drinks, pretzels, or ash-trays in the middle of the poker table. It's basically empty. I didn't want that. I started pushing everything in toward the center—the cards, the cigarettes, the watch, the dice. I have a believable center but that is all part of the composing. Then I get my slide of the composition and it's projected and I begin to paint in the light and recompose at the same time. For example, I made that cigar wrapper bluish; it's not.

C.N.   So there is a great deal of invention in your work; it isn't just copied or rendered?

A.F.   Even if you *think* you are merely rendering a photograph without feeling, you can't do it. I remember Marisol saying that if you pose for a photographic portrait, the portrait always comes out looking like the photographer. That goes for Photorealism too. My attitude toward *Royal Flush* has to do with me. I have lived with gamblers, real compulsive gamblers who play for real money. Notice the clock in the painting says 4:50. They have been playing all night. They play for days on end, taking out time for a nap, but they don't sleep. It's not just a still life; it comes out of my personal background. And I feel this painting is as universal as the ones I did of the *David* and the *Macarena.* Gambling is related to life—a Royal Flush is symbolic. It's the biggest winner; who wouldn't want it?

C.N.   There are also the symbols of passing time. The cigarette that has burned down.

A.F.   Yes, and the ice cubes have melted down into water and there are half-empty glasses. Then there is the ace of spades which is not in the center, but off to the side and seen through a glass. The presence of death is in all our lives but I wanted to push it back because it has been very up-front in my life for too many years.

C.N.   I also notice that you use a close-up vantage point more and more frequently in your paintings. Why do you gravitate to the close-up view?

A.F.   I have always seen larger than life. Then when I started to project, I really began to see details. It's like looking into a magnifying glass and seeing things break down into their components. There is also an intimacy. I bring you right into the poker game. In *Jolie Madame* my table becomes your table. I get you involved through large scale. And I want you involved. Though there are again certain affinities in my work to that of Chuck Close, I doubt if he is involved with this kind of intimacy. We both work very large but I don't get involved psychologically with his big heads—with who the person is. I only get involved with his technique.

C.N.   I think Close uses scale and detail to distract the viewers and keep them from getting involved with the subject in an intimate way. His size makes the image intimidating. On the contrary, your use of scale reinforces one's involvement with the subject. It acts to bring the viewers into the picture space. The way you have painted certain objects—as if they were breaking out of the picture plane and projecting outward into the viewer's space—also creates a sense of intimacy.

A.F.   I tilted the table top to achieve that effect.

C.N.   If you feel so strongly about the personal aspect of your subject matter, why did you accept a commission to do a painting like *Spitfire* where the subject was given to you?

A.F.   I liked the way the subject was presented to me by Louis Meisel who was asked by Stewart Speizer to commission artists to paint pictures of airplanes for his collection. At first I rejected the proposal saying, "I don't do airplanes," but I was told I could do anything with the subject that I wanted to. I could paint any kind of airplane. It could be a still life with an airplane on a table. I found that kind of freedom quite acceptable and exciting. The airplane on the left is a plastic toy bomber and the one down on the right is a Douglas jet trainer. The other is a Pan American passenger plane. I chose model boxes because I spent many hours as a child making models out of balsa wood and I also liked the volumetric aspect of them.

C.N.   I see you also put yourself in the painting overtly by including images of your paint jars and your necklace.

A.F.   Well, these still lifes all have to do with me. I made model airplanes, I wear *Jolie Madame,* my family gambled, and I play solitaire, which, by the way, is going to be my next painting.

C.N.   Both *Spitfire* and *Royal Flush* are very ambitiously composed paintings. There is so much movement in them—so much representation of pure energy.

A.F.   Yes. I have looked at my work as opposed to the work of Photorealists who were not Abstract Expressionists and I really can see its influence. Look at *Royal Flush* on the abstract level. Those two cigars, both diagonals, are a powerful force. So is the cigarette. The ace of spades is on that angle so there is an abstract balance that is taking place. These are monumental opposing forces which are carefully placed. I wanted to get a feeling of the tremendous motion of these forces that are flying against each other.

C.N.   This painting also has a tremendously expansive field which seems to suggest the image could extend past the canvas space in the same way as in a Morris Louis painting. Yet I think your work relates to the past as well as to contemporary art. For instance, do you feel any affinity with the Dutch still lifes that reveal a joy in material existence?

A.F.   Yes. The Dutch were interested in beauty and didn't just paint the ugly things around them. They were affirmative and would paint the full substance of their own lives. This includes the beautiful as well as the commonplace. But their attitude is one of acceptance rather than derision. Did you read the reviews of *Jolie Madame*? Rosalyn Drexler, in the *New York Times,* set the pattern for the interpretations. "Audrey Flack's painting *Jolie Madame* is a wholly satisfying painting 'in drag.' It is gorgeous, decadent, oppulent and jeweled. It is vulgar and risky: a powerful comment on the artificiality and absurdity of the good life. This painting is one of the most beautiful-ugly paintings I have ever seen." We should reexamine the current attitudes toward the concepts of beauty and ugliness. I think we have been brainwashed into believing that *beauty* is a bad word and *ugly* is a terrific word. *Cool* is desirable while *feeling* and *emotion* are put down. One must not paint beautiful objects. If you do you are labeled bourgeois and the bourgeois is scorned in the art world. I am not making any statement about bourgeois vulgarity. I paint the things that interest me—some are expensive, some are very cheap. How much is a rose? Why should a painting of a beautiful flower and jewels be ugly? But this painting was powerful and the art world had to deal with it, so it became the most beautiful-ugly painting. Not that I believe that beauty can't come out of a variety of subject matter. Grünewald's Isenheim altarpiece is a classic example. Although Christ is all gangrenous, pockmarked, and bleeding, it's a beautiful work because it's painted exquisitely. If you are out for beauty you can take any subject and make it so.

C.N.   It's a matter of where you choose to turn your eyes.

A.F.   I'm tired of put-downs. If we can have some kind of reaffirmation and help other people, or add a touch of beauty to the world, why not?

Kennedy Motorcade—Nov. 22, 1963, 1963–64.

Harry Truman's Teachers, ca. 1965.

The Farb Family, 1969–70.

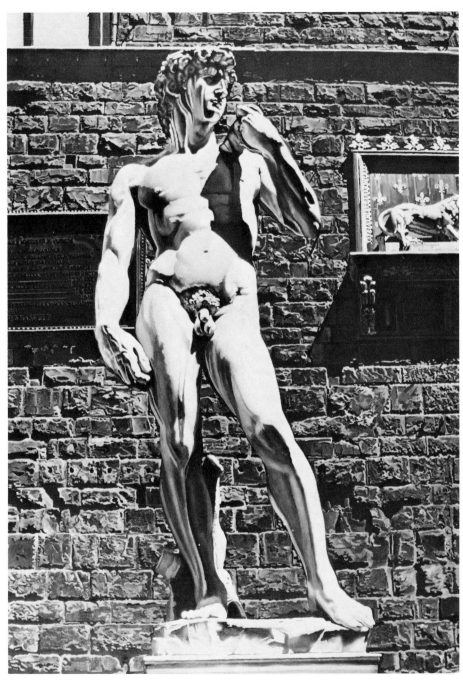

Michelangelo's David, 1971.

Macarena Esperanza, 1971.

Royal Flush, 1974.

Strawberry Tart, 1974.

Nancy Grossman, 1974.

ANCY GROSSMAN was born in New York City in 1940 and grew up in Oneonta, New York. Later she returned to New York to study art and graduated from Pratt Institute with a B.F.A. in 1962.

Grossman began as a painter in 1963 doing landscapes and female figures in an Abstract Expressionist manner. Her large, centrally placed forms, created out of brilliantly colored, ragged strokes of paint, seem to explode off the canvas surface. They resemble primal, matriarchal forces merging with the earth and vegetation as they struggle toward individuation.

Concerned with the relationships between men and women as well as between woman and nature, Grossman produced a series of lithographs, also in 1963, dealing rather explicitly with heterosexual tensions. From then on her works became more abstract, focusing on internal visceral elements. Her drawings of 1965–67 grouped intestine-like coils together with motor-like cogs and wheels to evoke the inner workings of some strange, anthropomorphized machines. Along with these drawings, the artist constructed collages out of "found objects," as well as metal and leather pieces, in which visceral and sexual imagery abound. Among these works, there are what the artist calls "women landscapes"; *The Bride* (1966), with its tondo format and unlaced slit suggests vaginal symbolism while *Yuma* or *Rust and Blue* (1967) with its more tubular extrusions are phallic in imagery. The seemingly casual placement of the materials, the frontal composition, the successions of planes created by the varying dimensions of the shapes, reveal a basic Cubist structure sifted through an Abstract Expressionist sensibility.

Then in 1968, Grossman shifted once more from abstractions of internal configurations to depictions of exterior human physiognomy. Instead of tortured leather insides spilling forth, leather enshrouds decapitated heads, covering eyes and binding mouths. These first sculptures are dumb and blind images of anguish. Others grow in size, develop necks, and reveal gnashing teeth. The sex of these creatures remains indeterminate until 1972. At an exhibition that year at the Cordier and Ekstrom Gallery, a distraught figure of a man, zippered and strapped into a clinging leather suit, reveals the sexual identity of the heretofore neuter images. Head thrown back, arms up-raised, a trapped human being struggles in his death throes. In his beautifully molded form and tragic situation he is a descendant of Michelangelo's *Dying Slave*.

Indeed, in Grossman's recent 1973 exhibition, images of death and distruction are prevalent. Drawings of men with horns or guns protruding from their foreheads, sometimes echoed by the depiction of an erect penis, suggest metaphors for the violence males do simultaneously to themselves and to others. Yet while Grossman is a feminist, she is not a man-hater. Her exquisite portrayal of the male body, along with her empathetic treatment of the male as both victim and victimizer, can be interpreted as an outcry transcending sexual bounds against all forms of human degradation.

CINDY NEMSER   What was your earlier work like?

NANCY GROSSMAN   In 1962 I did a whole series of landscapes but they were internal landscapes. I would ride along a road in the country and imagine I was seeing the landscape underneath the ground. Here is an example. It's a thundering, moving, underground landscape, almost volcanic. I used a lot of color, very arbitrarily. Next, in 1963, come paintings of mostly female figures. They are part of the landscape, merging with it. I would imagine that some of these figurative paintings were buried in the ground like seeds. I was using the figure like a plant, a tree.

C.N.   What you are saying is that the human and the landscape are not separate but are part of each other?

N.G.   Yes. But these figures also look as if they are worried to death. They are part of the landscape but something outside is attacking them. Birds are attacking them. I was not conscious of that when I did the paintings. When I work I just know if it is right or wrong. It has to do with the way I feel. If I have an honest feeling about what I am doing then it is a better work. But I don't verbalize it. I have a terrific need to do whatever I am doing at the time. There is a difference in making a work from the outside in rather than from the inside out. We use our brains in either case but in a different way. When you work from the outside of a thing you make yourself a problem, formalize it. It limits your feelings.

C.N.   Here's another painting of a woman. It has such brilliant color and very heavy, thick paint strokes. But I don't think these paintings are uncontrolled. They are in an expressionist vein but the subject and the handling are very much in harmony. You are not just throwing color around.

N.G.   That's a woman who is dancing. She is strutting, really strutting.

C.N.   She is part of the vegetation or landscape around her. Lee Krasner did a painting called *Visitation.* It is very abstract but there is a woman in it. This would be a marvelous companion piece for it. It would be interesting to see those two paintings in conjunction with Willem de Kooning's paintings of women. He seems to hate women.

N.G.   Did you ever think that was a subjective feeling on your part?

C.N.   I look at the way he portrays women. They are witches with gaping mouths.

N.G.   But these are too. It's a funny thing. Do you choose a thing or does it choose you? I have a feeling that whatever you become fixated on becomes your subject. It's significant for you. You're involved with it because you are acting on it. It can be very ambivalent. It can be terrifying. For myself, I was a woman, but what women did I know? Who were these paintings? Were they my mother? Were they me? I never have had that distance.

C.N.   We are into the problem of the artist's intentions versus the end result of his or her work. Often there may be things in the work that the artist never consciously put there. Then the viewer may read things into the work that come out of his or her own needs. All I know is that I see hostility in de Kooning's portrayal of women. I see other things in your work—a certain wildness, excitement.

N.G.   I looked at these works after many years of not looking at them. It was absolutely right for me to be doing them that way then, but it was wild and frenzied.

C.N.   It's very hard to categorize these paintings. They are intense but there is about them a sense of release, a certain celebration.

N.G.   This one is a bit of a Medusa. She is alone with these flowers and she is very tough.

C.N.   But you are not making her evil or demonic. It's a positive presentation.

N.G.   I am a woman. I could never feel that a woman is a strange creature in a way that a man could—but that's not true! Some of my work is frightening. My own work has the power to make me ill sometimes, when I get close to whatever I don't know about myself inside.

C.N.   How did you personally feel about being a woman?

N.G.   I was always rebellious. I wanted to consider myself a woman rather than a property, my father's or my mother's. I learned the way women are supposed to be from my mother but I didn't want to be an extension of her. Even now I spar with my mother.

C.N.   How old were you when you did these paintings?

N.G.   I was twenty-two.

C.N.   How old are you now?

N.G.   Thirty-three.

C.N.   That was in '63 before there was what we now call a woman's consciousness.

N.G.   I wanted to be a woman—to make myself.

C.N.   But there was no role model around for you. You had to invent her.

N.G.   I found a way but it was hard. It caused me terrible pain and anxiety. I had a hard time with it and with other people. I had a hard time with men. I saw myself as failing to be the prescription woman. I was not typical and there was no support. I couldn't find a model. Everybody has to have somebody to look up to. Who was I going to follow? I knew how my mother did it and what I had to do to be my mother but that's not what I was looking for. I was looking for somebody else and I would watch with bated breath. If I knew of any woman artist (I never knew any personally), I would watch to see what she did. In the end I could never relate to the existing ones.

C.N.   Well there was really no way. All the women artists were so separated from each other. They weren't even acknowledging themselves as women. It wasn't thought out or conscious.

N.G.   I had consciousness-raising way back in those days in the sense that I did find an ally who was a woman and an artist. There was nobody to say, "Gee, you are great," and to give you a kiss on both cheeks, but we used to shiver together. And we hurrahed each other. We dared ourselves and each other. It was the saving grace. We would go to the artists' bars, Old Stanley's Tavern on the East Side and to Max's Kansas City when it first opened. We would pretend we didn't know anything about art because we knew how unsafe it would be for us to say we were artists. You always had to be combative unless there were people you knew there. We would pretend to be hairdressers or manicurists. Our real life as artists was a secret.

C.N.   What did you think of the art world?

N.G.   There was a time I felt there was such a camaraderie, a closeness, a mutual admiration between artists, but then I withdrew from artists and the art world about the time Soho was coming into being. The men your own age were always out to get you. If they couldn't get something out of you they wanted to put something in. If you admire somebody, how are you going to admire them? Are you going to devour them to make yourself bigger and fatter with them inside you? I got very cynical about it. That's why I stayed away from artists entirely then.

C.N.   That's why I had to stay away from the women artists' groups. They wanted to devour everyone.

N.G.   Maybe someday they will become human and realize that without ego there wouldn't be life. When I went to the women's groups no one ever said, "How do you do sister." They didn't know anything about me.

C.N.   Did you go to the meetings?

N.G.   Sure I did. One day they were writing proposals to send to all the museums in New York, to the Guggenheim, the Museum of Modern Art, and so on. I sat there quietly listening. They were writing proposals, okaying them, changing them. Then I said, "It sounds good to me but what if all the museums accept your proposals? Do you all have the work to show in those places?" I was thinking about it in real terms. They looked at me. "What do you mean?" I got hot under the collar because they looked at me as if I were being subversive. They got into a whole discussion about juries, how work is judged, and how it shouldn't be judged. The whole idea of quality disappeared. Then Nancy disappeared. I couldn't identify with that. I had worked so hard in my life. The whole idea of being good doesn't have to do with being as good as Joe Schmoe. You have to compare yourself with everything that has gone before and everything that is contemporary.

C.N.   Many of those women don't have anything of their own and it's too painful to have people in their midst who are really gifted. It means they have to admit their own inadequacies.

N.G.   But they could support each other. Their work could be the thing they have in common with a fellow creative person. We are all trying to make something. There is a common ground on which to communicate and feel stronger. You can be bolstered by the existence of other people doing the same thing—even in a different discipline. But these women didn't want that. Their politics was only a fashionable, ridiculous, passing thing. As a woman I am very suspicious of the gains made by the movement across the board. I know it has to be carried by individuals.

C.N.   But in relating your attitudes as a woman to these women, in your paintings wouldn't you say they are the strong women that you wanted to find? Each is big and powerful.

N.G.   Some of them are frightening. I didn't assume it was my own life, but maybe I acted out my stress. Yet some of the women are very tender and the men too. I felt for them. I felt for people. But I wasn't conscious. I never separated it out in that way.

C.N.   But you are trying now to be as honest as you can about the way you felt then. Art done in the past is always being judged from the present and reinterpreted. It really doesn't matter if you weren't consciously articulating those motivations. They were there. But let's go back to your beginnings. When did you decide you wanted to be an artist?

N.G.   When I was a little kid I always drew on the walls, on books, on scrap paper. I loved to draw. It was something to rejoice upon. It was magical. That was the first power. But nobody ever made much of the fact.

C.N.   You come from a Jewish family, don't you?

N.G.   Italian and Jewish. My mother is Italian, my father Jewish. I was the oldest of five children, I have three sisters and one brother, and I feel as if I had raised them. I was responsible for them most of the time since both my parents worked. We went through some really poor times.

C.N.   Where did you grow up?

N.G.   I was born in New York City but when I was six my mother, her two sisters, and their husbands all bought a farm in Oneonta, New York. There were sixteen kids in the house.

C.N.   So you really lived a rural life in the midst of the country surrounded by all the mountains in upstate New York. That isn't a place where people are encouraged to be artists. When did you actually decide that would be your profession?

N.G.   It had to do with my life. I was very unhappy when I was an adolescent. I was always in hot water. I couldn't wait to get away from that town. I said I wanted to go to art school but it was just an arbitrary choice on my part. I thought when I was in high school that if you had a career as an artist it meant you made pictures for magazines and books that you sold. I never knew until I was in art school that I could actually go back to my childhood. I never knew people were free to do that. I didn't know that I could be a painter—that there was such a profession.

C.N.   Where did you go to study art?

N.G.   I went to Pratt. The first year I was very naive. I took the basic courses and felt very backwards. During that first year my family was having a hard time and they moved to Arizona. I was seventeen. In the summer I went back to my family in Arizona and my father said, "Now we need you here." I said, "Dad, I have to go back to school." He didn't talk to me. He would not physically give me his ear. He would just disappear, go to work, come home. I couldn't talk to him. I was very upset and depressed. I was afraid that that was the end. My father didn't speak to me that whole summer. I had a friend at Pratt with whom I had talked about taking an apartment. I wrote and told her it was all over. She said, "Don't give up like that. I'll talk to the department chairman."

C.N.   Where did you get money to live on?

N.G.   My father said he didn't have it. But my friend found out about student government loans and I submitted drawings for a competitive scholarship and I won. I also had three different jobs. I worked my way through school. And I was so scared. It was terrifying. That is why I mentioned my father not talking to me. It was so terrible to go against his will. He would always say, "Are you asking me or telling me?" I wasn't ready to be the child who stands alone. I terrified myself by making that move. But I did it.

C.N.   It's amazing that you had the will.

N.G.   I paid for it in a lot of ways. I was always terrified and anxious and guilty too.

C.N.   Did your parents have a different attitude about your brother's education?

N.G.   My brother is the person who is most like me. We have the same kind of personality and got into the same kind of trouble—wanting too much.

C.N.   Usually Jewish parents want their children to move ahead and be educated and successful.

N.G.   But I wasn't going to be the son, the doctor, and neither was my brother.

C.N.   They didn't take the idea of your being an artist seriously?

N.G.   It was never taken seriously and until very recently whenever I would see my family they would say, "Gee honey, can't you do that on the side?" That's still how it is.

C.N.   But I saw your aunt at your opening at the Cordier and Ekstrom Gallery.

N.G.   Now it is okay because, as in everything else in America, it's alright if you can make some kind of a success.

C.N.   I know even if you were going to be a doctor it would have been tough for you. But as a woman wanting to be an artist it was worse.

N.G. It was "When are you going to do real things? Like getting married and making grandchildren for us?" Then they stopped.

C.N. But you are not married.

N.G. No.

C.N. Do you think that marriage would be a problem? That a woman can't be married and be an artist?

N.G. I think there are as many arrangements as there are human beings. Now I look back and I realize that much of my problem was getting rid of what my parents dictated to me unconsciously. I was overly handled. I was a kid who was quite difficult so I was smacked around a lot. The body can be violated in one way or another. It begins a chain of circumstances in which it feels very natural to be violated, for people to violate your head, to take advantage of you. I have really suffered a great deal.

C.N. I hope you will get past that.

N.G. I want to. I stake my whole life on it.

C.N. You have done a lot to overcome all that already.

N.G. It's hard work and it has taken such a long time. I'll tell you something. It isn't a matter of work. I wouldn't have survived without it. But violence has not been invaluable. It's energy. I have a lot of energy.

C.N. Some people are threatened by it. But I guess it can be used.

N.G. Before it was working against me. But if I couldn't tolerate the way I was and chopped that part away, I would have had to sacrifice my whole self. Well I didn't hate all of myself but it was very hard not to be angry and not to distrust myself.

C.N. Your anger shouldn't be directed at yourself.

N.G. It started that way. There was no place else for it to go. People have children and the children make noise, ask questions, bring undue attention to their parents in public, make them furious, make them confront themselves. This makes the parents crazy. They don't know what they are going to do. Stomp on it. Stop it before it multiplies. They become very brutal in trying to stop it, to keep it down. When it is your own aliveness that has been set upon, what are you going to do? It takes a long time to undo what many people have done to you.

C.N. It's a marvelous thing to stop feeling guilty. Eva Hesse knew that in the end. She said she learned she had a right to live even if she wasn't an artist. Often we keep on paying and we don't know what we are paying for.

C.N.   Like in Duchamp's *Great Glass*—Duchamp and Picabia were using that imagery. But your works have none of that biting humor that twists in on itself. There is no irony. The sensibility is different.

N.G.   You could say I am lacking in male critical intelligence.

C.N.   I could never say that.

N.G.   I mean the irony which stands outside something, stating it, surrounding it with words, so as to make it more valid, less of a necessity for you to have done the thing.

C.N.   I know what you are talking about. As a writer of art criticism I have been told I was not cerebral enough, that I was too personal, that writing must be kept formal, distanced, cerebral.

N.G.   That's outrageous.

C.N.   Yes, but your comment about your own work is equally outrageous. It would never have entered my mind to say your work lacked critical intelligence. Is that an attribute only given to male minds?

N.G.   I feel anyone who does anything great in art and culture is out of control. It is done by people who are possessed. Anyone who is going to practice on the piano twenty-two hours a day is crazy. He or she has to be crazy and it is an embarrassment to deal with crazy people. So there is a great attempt to formalize art, to contain it, to hold its bowels. Everyone is trying to hold their bowels, to be properly toilet trained. Yet the whole exciting thing about art has to do with being out of control. It has to do with real things.

C.N.   Yet there is always control when there is art because if one articulates, makes form, one cannot really be out of control.

N.G.   I don't mean insanity. I mean the powerful impulse to do a thing. Then after that impulse is sifted through the discipline still something of its beginnings are showing and exciting people. But there is a terror too. And it is always met with great ambivalence. Sometimes with blindness. But if we can sing a catchy tune about it or if it can be described in twenty-six words—then you are *in,* kid. But I don't have to stand and look at it.

C.N.   Yes. It's frightening. You are articulating things that people don't want to think about or deal with. Then they react with hostility. They don't want to look your way. They'd rather pretend you are not there. But ultimately they can't.

N.G.   But they can. Even though there have been great women artists in Western history, even if they made a loud noise and were impossible to ignore, people couldn't wait to forget them, to throw dirt on their faces, on their graves. That's one way of revenge.

C.N.   We can only try to go on. A large part of getting recognition is what you do for yourself. What made you decide to use leather in your collages?

N.G.   I always liked it. It lent itself to whatever I wanted to do with it. If there had been some other material available I might have used it.

C.N.   But leather has certain connotations.

N.G.   In earlier days leather meant aviators and football players, later it was motorcyclists. It is a tough material yet it is flexible. I use leather as lines in these collages. The straps are linear elements. In this one the straps are very heavy and cumbersome. I use these straps as if I were drawing with lines. I made them come out in the same way as one uses steel rods in a steel sculpture—as a linear element as opposed to a sheet of steel.

C.N.   Your sensibility is related to that of the Abstract Expressionists?

N.G.   Absolutely. Maybe it was because I was a kid then and it was the first art in the world that I was confronted with that I understood something about. I made these constructions like an Abstract Expressionist painting. I never made a sketch. I never had a preconceived idea. I just put it down and followed it through. It seems a funny thing to do with such cumbersome material but when I am working this way those materials are nothing to me. I could draw with straps, I could draw with thirty-pound pieces of steel, if I had to. I set them in place and it becomes a great challenge to me that they be well made and solid. I do it quickly with no sweat. I was always good with my hands in terms of drawing.

   This collage is kind of obscene. It's called *The Bride*.

C.N.   I see it's a tondo and it has sewing on it. Did you see it as a woman's sexual organ, a vagina?

N.G.   I was unconscious of that. I have a couple of others like that. The others are landscapes—women landscapes.

C.N.   This black tubular piece is even more threatening than the women landscapes. I see them as something torn, as if someone's insides were being pulled apart.

N.G.   In 1966 I didn't even see the outside of the skin. It didn't even occur to me that there was an outside or an inside. When something came toward me I saw it with an x-ray vision. I was concerned with the activity of it but that activity took form like the earlier landscapes. We know what is on top of the ground but if we want to evoke the real landscape it is underneath the ground.

C.N.   I remember Eva Hesse talked about how she got into sculpture from painting. She wanted to go beyond the canvas and to draw in space. Were you after the same thing?

N.G.   Yes.

C.N.   I'm surprised you and Eva never met.

N.G.   It is shocking. People always asked me about it. They would swear that we talked together.

C.N.   You have much in common but there were things about Eva you might not have liked. She could play games. She wanted to be with the right people and was anxious to be accepted in the right art circles. After she became ill she put a lot of that aside. But she was terribly insecure.

N.G.   I was always terribly insecure too.

C.N.   But you don't behave as Eva did. She referred to herself as either the cockroach or the queen. You don't see yourself that way.

N.G.   No, there has to be some consistency inside and outside.

C.N.   How did you come to do the kind of leather-bound heads that you have become known for?

N.G.   I had to stop working all during the sixties to get any kind of job I could. I had done things like painting butcher shops and the amount of money I was getting for it was ridiculous. Later I discovered I could illustrate children's books. Then in 1965 I won a Guggenheim and I worked wonderfully that year. A lot of this work I have been showing you.was done in 1965. After that I had to get work. I had trouble getting freelance illustration jobs and finally I decided that instead of taking jobs on and off and having to tear myself away from my own work I would take three or four jobs at a time and buy myself a year. I would provide myself with my own scholarship. I started to illustrate books and I locked myself out of my own studio. This was a terrible thing for me to do because if there is one concentration of ego in my whole self it is in my work. My work is my worth to myself. I loved it. It was my life. Without it I would have been stepped on, blotted out completely. The illustrations took me about three or four months longer than I had imagined they would. Doing them changed me totally. From being all action and little reflection I was stuck with my legs chained to the table night and day. It changed my metabolism. I used to dance; I stopped dancing. I didn't walk. I just sat there and illustrated children's books. I was depressed. When I finally came back to my studio I couldn't relate to my work at all. Energy itself was terrifying to me. I had so quieted down from my imprisonment that I was in despair. I couldn't find myself. I associated objects, materials, leather with my work, not with the repeatograph pen that I used to do the illustrations. But when I came to the studio I had the pen in my hand and it was like an extension of my arm. I started making drawings. The first one is right there. It was the drawing of a head, belted up, closed up, and I felt as if I had done something dirty and secret. My work had not been specifically figurative like that for years and years since I was a student. But now it was necessary and I made another one and another one. I didn't show this work to anyone at first. But these drawings were so right to me that I decided to make them even more real. I decided to make them more physically there. Then I started to make the sculptures of heads and it seemed natural after my drawing with leather that the coverings of the heads should be leather. I never showed my work to anyone. Not even my dealer Krasner knew what I was doing. I thought of it as something that I was doing in secret. Then after a year and a half a friend of mine saw the heads and said, "These are wonderful." Then another friend saw them and said, "Oh I didn't know you went in for that kind of thing." I said, "What kind of thing?" He said, "Stop by my store. I have some photographs for you to see." He had these photographs of S and M people. I got so upset. I had never heard of such a thing, never seen anything like that. Now a few years have passed and I have had time to reflect on it. But that is everywhere whether it is dressed in chiffon or leather. This is the way human beings are. Everything in the world seems to be that way. But coming up against that so suddenly was really a terrible crisis for me.

C.N.   It is as if you had to say "What am I?"

N.G.   That is precisely what the crisis was. I said, "I must be one of those people." Yet those things I did were so private and felt so right. Then I thought there must be a whole bunch of people just like me. I was terrified of whoever they were. It was very strange and very shocking. I realized there were such things but I didn't go looking for those people, looking in S and M bars. I asked myself if it had to do with honesty. I have to have honesty because there is no other way for me to survive. But who feels like vomiting? Who likes unpleasantness? Yet I feel that if I hadn't made that work I wouldn't have been able to survive. I am always thrown up against something that threatens to kill me.

C.N.   You must get it out.

N.G.   I have to work it through and then I realize it was what I had to find out.

C.N.   How did this work come to be shown in the Cordier and Ekstrom Gallery?

N.G.   I started to make the head sculptures during that later part of '67 and the beginning of '68. I knew I wanted someone who could do something with the work when I decided to show it. I had a friend who saw the work and said, "I think I know who would be interested." He spoke to Mr. Ekstrom. One day I brought in two shopping bags with some head sculptures and a few drawings in them. Mr. Ekstrom was in the process of moving from one gallery to another. He was distracted and had a friend there too but he said, "I will call you." He did call and said he would like to come to my studio and see more work. He came and said, "Well I don't know if I could live with these things." Mr. Ekstrom has very strong convictions about what he shows, very personal feelings. I think he's a wonderful dealer because of that. If he decides to show something he really believes in it. Well after a few weeks he decided that he did want to show my work. It was a wonderful break that changed my fortune in the world.

C.N.   Your latest drawings are even more aggressive than before.

N.G.   I am not self-conscious about it anymore. They feel so natural to me.

C.N.   They are filled with guns and horns.

N.G.   The gun is an extension of the person. It is always coming out of the head. People scream at you. They shoot you with their words.

C.N.   It's interesting that it's males who are being tied up in your drawings.

N.G.   They are not *being* tied up. They are tied up. When I had made these sculptures for a year and then found out about S and M, I asked myself, "Are these voodoo dolls? Am I sticking pins in and tying them up or am I making something that is already there?" It was natural for me to feel that way for personal reasons.

C.N.   Are you saying that that is where you are?

N.G.   I see things that way.

C.N.   This is part of the human condition, but it's only one part of it.

N.G.   It's personal. If someone says something terrible or wonderful about your work, it's paralyzing. That happened after I showed these sculptures. They got a wonderful response, wonderful reviews, but it was so controversial that I became self-conscious. I had to start investigating why it looked this way. "Who am I?" "What state am I in in my life?" "Where is my head at?" "Is it tied down?" And it was. I can see that now.

C.N. That strikes me as strange because when I speak with you I don't feel you are tied up.

N.G. But how do you know how people really live? I can talk about it because I decided to go into analysis. Many people are afraid of such things but I forced myself to articulate some of them.

C.N. And by giving external form to your internal feeling you articulate feelings we all have? When people see your work they immediately relate to it on a gut level. It touches a universal cord.

N.G. But I didn't set out to do social work for myself or for anybody else. If I could articulate all this in words and make the same thing happen for myself, I would. Why bother with the studio, all this junk, wood, splinters? I would just carry a piece of paper with me and would write it down. I would love to do that, but I can't.

C.N. Who's to say your way is not as communicative. There is a great response to and fascination with your encased, zippered-up heads. At the time they appeared they articulated the isolation people were feeling but couldn't express.

N.G. You asked me about using leather before. Someone else asked why I use leather and I said, "I always liked it. I used to wear leather. I like how it feels. It is very sensuous and it breathes and you never get too warm. If you fall while you are wearing it you don't get scratched. For these reasons it is a wonderful material." Then this person said something that really struck home. "Why do you have to wear another skin? Isn't your own thick enough?" I was stunned. That's what it was. I was walking around with my own skin and another one just to be safe.

C.N. It's interesting that the figures you have been doing for the last few years are all men.

N.G. Whenever I wanted to say something specific, personal, to the effect that I am a woman, I would use a woman's image if the work were figurative. It seemed natural. But if I wanted to say something in general, I would use a man. It's as if man was our society. Yet I don't feel that the male forms are outside of me. I don't feel I have to conform to a political identification although, naturally, I'm a feminist. But if we have to split hairs, I'm a humanist.

C.N. That's what feminism is all about—being treated like a human being.

N.G. I've always had a tremendous problem fulfilling the perscription for being a woman with a capital W. But my heart always went out to the men too and the pressures they have felt. I have known the most macho men, the biggest phonies, the biggest latent homosexuals but also, happily for me, I have also known very gentle, feeling, human men. I have been both very unlucky and very lucky in that. I could never honestly slice the cake one way and say, "This is how it is, red on this side, black on that side."

C.N.   But it's men you tied up.

N.G.   Yes, they are men. On the other hand, I use the word figure. Even when you tried to dissect the things that look like machine parts. I always said these are figures too.

C.N.   But a gun is usually equated with a phallus.

N.G.   So is an erect person. An erect woman is phallic, standing straight up. She is a figure. Anything that is higher than it is wide is a figure. Human beings read that way, animals too. If we stand up, we are erections. Then when we back into the earth we are all female. The earth is female and we become part of it again. The life force is an erection. Is that a very sexist male way of looking at things?

C.N.   These drawings of men with horns coming out of their heads and guns where their penises should be can be read as anti-male statements. The male organ is equated with a weapon of violence and aggression.

N.G.   I don't make that equation. The figure, male or female, is an erect phallus since it is walking upright on the earth. Its head, which is equivalent to the head of the phallus, is its most aggressive part. After all, your head which is the seat of your hang-ups is also your most powerful organ, not your penis or your vagina. I know male artists experience making art in a so-called very female way. It is not about getting a hard-on. The whole concept of inspiration is about being filled. Actually in this act of art-making we are really bi-sexual and it's too bad the word is so distorted and politicized at this point. People feel so fugitive about saying it and will insist everything is black and white while the world is graying all around them.

C.N.   So you are insisting that the head as well as the sexual parts, the intellect as well as the instinct, are both male and female attributes.

N.G.   I don't believe in acting dumb.

C.N.   That's why I resent people like Judy Chicago insisting women are asserting their identity by painting their vaginas. I'm not only a vagina. I want to be able to write about my feelings and not be put down for doing it, but I am not about to disallow my intellect. I have a brain and I have worked hard to learn how to use it.

N.G.   And the head is where the power is.

C.N.   Why should it be either-or? Someone like Chicago is working for the worst kind of sexist male who wants to continue to stereotype women. There is a pseudo-masculine cult that denies feeling, emotions, and personal experience, but that's not what real masculinity is all about.

N.G.   Yes, those men are tied up. Wherever there is a taboo against living; to have a head and no feelings, to have a vagina and not fill it, to have a penis and not to stick it in—that is not living. To be a woman and not to be able to experience your power, your aggression, or your passivity, is not to be alive.

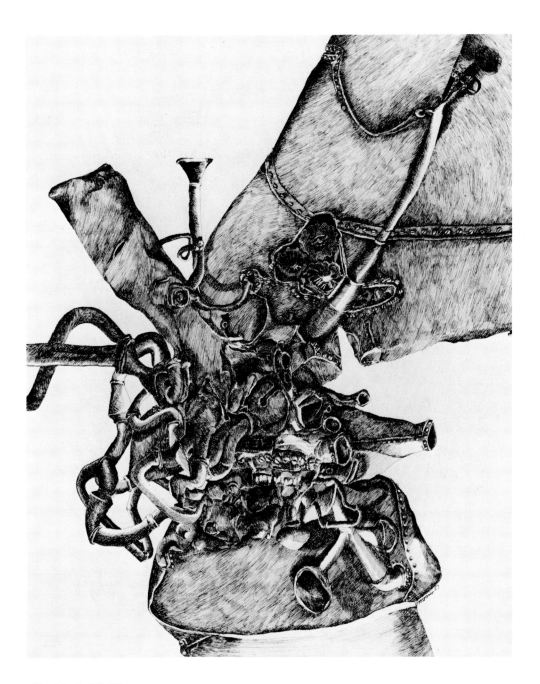

Untitled, 1967.

Yum (or Rust and Blue), 1967.

Bride, 1966.

Unfinished—Andro Series, 1969–71.

Slave 2, 1967.

Male Figure Study, 1969.

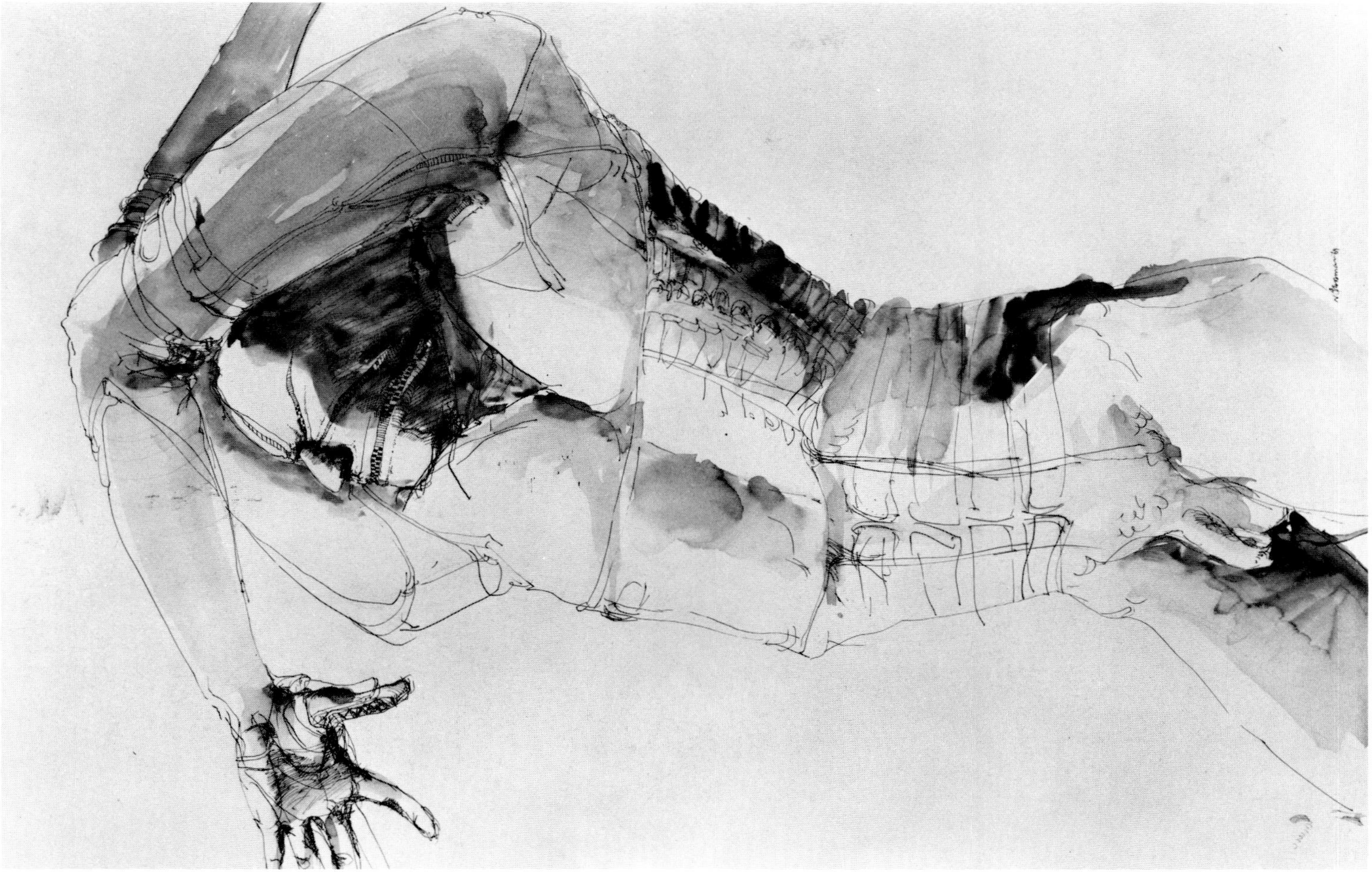

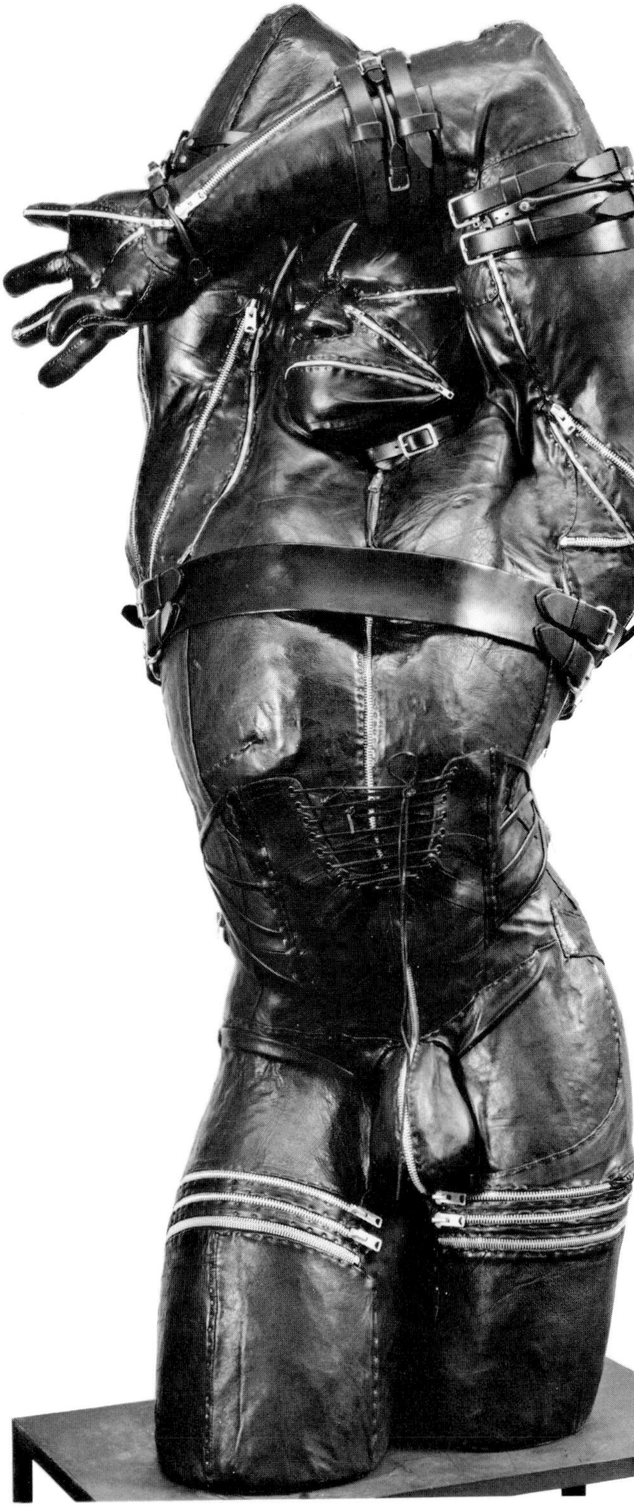

Figure Sculpture, 1971.

Portrait of A.E., 1973.

Head. "Kazakh." 1971.

Selected Bibliography

BOOKS AND PUBLICATIONS ON WOMEN ARTISTS

Baker, Elizabeth, and Hess, Thomas B., eds. *Art and Sexual Politics.* Art News Service, Macmillan Pub. Co., Inc. New York: Viking Press Paperback, 1973.

A Documentary History of Women Artists in Revolution, Jacqueline Skiles and Janet McDevitt, eds. New York: Women's Interart Center, 549 W. 52 St., 1971.

Female Artists Past and Present. Coordinator, Vicki Lynn Hill. Berkeley, Calif.: Women's History Research Center., Inc., 2325 Oak St., 1974.

The Feminist Art Journal, ed. Cindy Nemser, 41 Montgomery Place, Brooklyn, New York 11215.

Sex Differentials in Art Exhibition Reviews: A Statistical Survey, Rosalie Brauetigan, Bettye Fiske, and June Wayne, eds. Los Angeles, Calif.: Tamarind Lithography Workshop, Inc., 112 N. Tamarind Ave., 1972.

Sheehan, Valerie Harms, ed. *Unmasking: Ten Women in Metamorphosis.* Chicago: Swallow Press, 1973.

Woman Space Journal, ed. Ruth Iskin, 793 South Grandview, Los Angeles.

EXHIBITIONS, CATALOGUES, MONOGRAPHS

BARBARA HEPWORTH (1903–)

1950   "Retrospective: Barbara Hepworth," XXV Biennale, Venice, organized by the British Council.

1954   "Barbara Hepworth Retrospective: 1927–54," Whitechapel Art Gallery, London.

1955–56   "Barbara Hepworth, Retrospective Exhibition," touring the United States and Canada. Walker Art Center, Minneapolis; University of Nebraska Galleries; San Francisco Museum of Art; Albright-Knox Art Gallery, Buffalo; Art Gallery of Toronto; Montreal Museum of Fine Art; Baltimore Museum of Art.

1963   *Single Form,* United Nations, New York, comm. by Blaustein Foundation as a Memorial to Dag Hammarskjold, H. 252".

1965–66   "Barbara Hepworth: Retrospective," Rijksmuseum Kröller-Müller, Otterlo, The Netherlands.

1970   "Barbara Hepworth: Retrospective," Tate Gallery, London.

1970   "Barbara Hepworth," Marlborough Fine Art Ltd. (London) and Marlborough Gallery, Inc., New York.

1970–71   *Theme and Variations,* comm. by Cheltenham and Gloucester Building Society, Head Office, Cheltenham, England, L 300".

1972   "Barbara Hepworth, The Family of Man: Nine Bronzes," Marlborough Gallery, New York.

1974   "Barbara Hepworth: Conversations," Marlborough Gallery, Inc., New York.

Bowness, Alan, *Barbara Hepworth—Drawings from a Sculptor's Landscape.* Bath: Cory, Adams and Mackay, 1966.

_____, *Barbara Hepworth,* 1960–69. London: Lund Humphries, 1971.

Hammacher, A.M., *Barbara Hepworth.* London: Modern Sculpture Series, A. Zwemmer, 1958.

_____, *Barbara Hepworth.* London: World of Art Series, Thames and Hudson, 1968.

Hepworth, Barbara, *Barbara Hepworth—A Pictorial Autobiography.* Bath: Adams and Dart, 1970.

Hodin, J. P., *Barbara Hepworth, Life and Work.* London: Lund Humphries, 1961.

Marlborough, New York, *Barbara Hepworth: 'Conversations,'* March-April, 1974. (Intro. by Dore Ashton.)

Read, Herbert, *Barbara Hepworth, Carvings and Drawings.* London: Lund Humphries, 1952. (Intro. by Herbert Read, notes by the artist.)

SONIA DELAUNAY (1885–   )

1964	"Exhibition of the Delaunay Donation," National Museum of Modern Art, Louvre, Paris.
1965	"Robert and Sonia Delaunay," Traveling Exhibition in Canada: Ottawa, Toronto, Montreal, Winnipeg, Regina and Quebec.
1967	"Sonia Delaunay" (Retrospective), National Museum of Modern Art, Louvre, Paris.
1969	"Sonia Delaunay," Gimpel and Weitzenhoffer Gallery, New York.
1972	"Robert and Sonia Delaunay," Museum of Fine Arts, Nancy, France.
1972	"The Aubusson Tapestries of Sonia Delaunay," Corcoran Gallery, Washington, D.C.; Museum of Modern Art of The City of Paris.
1973	"Sonia Delaunay," Museum of La Rochelle, France.
1973	"Sonia Delaunay, Tapestries," Museum of Angers.
1973–74	"Sonia Delaunay, Tapestries, Gouaches, Lithographs," Aberbach Fine Art, New York.
1974	"Sonia Delaunay" (Retrospective), Museum of Grenoble, France.

Cohen, Arthur, *Sonia Delaunay.* New York: Harry N. Abrams Inc., 1975.

Delaunay, Sonia, *Sonia Delaunay, ses peintures, ses objets, ses modes.,* foreword by André l'Hote, poems by Cendrars, Delteil, Tzara, Soupault. Paris: Librairie des Arts Décoratifs, 1925.

Delaunay, Sonia, *Alphabet and Robes-Poèmes,* text by Jacques Damase. Paris, 1969.

Damase, Jacques, *Sonia Delaunay: Rhythms and Colours,* preface by Michel Hoog. Greenwich Conn.: New York Graphic Society, 1971.

_____ *Sonia Delaunay,* biographical notes by Edouard Mustelier. Paris: Gallerie de Varenne, 1971.

Dorival, Bernard, "La Donation Delaunay au Musée National d'Art Moderne," *La Revue du Louvre,* Paris, 1963.

_____, *Retrospective S.D.,* National Museum of Modern Art, Paris, 1965.

Ferreira, Paulo, *Correspondance de quatre artistes portugais avec R. et S.D.,* Paris, 1972.

Gimpel Gallery, New York, *Sonia Delaunay,* intro. by Michel Hoog, Nov., 1967.

Hoog, Michel, *R. et S. Delaunay, Inventaire des Collections Publiques Francaises,* Paris, 1967.

Vriesen, Gustav, and Imdahl, Max, *Robert Delaunay.* New York: Harry N. Abrams, 1967.

LOUISE NEVELSON (1899–   )

1964, 1965, 1966, 1969, 1971, 1972, 1974 "Louise Nevelson," The Pace Gallery, New York.

1967	"Louise Nevelson" (Retrospective) Whitney Museum of American Art, New York.
1967	"Louise Nevelson," Rose Art Museum, Brandeis University, Waltham, Mass.

1969 "Louise Nevelson," Museo Civico di Torino, Torino, Italy.

1969 "Louise Nevelson, Sculptures, 1959–69," Rijksmuseum Kröller-Müller, Otterlo Netherlands.

1970 "Louise Nevelson," Whitney Museum of American Art, New York.

1973 "Louise Nevelson," Moderna Museet, Stockholm.

1973 "Louise Nevelson, Wood Sculpture," Walker Art Center, Minneapolis, traveled to San Francisco Museum of Art; Dallas Museum of Art; The High Museum of Art, Atlanta; William Rockhill Nelson Gallery of Art, Kansas City; The Cleveland Museum of Art.

1974 "Louise Nevelson," Palais des Beaux Arts, Brussels.

1974 "Louise Nevelson," Musée de la Ville de Paris.

1974 "Louise Nevelson," Neue National Galerie, Berlin.

Bongartz, Roy, " 'I Don't Want to Waste Time,' Says Louise Nevelson at 70," *The New York Times Magazine,* Jan. 24, 1971. Sect. 6.

Friedman, Martin, *Nevelson Wood Sculptures,* New York: E.P. Dutton, Inc., 1973.

Glimsher, Arnold B., *Louise Nevelson.* New York: Praeger Publishers, 1972.

Gordon, John, *Louise Nevelson,* Whitney Museum of Art, New York, 1967.

Johnson, Una E., *Louise Nevelson.* New York: Shorewood Publishers Inc., 1967.

Martha Jackson Gallery, New York, *Nevelson,* 1961 (foreword by Kenneth Sawyer, poem by Jean Art, commentary by George Mathieu).

Rijksmuseum Kröller-Müller, Otterlo, Netherlands, *Louise Nevelson Sculptures, 1959–69,* 1969. (Intro. by R. Oxenaar.)

Robert, Collette, *Nevelson.* Paris: The Pocket Museum. Editions Georges Fall, 1964.

LEE KRASNER (1908–)

1951 "Lee Krasner," Betty Parsons Gallery, New York.

1955 "Lee Krasner," Stable Gallery, New York.

1958 "Lee Krasner, Recent Paintings," Martha Jackson Gallery, New York.

1960 "Lee Krasner," Howard Wise Gallery, New York.

1962 "New Work by Lee Krasner," Howard Wise, New York.

1965 "Lee Krasner, Paintings, Drawings and Collages" (Retrospective), Whitechapel Art Gallery, London.

1967 "Paintings by Lee Krasner," University Art Gallery, University of Alabama, Tuscaloosa.

1968 "Lee Krasner, Recent Paintings," Marlborough Gallery, New York.

1973 "Lee Krasner, Recent Paintings," Marlborough Gallery, New York.

1973–74 "Lee Krasner: Large Paintings," Whitney Museum of American Art, New York.

1974 "Lee Krasner: Works on Paper," Corcoran Gallery.

1974 "Woman's Work: American Art '74," Philadelphia Civic Center.

1974 "In Her Own Image," organized by Cindy Nemser, Fleisher Art Memorial, Philadelphia.

Campbell, Lawrence, "Of Lilith and Lettuce," *Art News,* Mar., 1968.

Marlborough-Gerson Gallery, New York. *Lee Krasner,* 1968.

Marlborough Gallery, New York. *Lee Krasner, Recent Paintings,* 1973.

Nemser, Cindy, "Lee Krasner's Paintings, 1946–49," *Artforum,* Dec., 1973.

Robertson, Bryan, "The Nature of Lee Krasner," *Art in America,* Nov.-Dec., 1973.

Rose, Barbara, "American Great: Lee Krasner," *Vogue,* June, 1972.

Wasserman, Emily, "Lee Krasner in Mid Career," *Artforum,* Mar., 1968.

Whitechapel Art Gallery. *Lee Krasner: Paintings, Drawings and Collages* (intro. by B.H. Friedman), London, 1965.

ALICE NEEL (1900–)

1964, 1966, 1968, 1970, 1973 "Alice Neel," Graham Gallery, New York.

      1967   "Alice Neel," Maxwell Gallery, San Francisco.

   1967–69   "Social Comment in America," circulating exhibition, Museum of Modern Art, New York.

      1969   "Harlem Artists '69," Studio Museum of Harlem, New York.

      1971   "Alice Neel" (Retrospective), Moore College of Art Gallery, Philadelphia.

      1972   "New Acquisitions, 1972 Annual Exhibition of Contemporary American Painting," Whitney Museum of American Art, New York.

      1974   "Alice Neel" (major exhibition), Whitney Museum of American Art, New York.

      1974   "Alice Neel," Summit Art Center, Inc., Summit, New Jersey.

      1974   "Woman's Work: American Art, '74," Philadelphia Civic Center.

      1974   "In Her Own Image," Fleisher Art Memorial, Philadelphia.

Alloway, Lawrence, "Art," *The Nation,* Mar. 9, 1974.

Berrigan, Ted, "The Portrait and its Double," *Art News,* Jan., 1966.

Cochrane, Diane, "Alice Neel; Collector of Souls," *American Artist,* Sept., 1973.

Crehan, Hubert, "Introducing the Portraits of Alice Neel," *Art News,* Oct., 1962.

_____, "A Different Breed of Portraitist," *San Francisco Sunday Examiner and Chronicle,* Mar. 7, 1971.

Halasz, Piri, "Alice Neel: I Have This Obsession With Life," *Art News,* Jan., 1974.

Leslie, Alfred, *The Hasty Papers, A One Shot Review.* New York, 1960.

Mainardi, Patricia, "Talking About Portraits," *Feminist Art Journal,* Summer, 1974.

Nochlin, Linda, "Some Women Realists," *Artsmagazine,* May, 1974.

Nemser, Cindy, "Portraits of Four Decades," *Ms.,* Oct., 1973.

Perreault, John, "Art; Alice Neel Show," *Village Voice,* Feb. 21, 1974.

Whitney Museum of American Art, New York, *Alice Neel,* Feb.-Mar., 1974. (Intro. by Elke Morger Soloman.)

GRACE HARTIGAN (1922–)

1962, 1964, 1967, 1970 "Grace Hartigan," Martha Jackson Gallery, New York.

      1962   "Carnegie International," Pittsburgh, Pa., one of six artists given entire room.

      1963   "Paintings, 1957–63," University Gallery, University of Minnesota.

      1967   "Grace Hartigan," University of Chicago.

      1972   "American Women 20th Century," Lakeview Center for the Arts, Peoria, Ill.

      1972   "Abstraction and Lyricism," Tokyo, Japan.

      1973   "Grace Hartigan," Gertrude Kasle Gallery, Detroit, Mich.

"Artists on Tape," *New York Times,* Apr. 26, 1968.

Barber, Alan, "Interview with Grace Hartigan," *Artsmagazine,* June, 1974.

Baur, John I.H., "Eastern Artists," *Art in America,* no. 1, 1954.

Dennis, Emily, "Grace Hartigan," *School of New York; Some Younger Artists,* ed. B.H. Friedman. New York: Grove Press, 1959.

Hakanson, Jay, "Robust Paintings at Hartigan Show," *The Sunday News-Detroit,* Apr. 28, 1974.

Hartigan, Grace, "An Artist Speaks," *The Arrow,* Dec. 9, 1960.

Hunter, Sam, *Art Since 1954.* New York: Abrams, 1959.

"Miss Hartigan and Her Canvas: The Rawness and the Vast," *Newsweek,* May 11, 1959.

Museum of Modern Art, *Twelve Americans,* New York, 1956.

Schwartz, D.M., "Hartigan at Tibor de Nagy," *Apollo,* Sept., 1959.

Soby, James Thrall, "Interview with Grace Hartigan," *Saturday Review,* Oct., 1957.

_____, "Non-Abstract Authorities," *Saturday Review,* Apr. 23, 1955.

"The Weather Vane," *Time,* Jan. 3, 1964.

"Women Artists in Ascendance," *Life,* May 13, 1957.

"Women of American Art," *Look,* 1960.

MARISOL (1930–   )

1964   "Marisol," Stable Gallery, New York.
1966   "Marisol," Sidney Janis Gallery, New York.
1967   "Marisol: Figures of State," Hanover Gallery, London; Sidney Janis Gallery, New York.
1968   "Marisol," Venezuelan Pavillion, Venice Biennale; Museum Boymans-Van Beuningen, Rotterdam.
1969   "Pop Art Redefined," Heyward Gallery, London.
1970   "Marisol," Moore College of Art, Philadelphia, Pa.
1971   "Marisol," Worcester Art Museum, Mass.
1972   "Colossal Scale," Sidney Janis Gallery, New York.
1973   "Marisol," Sidney Janis Gallery, New York.
1973   "Marisol: Prints 1961–73," The New York Cultural Center.
1974   "Marisol," Trisolini Gallery of Ohio University, Athens; Columbus Gallery of Fine Arts, Ohio.

"Art: Sculpture—The Dollmaker," *Time,* May 28, 1965.

Barrio-Garay, Jose, *Marisol,* Trisolini Gallery of Ohio University, Athens, Ohio, 1974.

Barnitz, Jacqueline, "The Marisol Mask," *Hispanic Arts,* Autumn, 1967.

Bernstein, Roberta, and Hersch, Susan, *Marisol,* Moore College of Art, Philadelphia, 1970.

Campbell, Lawrence, "Marisol's Magic Mixtures," *Art News,* March, 1964.

Chapman, Daniel, "Marisol . . . A Brilliant Sculptress Shapes the Heads of State," *Look,* Nov. 14, 1967.

Diament, Clara, *Marisol,* Venezuelan Pavillion, Venice Biennale, 1968.

Glueck, Grace, "It's Not Pop, It's Not Op- It's Marisol," *New York Times Magazine,* March 7, 1965.

Gold, Barbara, "Portrait of Marisol," *Interplay,* June, 1968.

Loring, John, *Marisol: Prints 1961–1973,* The New York Cultural Center, New York, 1973.

_____, "Marisol's Diptych," *Artsmagazine,* Apr., 1973.

O'Doherty, Brian, "Marisol: The Enigma of the SELF-Image," March, 1964.

Shulman, Leon, *Marisol,* Worcester Art Museum, Mass., 1971.

Sidney Janis Gallery, *Marisol,* New York, 1966.

———, *Marisol: Figures of State,* New York, 1967.

EVA HESSE (1936–1970)

1966   "Eccentric Abstraction," organized by Lucy Lippard, Fischbach Gallery, New York.

1967   "Art in Series," Finch College, New York.

1968   "Eva Hesse," Fischbach Gallery, New York.

1969   "Anti-Illusion: Procedures/Materials," Whitney Museum, New York.

1969   "Live in Your Head—When Attitude Becomes Form," Kunsthalle, Bern, Switzerland.

1969   "A Plastic Presence," The Milwaukee Art Center and the Jewish Museum, New York.

1969   "Art in Process IV," Finch College Museum, New York.

1969   "9 at Leo Castelli" (Warehouse Exhibition), New York.

1970   "String and Rope," Sidney Janis Gallery, New York.

1970   "Eva Hesse: Drawings," Fischbach Gallery, New York.

1971   "Eva Hesse," Visual Arts Gallery, School of Visual Arts, New York.

1972   "Eva Hesse: A Memorial Exhibition," Guggenheim Museum, New York; Albright-Knox Art Gallery, Buffalo, New York; Museum of Contemporary Art, Chicago; Pasadena Art Museum, Calif.

Davis, Douglas, "Cockroach or Queen," *Newsweek,* Jan. 15, 1973.

Guggenheim Museum, *Eva Hesse: A Memorial Exhibit* (text by Robert Pincus-Witten and Linda Shearer), New York, 1972.

Gula, Kasha Linville, "Eva Hesse: No Explanation," *Ms.,* Apr., 1973

Hesse, Eva, "Statement," *Art in Process IV: Exhibition Catalogue,* Finch College Museum of Art, 1969–70.

Hughes, Robert, "Vulnerable Ugliness," *Time* Magazine, Jan. 1, 1973.

Levin, Kim, "Eva Hesse: Notes on New Beginnings," *Art News,* Feb., 1973.

Lippard, Lucy, R., "Eva Hesse: The Circle," *Art in America,* May-June, 1973.

———, *Eva Hesse,* Paris: Paul Bianchini, 1974.

Nemser, Cindy, "Her Life," *The Feminist Art Journal,* Winter, 1973.

———, "My Memories of Eva Hesse," *The Feminist Art Journal,* Winter, 1973.

Pincus-Witten, Robert, "Eva Hesse: Post Minimalism Into Sublime," *Artforum,* Nov., 1971.

LILA KATZEN (1932–)

1968   "Directions 1: Options," organized by Lawrence Alloway, Milwaukee Art Center.

1968   "Lila Katzen: Light Floors," Architectural League, New York.

1969   "The Universe as Environment: Moon Markers," Loeb Student Center, New York University; Stonybrook State University, New York.

1969   "Lila Katzen" (Retrospective), University of Georgia, Georgia Museum of Art, Athens, Ga.

1970   "Expo '70" (Czech Theatre Facade and Exterior Lighting), Japan.

1970   "Light Floors," Centro Venezelano Americano Caracas, Venezuela.

1970   "Liquid and Solid," Max Hutchinson Gallery, New York.

1970   Explorations '70 ("Sao Paulo Biennale") ("Liquid Tunnel"), Smithsonian Institution, Washington, D.C.

1971	"Media Wall," commissioned by C & P Telephone Co., Inc., Baltimore, Md.
1973	"Whitney Biennial of American Painting and Sculpture," Whitney Museum of American Art, New York.
1973	"Storm King Art Center," Mountainville, N.Y.
1973	"Group Exhibition," World Trade Center and La Guardia Airport, New York.
1974	"Woman's Work: American Art, '74," Philadelphia Civic Center.
1974	"Sculptors' International-Invitational," South Houston Gallery, New York.

Crane, Catherine, "Kaleidoscope as Environment," *The Architectural Forum,* June, 1968.

Crichton, M., "People are Talking About . . .," *Vogue,* Sept. 15, 1970.

Georgia Museum of Art, *Lila Katzen,* Athens, Georgia, 1969. (Preface by William D. Paul, notes on the materiality of light by Lila Katzen.)

Glueck, Grace, "Lila Katzen's Floors," *New York Times,* May 4, 1968.

Hutchinson, Peter, "The Perception of Illusion, Object and Environment," *Artsmagazine,* Apr., 1968.

———, "Science Fiction: An Aesthetic For Science," *Art International,* Oct., 1968.

Jacobs, Jay, "Pertinent and Impertinent, All Systems Go," *The Art Gallery,* Mar., 1969.

Katzen, Lila, "How to be Seen and Counted," *The Feminist Art Journal,* Spring, 1973.

Nemser, Cindy, "Lila Katzen Defines Environment," *Artsmagazine,* Sept., 1970.

Tucker, Marcia, "Making it Big," *Ms.,* May, 1974.

ELEANOR ANTIN (1935–)

1970	"California Lives," Gain Ground Gallery, New York.
1970	"Portraits of 8 New York Women," Studio Exhibition, Chelsea Hotel, New York.
1971	"Library Science," Brand Library Art Center, Glendale, Calif.
1972	"Traditional Art," Henri Gallery, Washington, D.C.
1972	"Part of an Autobiography," Portland Center for the Visual Arts, Portland, Oregon.
1971–73	"Mail Exhibition—100 Boots" (51 serial postcards distributed through the U.S. Postal System).
1973	"100 Boots," Museum of Modern Art, New York.
1973	"I Dreamed I was a Ballerina," Orlando Gallery, Los Angeles, Calif.
1974	"The Ballerina and the King," Galleria Forma, Genoa, Italy.
1974	"Several Selves" (video), Everson Museum, Syracuse, New York.
1974	"Narratives," Centro di Arte y Communicacion, Buenos Aires, Argentina.
1974	"Woman's Work: American Art '74," Philadelphia Civic Center.
1974	"In Her Own Image," Fleisher Art Memorial, Philadelphia.

Antin, Eleanor, "Women Without Pathos," *Art and Sexual Politics,* edited by Thomas Hesse and Elizabeth Baker. New York: Collier-Macmillan, 1973.

———," On Self Transformation," *Flash Art,* March/Apr., 1974.

———, "The Red Bottle," Centro di Arte y Communicacion, Buenos Aires, Argentina, 1974.

Bethany, "100 Boots Head East," *Saturday Review of the Arts,* Mar., 1973.

"From Boot Hill to the Bronx," *Crawdaddy,* Sept., 1973.

Johnston, Laurie, "100 Boots End Cross-Country March," *New York Times,* May 16, 1973.

Lippard, Lucy, "Lucy Lippard Presents the Ideas of Eleanor Antin and Adrian Piper," *Art and Artists,* Mar., 1972.

_____, *Six Years: The Dematerialization of the Art Object from 1966–1972.* New York: Praeger, 1973.

Richards, Paul, "The Saga of the Empty Boots," *Washington Post,* Sept. 14, 1971.

AUDREY FLACK (1931–)

1959, 1963	"Audrey Flack," Roko Gallery, New York.
1963	"9 Realist Painters," Robert Schoellkopf Gallery, New York.
1965	"6 Women," Fischbach Gallery, New York.
1969	"Paintings From the Photograph," Riverside Museum, New York.
1970	"New Realism," St. Cloud State College, Minnesota.
1970	"22 Realists," Whitney Museum of American Art, New York.
1972	"Audrey Flack," French & Co., New York.
1972	"Whitney Annual," Whitney Museum of American Art, New York.
1972	"Women in Art," State University at Potsdam, New York.
1972	"Realism Now," New York Cultural Center.
1972	"Women Choose Women," New York Cultural Center.
1973	"The Super-Realist Vision," DeCordova Museum, Lincoln, Mass.
1973	"The Stewart Spiser Collection," Louis K. Meisel Gallery, New York; traveled to Brooks Memorial Art Gallery, Memphis, Tenn; University of Texas at Austin; Albrecht Gallery, St. Joseph, Miss.
1974	"Audrey Flack," Louis K. Meisel Gallery, New York.
1974	"Audrey Flack," Joselhoff Gallery, University of Hartford.
1974	"New-Photo Realism," Wadsworth Atheneum, Hartford, Conn.
1974	"Woman's Work: American Art '74," Philadelphia Civic Center.
1974	"In Her Own Image," Fleisher Art Memorial, Philadelphia.
1974	Tokyo Biennale.

Alloway, Lawrence, Forthcoming book on Realist Painting. New York: Praeger, Publishers, Spring 1975.

Coke, F. Van Deren, *The Painter and the Photograph.* Albuquerque, New Mexico: University of New Mexico Press, 2nd ed., 1972.

Cowart, Jack, *New-Photo Realism,* Wadsworth Atheneum, Hartford, Conn., 1974.

Farb, Oriole, *Paintings From the Photograph,* Riverside Museum, New York, 1969.

Filipacci, Daniel, *L'Hyperrealistes Americaine.* France: Filipacci Publications, 1974.

Kulterman, Udo, *New Realism.* Greenwich, Conn.: New York Graphic Society, 1972.

Levin, Kim, "Audrey Flack," *Art in America,* May/June 1974.

Monte, James, *22 Realists,* Whitney Museum of American Art, New York, 1970.

Perreault, John, "Glints of Glass, A Whiff of Poetry," *Village Voice,* Apr. 4, 1974.

NANCY GROSSMAN (1940–)

1964, 1965	"Nancy Grossman," Krasner Gallery, New York.
1967, 1971, 1973	"Nancy Grossman," Cordier and Ekstrom Gallery, New York.
1969	"Human Concern/Personal Torment," Whitney Museum of American Art, New York.

1969	"American Sculpture—Selection 2," Whitney Museum of American Art, New York.
1972	"Recent Figure Sculpture," Fogg Art Museum, Harvard University, Cambridge, Mass.
1973	"Biennial Exhibition," Whitney Museum of American Art, New York.
1974	"Invitational, American Academy of Letters," National Institute of Arts and Letters, New York.
1974	"Woman's Work: American Art '74," Philadelphia Civic Center.
1974	"In Her Own Image," Fleisher Art Memorial, Philadelphia.

Canaday, John, "Art: Nancy Grossman," *The New York Times,* Apr. 1, 1967.

_____, "Art: Surprise From Nancy Grossman: Her 3 Drawings Shine in Leading Show," *The New York Times,* May 30, 1970.

_____, "The Least Cruel Artist Alive," *The New York Times,* Nov. 28, 1971.

Diamondstein, Barbaralee, *Open Secrets.* New York: The Viking Press, 1972.

Doty, Robert, *Human Concern/Personal Torment,* Whitney Museum of American Art, New York, 1969.

Genauer, Emily, "Art and the Artist: Nancy Grossman," *New York Post,* Dec. 4, 1971.

_____, "Art and the Artist: Nancy Grossman," *New York Post,* Oct. 27, 1973.

Gruen, John, "Art Tour, The Galleries—A Critical Guide: Nancy Grossman," *New York Herald Tribune,* Apr. 3, 1965.

_____, "Art Tour, A Critical Guide to the Galleries: Nancy Grossman," *New York Herald Tribune,* Oct. 30, 1965.

Mayhall, Dorothy, *Highlights of the 1968–69 Art Season,* The Larry Aldrich Museum of Contemporary Art, Ridgefield, Conn., 1969.

O'Doherty, Brian, "This Week Around the Galleries: Nancy Grossman," *The New York Times,* Feb. 23, 1964.

Wasserman, J.L., *Recent Figure Sculpture,* Fogg Art Museum, Harvard University, Cambridge, Mass., 1972.